MW01617046

R<small>THE</small>osicrucian
Enlightenment

Frontispiece   The Invisible College of the Rose Cross Fraternity.
From Theophilus Schweighardt, *Speculum Sophicum Rhodo-Stauroticum*

R^{THE}osicrucian
THE
Rosicrucian
Enlightenment

Frances A. Yates

**BARNES
& NOBLE
BOOKS**
NEW YORK

CONTENTS

Frontispiece
The Invisible College of the Rose Cross Fraternity. From Theophilus Schweighardt, *Speculum Sophicum Rhodo-Stauroticum*, 1618

Between pages 8 and 9
1 Frederick V, Elector Palatine, and the Princess Elizabeth. Print, 1612. Sutherland Collection, Ashmolean Museum
2 Arch at Oppenheim, 1613. Designed and engraved by Johann Theodore de Bry. From *Beschreibung der Reiss*, Heidelberg, 1613
3 (a) Ship of the Argonauts, Pageant Car
(b) Arrival of the Princess Elizabeth at Heidelberg. From *Beschreibung der Reiss*
4 (a) Arch erected by Heidelberg University
(b) Arch erected in the courtyard of Heidelberg Castle
Triumphal Arches for the entry of the Princess Elizabeth, Heidelberg, 1613. From *Beschreibung der Reiss*

Between pages 24 and 25
5 Heidelberg Castle and Gardens, engraved by Matthieu Merian. From Salomon de Caus, *Hortus Palatinus*, Frankfurt, 1620
6 (a) Salomon de Caus, *Hortus Palatinus*, title-page
(b) Statue of Memnon. From Salomon de Caus, *Les raisons des forces mouvantes, Livre second*, Paris, 1624
7 (a) The Post Boy looking for a Missing King
(b) Frederick and Elizabeth in an Infernal Garden. German Prints, 1621 (the verses below the pictures have been omitted), British Museum, Print Room
8 Frederick and Elizabeth as King and Queen of Bohemia, with Four Lions. Print issued in Prague at the time of their coronation, 1619, National Portrait Gallery photograph (the explanatory verses below the picture have been omitted)

The title of this book may give rise to some misunderstanding. 'Rosicrucian' may suggest that this is going to be a book about modern groups of enquirers into various forms of occultism. 'Enlightenment' may suggest that the book will be about the period known as the *Aufklärung*, the emergence into the light of reason from the darkness of superstition with Voltaire, Diderot, and the eighteenth century. The two words together seem to make an impossibility, representing two opposite tendencies, the one towards strange forms of superstition, the other towards critical and rational opposition to superstition. How can a Rosicrucian be enlightened? The fact is that I am using 'Rosicrucian' in a strictly limited historical sense, and I am not using 'Enlightenment' in the usual strictly limited historical sense. The period covered by the book is almost entirely the early seventeenth century, though with excursions before and after. It is concerned with certain documents published in Germany in the early seventeenth century, generally known as 'the Rosicrucian manifestos', and with the historical setting of those documents. Later movements calling themselves 'Rosicrucian' up to, and including, the present, are entirely excluded. Since these documents, or manifestos, claim that new advances in man's knowledge are at hand, my title is historically correct. There was indeed a movement in the early seventeenth century which can be called a 'Rosicrucian Enlightenment', and that is what this book is about.

'Rosicrucian' in this purely historical sense represents a phase in the history of European culture which is intermediate between the Renaissance and the so-called scientific revolution of the seventeenth century. It is a phase in which the Renaissance Hermetic-Cabalist tradition has received the influx of another Hermetic tradition, that of alchemy. The 'Rosicrucian manifestos' are an expression of this phase, representing, as they do, the combination of 'Magia, Cabala,

xi

and Alchymia' as the influence making for the new enlightenment. In my book *Giordano Bruno and the Hermetic Tradition* (1964), I made an attempt to trace the Hermetic tradition in the Renaissance, from the time of its formulation in Italy by Marsilio Ficino and Pico della Mirandola onwards. Far from losing its power in the early seventeenth century (as I believed when writing that book), or losing its influence over cultural movements of major importance, I now realize that there was actually a renaissance of it in the early seventeenth century, fresh manifestations of it in new forms which had absorbed alchemical influences, and which were particularly important in relation to the development of the mathematical approach to nature.

A major 'Rosicrucian' figure was John Dee, who, as I said in an article published in 1968, 'seems obviously placeable historically as a Renaissance magus of the later Rosicrucian type'. In my book *Theatre of the World* (1969) I emphasized the importance of Dee as an influence behind the Elizabethan Renaissance, and in an excellent book, *John Dee* (1972), Peter French has filled a great gap in Renaissance studies by examining Dee's work and influence in England in a systematic way. Dee belonged emphatically to the Renaissance Hermetic tradition, brought up to date with new developments, and which he further expanded in original and important directions. Dee was, in his own right, a brilliant mathematician, and he related his study of number to the three worlds of the Cabalists. In the lower elemental world he studied number as technology and applied science and his *Preface* to Euclid provided a brilliant survey of the mathematical arts in general. In the celestial world, his study of number was related to astrology and alchemy, and in his *Monas hieroglyphica* he believed that he had discovered a formula for a combined cabalist, alchemical, and mathematical science which would enable its possessor to move up and down the scale of being from the lowest to the highest spheres. And in the supercelestial sphere, Dee believed that he had found the secret of conjuring angels by numerical computations in the cabalist tradition. Dee as 'Rosicrucian' is thus a figure typical of the late Renaissance magus who combined 'Magia, Cabala, and Alchymia' to achieve a world-view in which advancing science was strangely mingled with angelology.

Dee's striking and very influential career in Elizabethan England came to an end in 1583 when he left England for the continent, where he was extremely influential in stirring up new movements in central Europe. This half of Dee's career, the second or continental half, has not yet been studied in a systematic way and still remains in the world of rumour. It would seem that Dee was the leader in Bohemia, not only of an alchemical movement, but of a movement for religious reform, the nature of which has not yet been fully explored. Our knowledge of the world of culture surrounding the Emperor Rudolph II, upon which Dee's mission impinged, is still extremely scanty, and we await the publication of Robert Evans's important study of Rudolphine culture.

The present book—and I wish to emphasize this strongly—is basically a *historical* study. It is concerned with this 'Rosicrucian' phase of thought, culture, and religion, but its main attempt is directed towards indicating the *historical* channels through which the phase was distributed. These channels have been choked up and obscured through the disappearance out of history of a most important historical period.

It is true that we have learned from our history books that the Princess Elizabeth, daughter of James I, married Frederick V, Elector Palatine of the Rhine, who, a few years later, made a rash attempt to secure for himself the throne of Bohemia, which attempt ended in ignominious failure. The 'Winter King and Queen of Bohemia', as they were mockingly called, fled from Prague after the defeat of 1620, and passed the rest of their lives as poverty-stricken exiles, having lost both the Palatinate and Bohemia. What has slipped out of history is the fact that a 'Rosicrucian' phase of culture was attached to this episode, that the 'Rosicrucian manifestos' were connected with it, that the movements stirred up by John Dee in Bohemia in earlier years were behind those manifestos, that the brief reign of Frederick and Elizabeth in the Palatinate was a Hermetic golden age, nourished on the alchemical movement led by Michael Maier, on Dee's *Monas hiero-glyphica*, and all that that implied. Disowned by James I, the movement foundered, but its reconstruction is a most necessary preliminary for the tracing of 'Rosicrucian' survival in the later seventeenth century. The reconstruction by critical historical methods of this phase of European thought and history will, it is hoped, take this whole subject out of the range of uncritical and vaguely 'occultist' studies, and make of it a legitimate, and most important, field for research.

As a pioneer effort, the present book is bound to contain errors which scholars of the future will correct. The tools for working on this subject are in a rudimentary state and one is hampered at every turn by lack of accurate bibliographical work. Most of the literature on

'Rosicrucianism' is unusable by the critical historian, except as a means of leading to original material. The works of A. E. Waite are in a different category, and of these I have made much use, though, as G. Scholem has said, Waite's valuable work is marred by lack of critical sense. Paul Arnold's book has been useful for its large collection of material, though very confusingly arranged. Will-Erich Peuckert's study is fundamental for the German background. All these books, and others mentioned in the notes, have been of great assistance, though the attempt made in the present book to relate Rosicrucianism to contemporary situations is on entirely new lines.

As already said, I have completely omitted the later history of so-called 'Rosicrucianism' and the strange vagaries in which the use of the word became involved. It might now be possible to clarify the later history, though I shall not make the attempt. That is a subject in itself, and a different subject, though survivals from the imagery of the early period can be detected in, for example, such a work as *Geheime Figuren der Rosenkreuzer*, published at Altona in 1785; what the figures may mean in the later context it would require new research to discover. In order to keep this book within bounds, it has been necessary to curtail or omit much material, and to resist the temptation to turn every stone, or to follow every avenue branching out from this fundamental subject.

The subject is fundamental because, basically, it is concerned with a striving for illumination, in the sense of vision, as well as for enlightenment in the sense of advancement in intellectual or scientific knowledge. Though I do not know exactly what a Rosicrucian was, nor whether there were any, the doubt and uncertainty which beset the seeker after the invisible Rose Cross Brothers are themselves the inevitable accompaniment of the search for the Invisible.

The themes of some of the earlier chapters of this book formed the basis of a lecture on 'James I and the Palatinate: a forgotten chapter in the history of ideas' delivered as the James Ford Special Lecture in English History at Oxford in October 1970. The encouragement generously given by H. Trevor-Roper on that occasion helped me to tackle the book.

As always, the Warburg Institute has been my mainstay and my home and to the Director and to all my good friends there I am deeply grateful. D. P. Walker most kindly read a draft of the manuscript and there have been many valuable discussions of its themes with him.

Jennifer Montague and the staff of the Photographic Collection have been most helpful in collecting the photographs for the illustrations. I am indebted to Maurice Evans for drawing the sketch map for the figure in the text.

Peter French kindly allowed me, with the permission of the publishers, to see the page proofs of his book on Dee before its publication.

To the staff of the London Library I offer my most sincere thanks. I have also received kind help from the staff of the Dr Williams Library. I am indebted to the directors of the National Portrait Gallery, the Ashmolean Museum, and the British Museum for permission to reproduce portraits and engravings. The director of the Württemberg Landesbibliothek at Stuttgart gave permission for a microfilm of a manuscript to be made. The quotations from E. A. Beller, *Caricatures of the Winter King of Bohemia*, 1928, are made by permission of the Clarendon Press, Oxford.

This book belongs to the series which began with *Giordano Bruno and the Hermetic Tradition*. Throughout all the time of the writing of these books, my sister has sustained me in countless ways. It has been her constant practical help, unfailing encouragement, intelligent understanding, and lively critical sense which have made the work possible.

Warburg Institute,
University of London

CHAPTER I

A ROYAL WEDDING
The Marriage of Princess Elizabeth with the Elector Palatine

In the old Europe, a royal wedding was a diplomatic event of the first importance, and royal wedding festivities were a statement of policy. For the marriage in February 1613 of the Princess Elizabeth, daughter of James I, with Frederick V, Elector Palatine of the Rhine, all the treasures of the English Renaissance were outpoured, and London went wild with joy at what seemed a continuation of the Elizabethan age in this alliance of a new, young Elizabeth with the leader of the German Protestants and a grandson of William the Silent.

Earlier patterns, the patterns of the old Queen's times, were indeed implicit in this happy event. The old Elizabeth had been the support of Europe against Hapsburg aggression, allied to Catholic reaction; her foreign alliances had been with the rebellious Netherlands and their leader and with German and French Protestants. Ideally, she had represented in religion a reformed and purified imperialism, typified in the name Astraea, the Just Virgin of the Golden Age, which her poets gave her.[1] There was a certain piquancy in the fact that the young Elizabeth, unlike the old Elizabethan ·Virgin, was to cement these sacred policies through her marriage. The court bankrupted itself through the vast expenditure in clothes, jewellery, entertainments, and feasting for this marriage. And there was also accumulated wealth of genius and poetry available for expenditure on the shows devised for this fortunate pair. Shakespeare was still alive and in London; the Globe theatre was not yet burned down; Inigo Jones was perfecting the court masque; Francis Bacon had published *The Advancement of Learning*. The English Renaissance was at a high point of splendour, developing into the dawning intellectual promise of the seventeenth century.

But would that promise be allowed to develop peacefully or would

[1] See my article, 'Queen Elizabeth as Astraea', *Journal of the Warburg and Courtauld Institutes*, X (1947), pp. 27–82.

disasters intervene? The auguries were not good. The war between Spain and the Netherlands had been ended by a truce which was due to expire in 1621. The forces of Catholic reaction were preparing for a new assault on heresy, an objective which was connected with the aggrandisement of the House of Hapsburg. Those on the other side were everywhere on the watch. Most informed people believed that war was inevitable and that it would break out in Germany. There were thus dark shadows behind the splendours of this wedding, and these rather charming and innocent young people, Frederick and Elizabeth (Pl. 1), would in a few years' time find themselves at the very heart of the whirlwind.

The young German prince landed at Gravesend on 16 October 1612.[1] Handsome and gentle, he made a good impression on the court and people and on his bride-to-be. Frederick and Elizabeth really fell in love with one another and this romance was to endure throughout the vicissitudes to come. The happiness of the courtship period was marred by the illness and death of the bride's brother, Henry, Prince of Wales. Young though he was, Prince Henry had already made his mark as a leader, a possible successor to Henri IV of France (who had been assassinated in 1610) as representative of opposition to the Hapsburg powers. Henry had planned to accompany his sister into Germany, to choose a wife for himself there, and was said to entertain very large schemes for ending 'the jars in religion'.[2] His sudden early death removed an influence on his father which would certainly have been used in the interest of his sister and her husband. This fatal event did not for long interfere with the court amusements, though it caused the wedding to be postponed.

Elizabeth loved the theatre and had her own company of players, the Lady Elizabeth's men, who gave performances before her and her fiancé.[3] And about Christmas time the King's Men, Shakespeare's company, gave twenty plays at court. John Heminges, later to be co-editor with Henry Condell of the first folio edition of Shakespeare's plays, was paid for presenting before the Lady Elizabeth and the Prince Palatine a list of plays which included *Much Ado About Nothing*, *Othello*, *Julius Caesar*, and *The Tempest*.[4] It has been suggested that the

---

[1] For full accounts of events, ceremonial, and festivities in connection with the betrothal and marriage of Frederick and Elizabeth, see John Nichols, *The Progresses of James I*, II, 1826.

[2] Nichols, p. 474 n.

[3] E. K. Chambers, *Elizabethan Stage*, II, p. 248.

[4] E. K. Chambers, *William Shakespeare*, II, p. 343.

masque in *The Tempest* was added to the play to make it suitable for performance before this princely pair, perhaps on the betrothal night, 27 December 1612.[1] There is no evidence to support this interesting theory, beyond the fact that this play about the love story of an island princess and containing a nuptial masque was one of the plays by Shakespeare known to have been performed before Frederick and Elizabeth, who, at this comic moment in their history—comic in the sense that their lives seem now a comedy with a happy ending—have something of the air of a Shakespearean hero and heroine.

As a necessary appendage to his future status as husband of the daughter of the King of Great Britain, the Elector Palatine (or the Palsgrave as he is called in the English records) was invested with the Order of the Garter. He and his uncle, Maurice of Nassau, were elected to the Order on 7 December, and on 7 February, a week before the wedding, the Palsgrave was solemnly invested at Windsor.[2] A jewel-studded George—the pendant of St George and the Dragon which depends from the great collar of the Order—was presented by the King to his future son-in-law, and his fiancée also presented him with a George,[3] probably a Lesser George or the smaller version of the pendant worn on a ribbon on occasions when the full regalia of the Order were not worn. The very special significance attached to the Order of the Garter was again an Elizabethan tradition. There had been a great revival of the Order, its ceremonies, processions, and ethos, during the reign of Elizabeth, who had used it as a means of drawing the noblemen together in common service to the Crown.[4] When the Palsgrave became a Garter Knight he enlisted under the banner of the Red Cross of St George in defence of the causes for which the Order stood, the fighting of the Dragon of Wrong and the defence of the Monarch.

The story of St George and the Dragon and of his romantic adventures in attacking wrongs and defending the oppressed was blazoned in fire in the firework display given by the King's gunners shortly

---

[1] *The Tempest* was first performed in 1611. Some scholars have supported the view that the nuptial masque in the play was an addition to the original version made for the performance before Frederick and Elizabeth. See *The Tempest*, ed. F. Kermode, Arden Shakespeare, 1954, pp. xxi–xxii.

[2] Nichols, p. 512.

[3] M. A. Everett Green, *Elizabeth Electress Palatine and Queen of Bohemia*, revised edition, London, 1909, p. 47.

[4] See Yates, 'Elizabethan Chivalry: The Romance of the Accession Day Tilts', *Journal of the Warburg and Courtauld Institutes*, XX (1957), pp. 4–24; R. C. Strong, 'Queen Elizabeth and the Order of the Garter', *Archaeological Journal*, CXLX (1964), pp. 245–69.

before the wedding, on the night of 11 February. These fireworks are fully described in a printed account[1] and are illustrated in a manuscript in the British Museum.[2] A queen, imprisoned by a necromancer, was delivered by the great champion of the world, St George. One fiery scene showed the champion riding over the bridge between the queen's pavilion and the necromancer's tower; on this bridge he slew the dragon. Then he entered the tower and captured the necromancer. The display concluded with the firing of the necromancer's tower 'with reports thwacking and lights burning'.

Though enthusiastically described by the gunners, it appears that this show did not go off very well, and some people were injured.[3] Coming between the investiture and the wedding it was clearly intended as an allegory of the Elector Palatine as St George, patron of the Order of the Garter, clearing the world of evil enchantment. Readers of Spenser's *Faerie Queene*, if there were any amongst those who watched this show, might have been reminded of the Red Cross Knight who championed Una in that chivalrous allegory in honour of the old Virgin Elizabeth. Now the young married Elizabeth has a St George allegory written in fire as one of the celebrations of her marriage to her Garter Knight.

At last, on 14 February, came the wedding, in the royal chapel at Whitehall. The bride wore 'a crown of refined golde, made imperiall by the pearles and diamonds thereupon placed, which were so thicke beset that they stood like shining pinnacles upon her amber-coloured haire, dependently hanging playted downe over her shoylders to her waste.'[4] They were married by George Abbot, Archbishop of Canterbury. The bridegroom was a Calvinist but the ceremony was Anglican, 'the Prince Palatine speaking the words of marriage in English after the Archbishop'.[5] This was important, that the day was a triumph for the Church of England which was extending its influence into foreign lands through this marriage. Abbot regarded this marriage as in the nature of a religious mission, Puritan and purifying in its influence.[6] Music and anthems followed the ceremony. The Garter King at Arms

---

[1] Nichols, pp. 527–35, 536–41.

[2] 'A description of the seuerall fireworkes inuented and wrought by His Maiesties Gunners', British Museum, Kings MSS., 17, c. xxxv.

[3] Nichols, p. 587.

[4] *Ibid.*, pp. 542–3.

[5] *Ibid.*, p. 547.

[6] On Abbot's enthusiasm for the Palatinate match, see Paul A. Welsby, *George Abbot the Unwanted Archbishop*, London, 1962, pp. 51–3. Lancelot Andrewes was also an enthusiastic supporter.

published the styles of the bride and bridegroom. As the latter left the chapel six of his own men went before him bearing silver trumpets on which they flourished so delightfully that it rejoiced the whole court, and caused thousands to say 'God give them joy'.[1] So the Royal Wedding ended on this note of the German trumpets.

That night a masque was presented in the banqueting house at Whitehall before the newly wedded pair and the whole court. The words were by Thomas Campion, the production by Inigo Jones.[2] The theme of the first scene was the power of the music of Orpheus to charm away melancholy and madness. Choral episodes between Orpheus, the 'franticks', and poetic frenzy followed. Then the upper part of the scene was discovered in which were clouds and large stars. The harmony of the spheres blended with the harmony of the royal wedding:[3]

> Advance your chorall motions now,
>> You musick-loving lights,
> This night concludes the Nuptiall vow,
>> Make this the best of nights;
> So bravely crowne it with your beames,
>> That it may live in fame,
> So long as Rhenus or the Thames
>> Are knowne by either name.

The Rhine is joining with the Thames, Germany unites with Great Britain, the stars in their courses rain down harmonies on this marriage.[4]

According to the humour of this Song, the starres mooved in an exceeding strange and delightfull manner, and I suppose fewe have ever seene more neate artifice than Master Inigoe Jones shewed in contriving their motion, who in all the rest of the workmanship, which belonged to the whole invention shewed extraordinarie industrie and skill.

Later a deep perspective scene was disclosed, in the midst of which was a silver obelisk, and beside it golden statues of the bride and bridegroom. Old Sybilla advanced to prophesy in Latin verses the great race of Kings and Emperors which would spring from this union of the

[1] Nichols, p. 548.
[2] Thomas Campion, *The Lords' Masque*, reprinted in Nichols, pp. 554–65.
[3] Nichols, p. 558.
[4] *Ibid.*, pp. 558–9.

strength of Germany with that of Great Britain, and of the joining of peoples in one religious cult and in simple love.[1]

On the following night, 15 February, the members of the Inner Temple and Gray's Inn put on a masque by Francis Beaumont,[2] which again circles round the theme of the union of the Rhine and the Thames. The text is dedicated to Sir Francis Bacon, described as 'You that spared no time nor travail in the setting forth, ordering, and furnishing of this masque.'[3] This show had been somewhat rebuffed by King James who had ordered it to be deferred. Its main scene showed a splendid vision of Knights and Priests on a hill whence they descended to dance a solemn measure, a tremendous affirmation of the aims of Religious Chivalry. At the wedding of such a pair, sing the Priests,[4]

> Each Dance is taken for a prayer,
> Each Song a sacrifice.

If Francis Bacon devised the whole of this entertainment, he must have taken the marriage of Frederick and Elizabeth very seriously and have been profoundly in sympathy with the alliance which it represented. That the author of *The Advancement of Learning*, which had been published eight years previously, in 1605, took time off from his other studies to work for this wedding adds the final touch to the extraordinary galaxy of poetic, artistic, and scientific genius whose united efforts made the Princess Elizabeth's last days in England a blaze of glory.

The bridegroom had still to pay visits to the universities, where he was welcomed by erudite Latin poems, including one by George Herbert.[5] And the air was still thick with congratulatory verses pouring from the press, including some by John Donne,[6] in many of which rejoicing for Elizabeth's wedding was mingled with mourning for her brother's death.

---

[1] *Ibid.*, p. 563.

[2] Francis Beaumont, 'Masque of the Middle Temple and Lincoln's Inn', reprinted in Nichols, pp. 566–90.

[3] *Ibid.*, p. 591.

[4] *Ibid.*, p. 600.

[5] P. O. Kristeller notes in his *Iter Italicum*, II, p. 399, that the Vatican manuscript, Pal. lat. 1738, contains Latin poems addressed to the Elector Palatine on his visit to Cambridge, including one by George Herbert. I am indebted to Professor Kristeller for this reference.

This manuscript would have been amongst the material carried off to Rome with the *Bibliotheca Palatina* after the fall of Heidelberg; see below, p. 28.

[6] See below, p. 139.

'All well-affected people take great pleasure and contentment in this Match', says a contemporary letter-writer, 'as being a firm foundation and stablishing of religion.'[1] That is to say, the wedding and the wedding festivals were seen as a statement of religious policy, a firm indication that Great Britain would support the Elector Palatine as leader against the reactionary Catholic powers now massing in preparation for the end of the truce. Ambassadors from the Dutch states attended the wedding and shows. The French and Venetian ambassadors also came, the latter expressing warm admiration for some of Inigo Jones's effects. Conspicuously absent were the ambassadors of the Hapsburg powers. 'The Spanish (ambassador) was, or would be, sick; and the Archduke's Ambassador being invited for the second day, made a sullen excuse.'[2] It was thought by friends and enemies alike, that this wedding—in accordance with European custom—was a statement of policy, that England was continuing her old Elizabethan role of supporter of the European Protestant powers, that the Elector Palatine was being built up as leader of that policy, with the strong encouragement of his father-in-law.

It was not fully realized at the time that this view of the alliance was not that of James himself. James did not see himself as the continuer of the policies of his mother's executioner. His idea, as he developed it later, was to balance the marriage of his daughter to a German Protestant prince with the marriage of his son, Charles, to a Spanish Catholic princess, and so, at all costs, to avoid war with the Hapsburg powers, his great dread. This side of James was not understood by the Elector Palatine and his advisers who were to rush into dangerous anti-Hapsburg policies under a profound misapprehension.

Elizabeth with her husband and their trains left England on 25 April 1613, when they sailed from Margate for The Hague,[3] there to be warmly welcomed by the Palsgrave's maternal uncle, Maurice of Nassau, the son of William the Silent.

The arrival of a British princess on Dutch soil—a princess actually named Elizabeth—must have awakened memories of deeply ingrained historical, political, and religious patterns of the previous century. William the Silent had longed to build a close alliance with England against Spanish aggression, and to cement it with a marriage. He had installed the French prince, François d'Anjou, as governor of Flanders

[1] Nichols, pp. 601–2.
[2] *Ibid.*, p. 603.
[3] *Ibid.*, p. 611.

7

and Brabant, hoping that Queen Elizabeth would marry this prince, and so he would have a Franco-Anglo alliance in his hand. This plan failed; the Anjou rule collapsed in ignominy; and the Spaniards returned to Antwerp. This was in 1584.[1] Then, in 1586, Robert Earl of Leicester seemed to promise English help, was hailed as a deliverer, and had a triumphal progress through the Provinces, one feature of which was the great Garter Feast which he held in Utrecht,[2] which made Garter symbolism familiar as a symbol of liberation.

Now there arrives from England a princess, wedded to a Garter Knight, and that knight a relative of the Orange-Nassau house, the hereditary ruler of the Palatinate, chief lay Elector of the Empire, and head of the union of German Protestant princes. This seemed an ideal alliance for the Netherlands, as the country anxiously awaited the end of the truce. No expense was spared in the reception given by the towns of the Netherlands to the Princess Elizabeth and the Elector Palatine.[3] They were regaled with costly banquets, given rich presents, and entertained with plays. The Elector left his wife at The Hague to go on into his country to prepare for her reception there.

The Princess followed in due course, floating up the Rhine in an expensive barge. Now began that marriage of the Thames and the Rhine foretold in the wedding masques. And it is possible that Inigo Jones himself, the chief deviser of their wondrous perspective scenes, may have been floating up the Rhine in her train. We know that the Earl of Arundel, art connoisseur and collector and patron of Inigo Jones, accompanied the Princess on her journey to her new country. And we know that Inigo Jones made his second visit to Italy in the train of the Earl of Arundel. The conclusion suggests itself—though there is no document to prove this—that Inigo, as well as his patron, may have travelled in the Princess's party from London to Heidelberg, whence he would have gone on with Arundel into Italy.[4] The formation of a half-English court at Heidelberg involved much coming and

---

[1] On the abortive attempt to establish François d'Anjou in the Netherlands, see Yates, *The Valois Tapestries*, Warburg Institute, 1959.

[2] See R. C. Strong and J. A. Van Dorsten, *Leicester's Triumph*, Leiden and Oxford, 1964.

[3] The reception in the Netherlands, and other events of Elizabeth's journey to Heidelberg, are described in a contemporary illustrated account: *Beschreibung der Reiss . . . des Herrn Frederick des V mit der Hochgebornen Fürstin und Königlichen Princessin Elizabethen, Jacob des Ersten Königs in Gross Britannien Einigen Tochter*, Heidelberg, 1613.

[4] See John Summerson, *Inigo Jones*, London (Penguin), 1966, p. 35. On the other hand, the article on Arundel in the *D.N.B.* maintains that the earl returned to England after the visit to Heidelberg and started out again for Italy later in the year. In that case, it would be very unlikely that Inigo had also accompanied him on the previous trip to Heidelberg.

1   Frederick V, Elector Palatine, and the Princess Elizabeth

2 Arch at Oppenheim,
1613. From *Beschreibung der
Reiss*

3a   Ship of the Argonauts, Pageant Car

3b   Arrival of the Princess Elizabeth at Heidelberg. From *Beschreibung der Reiss*

4a Arch erected by Heidelberg University
4b Arch erected in the courtyard of Heidelberg Castle
Triumphal Arches for the entry of the Princess Elizabeth, Heidelberg, 1613. From *Beschreibung der Reiss*

going between London and the Palatinate, and was opening up a new route for Englishmen into the continent.

The first Palatinate town that Elizabeth entered was Oppenheim, just within the border, where the loyal inhabitants had erected decorations in her honour. These are illustrated in the contemporary printed account of her journey from London to Heidelberg.[1] One of the Oppenheim triumphal arches (Pl. 2) was thickly painted with roses, an allusion, so it was stated, to the descent of Elizabeth from the Houses of York and Lancaster. The royal arms of Great Britain, surrounded by the Garter, are flanked by the Palatinate arms. The streets of Oppenheim were lined with guards in fancy dress costumes, and the citizens welcomed with frantic enthusiasm the royal bride from England.

The engraving of the Oppenheim rose arch is signed 'De Bry', as are other of the engravings in the printed account of the journey. This is the well-known engraver Johann Theodore De Bry who had recently moved his engraving and publishing business from Frankfurt to Oppenheim. During the whole of the reign of Frederick and Elizabeth in the Palatinate, that is from 1613 to 1619, Johann Theodore De Bry poured out a flood of publications from Oppenheim, on very abstruse subjects and notable for the high quality of their engraved illustrations. His son-in-law, Matthieu Merian, assisted with the engraving.

Chief among the works published by De Bry at Oppenheim were the great volumes of Robert Fludd's *Utriusque Cosmi Historia*, profusely illustrated. That this Palatinate town was now so closely connected with England undoubtedly facilitated the publication there of this vast philosophical work by an Englishman. I shall return later to discuss the significance of the publication of Fludd's work at Oppenheim during the reign of Frederick and Elizabeth.[2]

At last, on 7 June 1613, Elizabeth arrived at her capital city of Heidelberg, a scene illustrated in the account of her journey (Pl. 3b). A military review is in progress. Elizabeth, wearing a tall scarlet hat, lace ruff, and farthingale of cloth of gold, has just alighted from her coach. Her husband is hurrying to greet her. The crimson velvet coach in which she will ride into Heidelberg is waiting.

The Faculties of the University of Heidelberg, one of the chief centres of Protestant learning in Europe, had erected arches in her honour. The arch of the theological faculty (Pl. 4a) was decorated

---

[1] The *Beschreibung der Reiss* which gives a full account of the reception at Oppenheim.
[2] See below, pp. 73 ff.

with portraits of the Fathers, and of Luther, Melanchthon, and Beze (curiously enough, no Calvin).

Having passed through the town, the carriages bearing the party made the ascent to the castle of Heidelberg, a vast and romantic edifice impressively situated on a steep eminence overlooking the town and the river Neckar, tributary of the Rhine. In the courtyard of the castle was a triumphal arch, sixty-five feet high (Pl. 4b) covered with statues of former Palatinate rulers and their English wives. At the castle entrance stood the Elector's mother, Louise Juliane of Nassau, daughter of William the Silent, who had long anxiously hoped for this match for her son.

For some days after the arrival, Heidelberg castle was enlivened by tournaments and other festivities. Triumphal chariots containing mythological deities rolled by. In one of these was the Elector Palatine, attired as Jason, and sailing with the Argonauts in the quest of the Golden Fleece (Pl. 3a). This Franco-Burgundian style of mythological festival must have looked, one would think, rather archaic to those fresh from Inigo Jones's productions at the court of James I, and Inigo Jones may himself have been there to make the comparison. Nevertheless the theme of the Jason chariot was in agreement with the themes of the London productions. The allusion to the Elector as Jason was an allusion to the Order of the Golden Fleece, the pendant of which is seen hanging from the tree in the ship. As Elector of the Empire, Frederick was of course a member of this imperial order. And on the mast of the ship can be seen the Garter, alluding to the famous English order to which he belonged as husband of the King of Great Britain's daughter. He had appeared in the London fireworks as St George of the Order of the Garter; here he is Jason of the Order of the Golden Fleece. The role of paladin on some mystic adventure would seem to be one which suited him, or was thought to suit him.

At last all was ended. The English commissioners departed having performed their duty. The Earl and Countess of Arundel left. Lord and Lady Harrington went home to England. Elizabeth's last official connections with her former country were severed. Henceforth she was Electress Palatine of the Rhine, residing in splendour at Heidelberg until the fatal year of destiny, 1619.

No one in the Holy Roman Empire can have failed to know that the chief Elector had married the daughter of the King of Great Britain. Through the dense forests, in the cities, the news travelled, arousing satisfaction in some quarters that here was a great alliance, strengthening the German Protestant cause. In other quarters there would have been less satisfaction, particularly at Graz where the Austrian Hapsburgs kept their stately court.

Heidelberg castle was to become a centre whence strange and exciting influences were to emanate in the years following Elizabeth's arrival there. Her brother, Prince Henry, had been deeply interested in Renaissance garden design, in mechanical fountains which could play musical tunes, in speaking statues and other devices of this kind, the taste for which had been stimulated by the recovery of ancient texts describing such marvels by Hero of Alexandria and his school. In his employment, as his surveyor, was Salomon de Caus, a French Protestant and an extremely brilliant garden-architect, and hydraulic engineer.[1] He was on intimate terms with Inigo Jones, who also worked for Prince Henry. Nourished in the Renaissance revival of Vitruvius, these two men were versed in those accomplishments which Vitruvius recommends as necessary for the true architect to know, the arts and sciences based on number and proportion, music, perspective, painting, mechanics, and the like.[2] Vitruvius had stated that architecture was the queen of the mathematical sciences, and with it had grouped the other arts and sciences. Inigo Jones was concentrating on architecture and on theatrical design as intimately connected with architecture and its subsidiaries, perspective and mechanics.[3] Salomon de Caus concentrated on garden design, which, in the Renaissance, was closely affiliated to architecture, dependent, like the queen of the mathematical sciences, on proportion, perspective, geometry, and employing the newest refinements in mechanics for its decorative singing fountains and other embellishments.

On Prince Henry's death, Salomon de Caus entered the service of the Elector Palatine, and was established at Heidelberg as architect and engineer in charge of the amazing improvements to the castle and grounds, some idea of which can be gained from the engraving in the *Hortus Palatinus* by De Caus, published at Frankfurt in 1620 by Johann Theodore De Bry (Pl. 6a). De Caus had blasted away the rocky

[1] Amongst the published works by Salomon de Caus is *Les raisons des forces mouvantes*, Frankfurt, 1615. Inspired by Vitruvius, there is much important work in this book on mechanics and hydraulics. The dedication to the Princess Elizabeth reminds her of her brother's interest in these subjects. The work was reprinted at Paris in 1624, with an added second book: *Livre Second ou sont desseignees plusieurs Grotes & Fontaines*. It is stated that some of the grottoes, fountains, mechanical statues and so on illustrated in this book were designed for the Elector Palatine's grounds at Heidelberg (see Pls 6b, 25a).

[2] On the 'Vitruvian subjects', see Yates, *Theatre of the World*, London, 1969, pp. 20-59.

[3] See *ibid.*, pp. 80-91.

hillside to form a flat surface on which he developed geometrical garden designs of great complexity (Pl. 5). This marvellous garden, perched above the town and the valley of the Neckar, was talked of as an eighth wonder of the world.[1] The ancient castle, too, had been modernized with new extensions, lightened with many windows, said to have been planned in imitation of English houses or palaces. The vast building seen in the engraving certainly has something of the air of a Teutonic Nonesuch.

De Caus had constructed many grottoes (Pl. 25a) in the gardens, containing scenes enlivened with music from mechanical fountains and formed of mythological figures, Parnassus with the Muses, or Midas in a cave. Very striking was the statue of Memnon (Pl. 6b), a Hercules-Memnon with a club. This statue gave forth sounds when the sun's rays struck it, as in the classical story. The scientific magic by which this effect was achieved is shown in the engraving; it was derivative from the pneumatics of Hero of Alexandria.

Salomon de Caus believed in music as the chief of the sciences based on number, and he was an authority on organs.[2] He is said to have constructed a water-organ at Heidelberg (an ancient water-organ is described by Vitruvius). This, with the sounds from his statues, fountains, and grottoes, must have made Heidelberg as 'full of noises' as Prospero's island.

Inigo Jones, if he came to Heidelberg in the train of the Earl of Arundel, accompanying the Princess Elizabeth, would surely have been interested in the activities there of his former colleague, Salomon de Caus. And indeed, the scenic singing fountain or grotto, the garden group with its musical water-cadences, were but a slightly different application of Vitruvian techniques and sciences from those used by Inigo Jones for his production of masques. If we compare the Heidelberg 'Apollo and the Muses', or the Heidelberg 'Midas' grotto, with scenes designed by Inigo for the masques, it is clear that they are in the same theatrical atmosphere. The Elector Palatine surrounded his wife at Heidelberg with a continuation of the dream world which she had known in London.

Though the production of masques, or of musical grottoes, singing fountains, or pneumatically controlled speaking statues may not seem

[1] See Lili Fehrle-Burger, 'Der Hortus Palatinus als "achtes Weltwunder" ', in *Ruperto-Carola, Mitteilungen der Vereinigung der Freunde der Studentenschaft der Universität Heidelberg*, XIV (2). 1962. I am indebted to R. Strong for this reference.
[2] See Salomon de Caus, *Institution harmonique*, Frankfurt, 1615.

to us important applications of science to technology, it was in fact in such ways as these that Renaissance science, still involved in a magical atmosphere, began to use technical skills on a large scale.[1] De Caus is an important example of the development of science within this tradition; he is said to have invented the use of power from steam, anticipating the nineteenth century. And in his *Les raisons des forces mouvantes*, which was dedicated to the Princess Palatine in 1615 and contains illustrations of works done for Heidelberg, De Caus quotes Vitruvius on machines, illustrates the builders' machine described by Vitruvius, and is applying mathematical principles to mechanics. This core of advanced science in the architect-engineer employed by Frederick for his improvements at Heidelberg shows that the new culture in the Palatinate was abreast of the times, was developing towards the seventeenth century out of the Renaissance in a natural way.

Using the image employed by the poets in the masques, we may think of Jacobean Heidelberg as arising from the marriage of the Thames and the Rhine. Thought movements and cultural movements are passing from England into the Palatinate in the wake of the Princess Elizabeth. Inigo Jones perhaps visits Heidelberg. Salomon de Caus introduces Prince Henry's tastes into its gardens. The Shakespearean pair, Frederick and Elizabeth, continue the London drama of their lives in a new theatrical setting.

And amongst the influences already passing between England and this part of Germany were those of the travelling companies of English players. The presence of a drama-loving couple, familiar with the English dramatic scene, would be an encouragement for travelling English actors. There were English actors at Heidelberg in 1613,[2] who afterwards went on to the Frankfurt Fair, always the haunt of the travelling companies. Knowledge of the English stage and its conditions would be diffused through the presence of Princess Elizabeth, who had had her own company of players in London, and who was passionately addicted to drama in all forms.

There was much coming and going between the Palatinate and England as servants and other emissaries travelled to and from Heidelberg and London. In this way news, or new publications, could have percolated from England into the German state. Francis Bacon had

---

[1] See *Theatre of the World*, pp. 78–9.

[2] E. K. Chambers, *Elizabethan Stage*, II, pp. 288–9. The troupe was headed by John Spencer, an actor who travelled extensively in both Protestant and Catholic Germany.

shown himself very well disposed towards the Princess and her husband in his enthusiastic interest in a production for their wedding. It is probable that they had both read *The Advancement of Learning*. We know that Elizabeth was interested in Bacon's works in later life and read them with delight.[1] She was a woman of quick, though perhaps not profound, intelligence. The Elector was an intellectual and a mystic, and deeply interested in music and architecture. He passed on philosophical tastes to some of his children. His eldest daughter, another Princess Elizabeth, had the honour of having the *Principia* of Descartes dedicated to her.[2]

As we gaze at Matthieu Merian's fascinating engraving of the Heidelberg gardens, we may reflect that here, perched on this hillside in the heart of Germany, was an outpost of Jacobean England, a citadel of advanced seventeenth-century culture. But this most promising new growth, fertilized by the marriage of the Thames and the Rhine, was to have no future. The date, 1620, of the publication of the engraving, is the year of the brief reign of Frederick and Elizabeth in Prague as King and Queen of Bohemia, the year which ended with the events leading to the outbreak of the Thirty Years War which was to devastate the Palatinate and destroy the splendours of Jacobean Heidelberg. The Palatinate was in the front line of the battle and the devastating impact of the reaction can be clearly seen in the fate of Heidelberg.

The fierce propaganda war launched against Frederick of the Palatinate after his defeat used every weapon of ridicule and satire against him. Large numbers of satirical prints were circulated. These consisted of single sheets containing pictures, the meaning of which is explained in doggerel verse. The post boy riding through the countryside sounding his horn (Pl. 7a) is making a mock search for the runaway King of Bohemia. Most of these caricature-prints are much fiercer than this comparatively harmless one, and make sinister insinuations. In one of them, Frederick and his wife and child are shown in an elaborately laid out garden (Pl. 7b). They are given a degraded look and their garden leads to Hell and its flames. These representatives of an exquisite Renaissance culture are being turned by hostile propaganda into witches. It is difficult to recognize in this bitter parody the Frederick and Elizabeth who, in their happier days, had watched the magic of Shakespeare's *Tempest*.

---

[1] See Green, *Elizabeth of Bohemia*, p. 260 n.
[2] See below, p. 117.

CHAPTER II

THE BOHEMIAN TRAGEDY

In 1577 the young Philip Sidney was sent on a mission to the imperial court to convey to the new emperor, Rudolph II, the condolences of Queen Elizabeth on the death of the previous emperor, his father, Maximilian II. It was in the course of this journey that Sidney took occasion to visit German Protestant princes, particularly the Calvinist rulers of the Palatinate, in order to explore the possibility of a Protestant League in Europe. Sidney had already developed his political and religious position, based on that of his uncle, the Earl of Leicester. He believed in a policy of Protestant 'activism' against Spain, a policy more daring than Queen Elizabeth's caution was prepared to sanction. And he found a kindred spirit at Heidelberg in the person of John Casimir, brother of the then Elector Palatine. Sidney reported to Walsingham that the Protestant princes of Germany were in general lukewarm about a Protestant League, the only keen ones being Casimir of the Palatinate and the Landgrave William of Hesse.[1]

After his early death, Philip Sidney became a legend as the *beau idéal* of Protestant chivalry. With him, too, were associated the romantic trappings of revived chivalry, the fantastic cult of Queen Elizabeth by her knights at the Accession Day Tilts. That Casimir of the Palatinate had been his close friend was a link between the court of Heidelberg and the Sidney tradition in England, and one which facilitated the build up of the young Elector Palatine as a paladin of Anglo-German Protestant chivalry.

The 'activist' tradition of the Palatinate[2] had been continued when active support had been offered to Henry IV of France in his plans for an invasion of Germany, those plans which were cut short by his

[1] Sidney's visit to the Palatinate is recounted by Fulke Greville who accompanied him; see F. Greville, *The Life of the Renowned Sir Philip Sidney*, ed. N. Smith, Oxford, 1907, pp. 41 ff. Cf. R. Howell, *Sir Philip Sidney The Shepherd Knight*, London, 1968, pp. 34–5; J. O. Osborn, *Young Philip Sidney*, Yale Univ. Press, 1972, pp. 450 ff.

[2] See Claus-Peter Clasen, *The Palatinate in European History*, Oxford, 1963.

assassination in 1610. This Palatinate support of the French king was a continuation of earlier Franco-Palatinate understanding in the time of Casimir, who had supported Henry, then Henry of Navarre, in his struggles as leader of the Huguenots.

Very important as the master mind behind Palatinate policy was Christian of Anhalt,[1] the chief adviser to the Heidelberg court, who had been eager to aid Henry IV in plans which were said to involve a large scale attempt to end Hapsburg power in Europe. When Henry's projects were interrupted by his death, the Palatinate policy, still inspired largely by Anhalt, turned to other means for the pursuit of these large aims.

It was then that the young Elector Palatine, Frederick V, began to be seen as destined to step into the vacant place of leader of Protestant resistance against the Hapsburg powers. There was much to mark him out for this position. He had inherited the rank of chief of the lay electors of the Empire. He had inherited a tradition of Protestant activism which indicated him as the natural leader and head of the Union of German Protestant Princes, formed to counteract the League of Catholic Princes. He had powerful connections with French Protestants, his uncle being the Huguenot leader, the Duc de Bouillon. With the Netherlands, the bulwark of Protestant leadership in Europe, he was closely connected by family ties. Finally—and it was this which put the crowning touch to the edifice of Frederick's position— he had married the daughter of the King of Great Britain, thus ensuring, so his supporters believed, that James I could be counted on to assist his daughter and son-in-law. It looked like an ideal set of alliances behind the young Elector Palatine, marking him out as destined to play a most important part in shaping the destiny of Europe in the critical years ahead.

In those years ahead, very much would depend on the person of the Emperor of Germany, and on whether the Hapsburgs could retain control of the imperial office.

In the tense atmosphere of Europe between the wars (between the sixteenth-century wars of religion and the Thirty Years War) the death of the Emperor Rudolph II in 1612 had marked a moment of crisis. Though a member of the House of Hapsburg, Rudolph had

---

[1] On Anhalt, see Clasen in the work just cited; Julius Krebs, *Christian von Anhalt und die Kurpfalsische Politik am beginn des Dreissigjährigen Krieges*, Leipzig, 1872; *Cambridge Modern History*, IV, Cambridge, 1906, pp. 3 ff.; David Ogg, *Europe in the Seventeenth Century*, ed. of London, 1943, pp. 126 ff.

held aloof from his nephew Philip II of Spain and had mysteriously buried himself in abstruse studies.[1] He moved the imperial court from Vienna to Prague, which became a centre for alchemical, astrological, magico-scientific studies of all kinds. Hiding himself in his great palace at Prague, with its libraries, its 'wonder rooms' of magico-mechanical marvels, Rudolph withdrew in alarm from the problems raised by the fanatical intolerance of his frightening nephew. Prague became a Mecca for those interested in esoteric and scientific studies from all over Europe. Hither came John Dee and Edward Kelly, Giordano Bruno and Johannes Kepler. However strange the reputation of Prague in the time of Rudolph it was yet a relatively tolerant city. Jews might pursue their cabalistic studies undisturbed (Rudolph's favourite religious adviser was Pistorius, a Cabalist) and the native church of Bohemia was tolerated by an official 'Letter of Majesty'. The Bohemian church, founded by John Huss, was the first of the reformed churches of Europe. Rudolph's toleration was extended to the Bohemian church and to the Bohemian Brethren, a mystical brotherhood attached to its teachings.

Prague under Rudolph was a Renaissance city, full of Renaissance influences as they had developed in Eastern Europe, a melting pot of ideas, mysteriously exciting in its potentiality for new developments. But for how long would this relative immunity from the forces of reaction continue after Rudolph was dead? The problem was postponed for a short time by the election to the Empire and to the crown of Bohemia of Rudolph's brother, Matthias, an old man and a nonentity, who soon died also, and then the problem could no longer be postponed. The forces of reaction were gathering; only a few years of the truce in the religious wars were left to run. The most likely next candidate for the imperial and Bohemian thrones was the fanatical Catholic-Hapsburg Archduke Ferdinand of Styria, a pupil of the Jesuits, determined to stamp out heresy.

In 1617 Ferdinand of Styria became King of Bohemia.[2] True to his training and nature, Ferdinand immediately put an end to Rudolph's policy of religious toleration by revoking the Letter of Majesty and beginning to set about the suppression of the Bohemian church. Some people have said that the true beginning of the Thirty Years War lay in the beginning of the application of intolerant policies in Bohemia.

[1] There is as yet no good book on Rudolph II.
[2] For a lucid account of events in Bohemia see C. V. Wedgwood, *The Thirty Years War*, paperback edition, 1968, pp. 69 ff.

An honourable attempt to stop this disastrous move was made by the Bohemian liberal Catholics. But Ferdinand and his Jesuit advisers could not be stopped and the attacks on the Bohemian church and clergy continued. Violent opposition was aroused and at a stormy meeting in Prague two Catholic leaders were thrown out of a window, the incident known as the Defenestration of Prague, another step in the train of events leading to the Thirty Years War. Bohemia was now in a state of open rebellion against its Hapsburg sovereign. According to the rebels the crown of Bohemia was an elective crown, to be offered to whomever they elected, and not hereditary in the House of Hapsburg as Ferdinand and his supporters claimed.

On 26 August 1619 the Bohemians decided to offer the crown of their country to Frederick, Elector Palatine.

The possibility that Frederick might become King of Bohemia had been in the air for some time; it is said that it was already talked of at the time of his wedding.[1] Anhalt had been eagerly canvassing it, and pushing Frederick's cause in Bohemia, for this move constituted a most important part of the anti-Hapsburg edifice which Anhalt was building up around Frederick.

According to the peculiar and elaborate rules of the imperial constitution, the King of Bohemia held one vote in the election of an emperor. Since Frederick was already an elector, if he became King of Bohemia, he would hold two votes in an imperial election, which might build up a majority against Hapsburg supporters and open a way towards breaking the Hapsburg control. It was along such lines that Anhalt and his friends were thinking and they may even have entertained the idea of eventually gaining the imperial office for Frederick himself. Such vistas of religious policy would lead in idealistic thinking to those hopes of a reform of the church through the empire which had been a European dream ever since the time of Dante.

The decision which Frederick had to make, of whether or not he would accept the proffered crown of Bohemia, was thus both a practical and a religious dilemma. Practical, because to accept it was dangerous; it would amount to a declaration of war against the Hapsburg powers. But then, had he not very powerful alliances? It was mainly because of those alliances—with German and French Protestants, with the Dutch, with the King of Great Britain whose daughter he had married—that the Bohemians had chosen him. Religious, because to refuse to walk in this way which God was show-

[1] *Cambridge Modern History*, IV, p. 17.

ing him might be a refusal to do the will of God. There is every reason to believe that it was the last consideration which weighed most with Frederick.

Some of those who saw Frederick at Heidelberg at about this time were impressed by his attitude. An English ambassador, writing to James from Heidelberg in June 1619, thinks that Frederick 'is much beyond his years religious, wise, active, and valiant', and his wife is still 'that same devoute, good, sweet, princess . . . obliging all hearts that come near her by her courtesy, and so dearly loving and beloved of the Prince her husband, that it is a joy to all that behold them'.[1] The Shakespearean pair are revealed here, for a moment. John Donne, the poet, who had preached before them at Heidelberg, as chaplain to the ambassador, accepted a small commission to be performed on their behalf, expressing himself with characteristic ecstasy. 'Yt ys so generall a business [the business about the Bohemian crown] that even so low and poore a man as I have a part in yt, and an office to do for yt, which is to promove yt with the same prayers as I present for myne own soule to the ears of Almighty God.'[2] Amongst those who proffered advice as to whether the Bohemian offer should be accepted, George Abbot, Archbishop of Canterbury, was warmly in favour of acceptance. Years afterwards, Elizabeth used to show visitors to The Hague the letter which the Archbishop of Canterbury had written advising the acceptance of the Bohemian crown as a religious duty.[3]

Others gave more cautious advice. The Union of Protestant Princes were on the whole against acceptance as too dangerous. And the Elector's mother implored him not to accept; the daughter of William the Silent knew too well the nature of the powers which her son was challenging.

On 28 September 1619 Frederick wrote to the Bohemian rebels that he would accept the crown. As C. V. Wedgwood has said, 'Whatever the suspicions of the world there is little doubt that Frederick expressed the sum of his intentions when he wrote to his uncle, the Duke of Bouillon, "It is a divine calling which I must not disobey . . . my only end is to serve God and His Church".'[4]

---

[1] Lord Doncaster to James I, June 1619, in S. R. Gardiner, *Letters and other Documents Illustrating Relations between England and Germany at the Commencement of the Thirty Years War*, Camden Society, 1865, I, p. 118.

[2] John Donne to Sir Dudley Carleton, August 1619; see Gardiner, II, p. 6.

[3] Green, *Elizabeth Electress Palatine*, p. 185.

[4] Wedgwood, *Thirty Years War*, p. 98.

But already the wider issues of the Bohemian adventure had been thrown into disarray. Ferdinand had been elected emperor at a meeting at Frankfurt in August. The Bohemian crown would not lead to the empire which was already given to the Hapsburg, Ferdinand, and Frederick was in the awkward position of having to put aside his duty to an emperor by supporting the rebels—ignoring a feudal obligation for what he regarded as a religious one. He chose to act on the religious issue, but many contemporaries would have thought his action legally wrong.

On 27 September Frederick and Elizabeth and their eldest son, Prince Henry, set out from Heidelberg on the journey to Prague. An enthusiastic observer tells in what a humble and pious spirit they began the journey, the young prince's bearing raising hopes that the dead Prince Henry would be revived in him, whilst Elizabeth is devoutly hailed as 'another Queen Elizabeth, for so now she is, and what more she may be in time, or her royal issue, is in God's hands to dispose to his glory and the good of his church.'[1] In England enthusiasm knew no bounds. 'With what great and general love' writes a contemporary. 'Britain burned towards Frederick and Elizabeth I can scarcely describe.'[2] It seemed as though the 'only Phoenix of the world', the old Queen Elizabeth, was returning and that some great new dispensation was at hand.

They had travelled through the Upper Palatinate to the Bohemian border (see Map, p. 26), where a deputation of Bohemian nobles awaited them, then on through their new kingdom to its wonderful capital. The coronation ceremony in Prague cathedral was conducted by the Hussite clergy. It was the last great public ceremony to be sponsored by the Bohemian church, soon to be completely suppressed.

On the day of the coronation a commemorative print was published (Pl. 8). It shows Frederick and Elizabeth as crowned king and queen of Bohemia. In the background, Reformers and peace have triumphed over Counter-Reformers and war. Four lions represent the alliances on which the new king and queen of Bohemia can count. The lion was Frederick's own heraldic animal, and the lion on the left is the lion of the Palatinate, holding an electoral crown. Then come the double-tailed lion of Bohemia, the British lion with his sword, and the lion of the Netherlands. German verses under the print explain these allusions.

[1] John Harrison, *A short relation of the departure*, London, 1619; quoted Green, p. 133.
[2] Harrison; quoted Green, *loc. cit.*

They were to be sung to a psalm tune and they begin (translated into English) as follows:[1]

> Good cheer, and let us be joyful,
> The red dawn of the morn is breaking,
> The sun can now be seen.
> God turns his face towards us,
> Honours us with a king
> The enemy cannot withstand.

Sunlike rays from the Divine Name, in Hebrew, are indeed falling on Frederick and Elizabeth, and this is the red dawn of a new morning. The verses lay particular stress on how this dawn depends on the new Queen. Wyclif came from England, they explain, from whom Huss took his teaching, alluding to Wyclif's influence on the Hussite reformation; and now a queen comes to us from England.[2]

> Jacobus, her lord father dear,
> Through her has become
> Our mightiest patron and support:
> He will not desert us,
> Otherwise we would suffer great distress.

Here we reach the heart of this great tragedy of misunderstanding. For James was not supporting his daughter and her husband; he was working for the other side in his frantic cult of Spanish friendship; he was even now, when this print was published, disowning all responsibility for his son-in-law's Bohemian enterprise to every court in Europe.[3] Not only had no military or naval preparations been made in Britain for the support of this enterprise, but James's diplomacy was working against it, disowning it, counteracting it, making every effort to curry favour with the Hapsburg powers. James's attitude, of course, immeasurably weakened Frederick's position and caused his other friends to doubt him. It had been assumed that James would be bound to support his daughter when the times of trial came. She was the hostage ensuring her father's good will. But when the time came

---

[1] Quoted as translated by E. A. Beller, *Caricatures of the 'Winter King' of Bohemia*, Oxford, 1928, plate I.

[2] Beller, *Caricatures, loc. cit.*

[3] 'The King of England celebrated his son-in-law's accession by officially denying to every sovereign in Europe that he had countenanced or even known of the project.' Wedgwood, p. 108.

it was revealed that James was perfectly willing to desert his daughter rather than risk incurring the Hapsburg anger.

The whole question is extremely complicated, and the rights and wrongs of it are complicated. James stood for peace at all costs; he had wanted to achieve this by marrying his children to opposite sides in the great conflict. Frederick and his supporters had interpreted the marriage as full support for their side. Many of James's subjects also interpreted it in this way and welcomed it with enthusiasm as a continuation of Elizabethan tradition. But even Queen Elizabeth might not have entirely approved of Frederick; she had carefully avoided doing what he did, namely taking sovereignty of a country claimed by another power. She had firmly refused to take the sovereignty of the Netherlands, though she supported its cause.

However, for the purposes of this study it is not necessary to argue these points nor to examine the complications of these events in detail. We need only the broad outline of what actually happened, and the general statement of the fact that James pursued a policy of appeasement of the Hapsburg powers whilst Frederick and his supporters hoped against hope that he would be actively on their side. The truth probably is that Frederick's chief crime was that he *failed*. If he had succeeded in establishing himself in Bohemia, all the waverers, including his father-in-law, would probably have wavered over to him.

The personage who should have been the informed arbiter of these affairs, the personage to whom liberal Europe was looking for guidance —James I of Great Britain—appears to have been rapidly falling into a state of senile incompetence and decay, incapable of taking decisions, avoiding serious business, at the mercy of unscrupulous favourites, despised and hoodwinked by Spanish agents.[1] So Europe rushed on, unguided and confused, into the Thirty Years War.

During the winter of 1619–20 those who were afterwards to be known as the 'Winter King and Queen of Bohemia' reigned in Prague, in that palace so full of memories of Rudolph II. Not very much seems to be known of what went on in Prague during the reign of this fantastic pair, and, as so often in history, the blank is filled by a few hoary anecdotes, repeated from historian to historian. Things that one would like to know are what were Frederick's reactions to the Rudolphine artistic and scientific collections, what the

[1] See the account of James's physical and mental decay from 1616 onwards in D. H. Wilson, *King James VI and I*, London, 1956, pp. 378 ff.

Prague Cabalists and alchemists thought of him, what plays were acted by the company of English players, under Robert Browne, who are said to have spent the winter in Prague,[1] what were the proposed reforms which an enemy satire accused him of having encouraged.[2] It would seem that the rabidly Calvinist court chaplain, Abraham Scultetus, created much annoyance by tactlessly destroying some images beloved by the people, and that the life style of Frederick and Elizabeth was unfamiliar and not entirely approved. Dresses which would have been fashionable at the court of James I seemed immodest in Prague.

As the year wore on the situation grew very menacing. Frederick's enemies were massing to expel him; his more important allies, the German Protestant princes, were not coming to his assistance. Anhalt was in command of Frederick's forces; the Duke of Bavaria commanded the Catholic armies. Frederick's forces were totally defeated at the Battle of the White Mountain, outside Prague, on 8 November 1620. This victory riveted the Hapsburg domination on Europe for another generation and initiated the Thirty Years War, which eventually whittled away the Hapsburg power.

The Battle of the White Mountain was thus a crucial event in European history. The defeat was total. Prague was in utter confusion, dreading the revenge which would fall on it, and frantic to get rid of the incriminating presence of Frederick. Elizabeth had given birth to another child in Prague (famous in the English civil wars as Prince Rupert of the Rhine), and Frederick with his wife and children escaped in such a hurry from Prague that most of their effects were left behind. Amongst the abandoned valuables which fell into the hands of the enemy were the insignia of the Order of the Garter.[3] The propaganda pamphlets against Frederick which were afterwards distributed by his enemies delighted to show him as a poor fugitive with one of his stockings coming down (Pl. 9)—an allusion to his loss of a Garter.[4] These satires rubbed in the fact that the support of his wife's father for the Garter knight had not been forthcoming, that his whole enterprise had been a most disastrous failure, ending in

---

[1] Chambers, *Elizabethan Stage*, II, p. 285. Browne was the leading organizer of English actors abroad, and constantly visited Germany. He was by now an old man and 1620 seems to be the last year of his appearance. The presence of Browne and his troupe in Prague in 1620 is not well documented.

[2] See below, p. 57.

[3] Wedgwood, p. 130.

[4] For other satirical prints on the 'Garterless' theme, see Beller, *Caricatures*.

this appallingly ignominious way in flight and the loss of all his possessions.

Meanwhile, the Palatinate had been invaded by Spanish armies under Spinola. On 5 September Spinola had crossed the Rhine; on the 14th, he took Oppenheim; other towns had already fallen. Frederick's mother and his two elder children who had been left in Heidelberg fled to relations in Berlin. Eventually, the whole family was reunited at The Hague where they were to hold their impoverished and exiled court for many years.

In Bohemia, mass executions or 'purges' exterminated all resistance. The Bohemian church was totally suppressed and the whole country reduced to misery. The Palatinate was devastated and was to suffer more than any other part of Germany in the terrible Thirty Years War.

Frederick, Elector Palatine, had turned out to be a mirage. No one knows, of course, what might have happened if he had won the Battle of the White Mountain. But as a failed deliverer of Bohemia and a failed candidate for a new anti-Hapsburg leadership in Europe, once he had lost that battle he was finished. The waverers wavered away from him. The German Protestant princes lifted not a finger to help him, only watching the devastation of the Palatinate with fascinated fear. And the famous King of England turned a deaf ear to all appeals from his daughter, his son-in-law, and their many enthusiastic friends in England.

Historians have noted the effect on the internal history of England of the extraordinary Bohemian enterprise and its failure. They have seen that James I, conducting his foreign policy by 'divine right' and without consulting Parliament, which was unanimously in favour of supporting the King of Bohemia, was beginning a train of events which would eventually destroy the Stuart Monarchy. It was not only the internal government of the country without consulting Parliament which aroused anger; it was the pursuit of a foreign policy against the wishes of Parliament, or without consulting Parliament, which also aroused deep anger, and that not only among members of Parliament but among the people generally, of all classes. Great noblemen like William Herbert, Earl of Pembroke, practically apologized, with shame, to Frederick's representative about the King's abandonment of what he considered his duty.[1] The people, eager to ring bells and light bonfires in honour of their beloved Elizabeth, were not allowed to do so. The

---

[1] Pembroke to Carleton, September 1619. Much first-hand evidence of the feeling in England in favour of assisting the King of Bohemia is quoted in Gardiner, *Letters*.

5 Heidelberg Castle and
Gardens, engraved by Matthieu
Merian.
From Salomon de Caus, *Hortus
Palatinus*

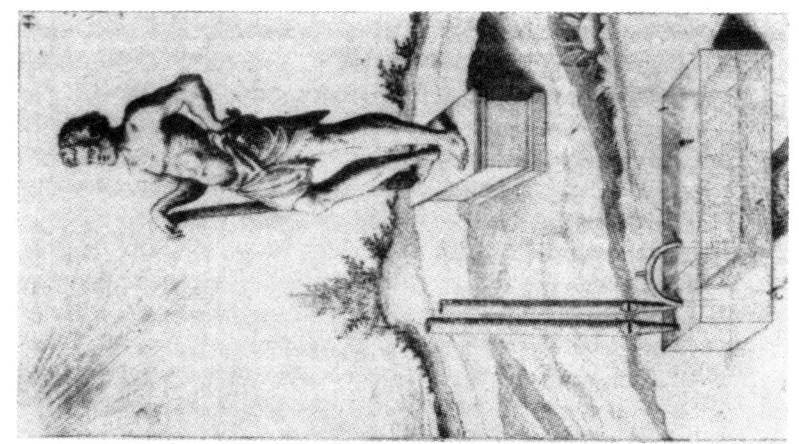

6a Salomon de Caus, *Hortus Palatinus*
6b Statue of Memnon. From Salomon de Caus, *Les raisons des forces mouvantes*

7a   The Post Boy looking for a Missing King

7b   Frederick and Elizabeth in an Infernal Garden

8 Frederick and Elizabeth as King and Queen of Bohemia, with Four Lions

split between the Monarchy on the one hand and the Parliament and nation on the other which was beginning to open was widened by James's unpopular foreign policy.

While readers of history are fairly familiar with this aspect of the Bohemian tragedy it would seem that not much, if any, enquiry has been made into what may have been the effect in Europe of the hopes raised by the supposed alliance of the King of England with the Elector Palatine. In those years of uneasy peace between the wars of religion the Elector Palatine had stood for something more than the traditional Calvinism of his house. He had transported the splendours of the Jacobean Renaissance into Germany through his marriage, and that great Renaissance movement had met and mingled with other powerful movements going on in the area to form a rich new culture which, although of such short duration, was, I believe, a very important element in the movement from Renaissance to Enlightenment. Here the forces of Renaissance met Reaction with a terrific, head-on impact. They are lost and disappear from view in the horrors of the Thirty Years War, but when, at last, those wars are ended, the Enlightenment arrives. The attempt to unravel thought movements in the Palatinate during the reign of Frederick and Elizabeth—the attempt which we are about to make—may help to throw light on one of the most important problems of intellectual and cultural history, the problem of trying to identify the stages by which Renaissance evolved into Enlightenment.

Though the Palatinate was a Calvinist state, the thought movements within the Palatinate with which we are to be concerned have little, indeed nothing, to do with Calvinist theology. These movements are a remarkable example of the trend to which H. Trevor-Roper has drawn attention,[1] namely that activist Calvinism attracted liberal thinkers of many different types—attracted because activist Calvinism represented a stand against the extreme forces of reaction, a guarantee that within its sphere of influence the writ of the Inquisition would not run. As a preparation for the chapters to come it will be useful to dwell for a moment, at the end of this chapter, on the map showing the position of the Palatinate in relation to neighbouring states.

In Venice, Paolo Sarpi had recently been making a stand against papal encroachment, and the liberal Venetian movement had been watched with extreme interest in England. Henry Wotton, the enthusiastic English ambassador to Venice, had even hoped to convert the

---

[1] H. Trevor-Roper, *Religion, the Reformation and Social Change*, London, 1967, pp. 204 ff.

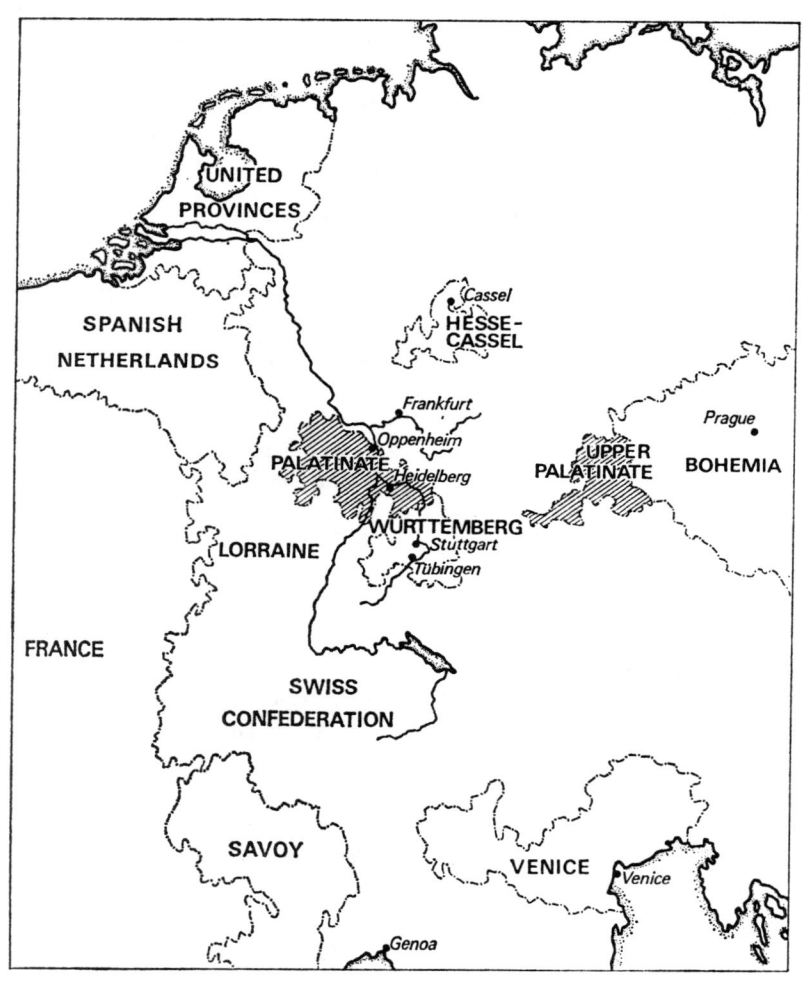

Map showing the position of the Palatinate in the early seventeenth century

Venetians to a kind of Anglicanism.[1] The excitements of the Interdict were a thing of the past by 1613 but Venice watched with interest Frederick's affairs; Anhalt was in touch with Sarpi;[2] Wotton called at Heidelberg on his journeys to and from Venice. Had Frederick succeeded in keeping open a liberal corridor from Holland to Venice through Germany, the advance of thought repression in Italy, from which Galileo was to suffer, might have been checked.

With Holland, the Elector's links were obviously very close. There were many Dutch scholars at Heidelberg, notably the famous Janus Gruter, humanist and poet, the centre of a very large circle of international correspondence.[3] Gruter was a professor at Heidelberg university, and also the librarian of the famous *Bibliotheca Palatina*, the very rich library of books and manuscripts collected by the Elector's forebears, and which was housed in the Church of the Holy Ghost in Heidelberg.

Closest to him of all Frederick's neighbours was the Duchy of Württemberg which adjoined his territory on the south. The religion here was Lutheran but there was much interest in attempting to unite Lutherans and Calvinists. Frederick of Württemberg, who had died in 1610, had been intensely Anglophil, had visited Elizabethan England, and in 1604 had obtained from James I the honour of the Garter, which Queen Elizabeth had promised him, and which was conferred on him by special embassy.[4] Lutheran and Anglophil, Württemberg was the centre of interesting thought movements going on around Johann Valentin Andreae, Lutheran pastor and mystic. The present Duke was very closely in touch with the Elector Palatine. Another close friend among the German Protestant princes was Maurice, Landgrave of Hesse, a cultivated man, great encourager of the travelling companies of English actors.

Above all, it was from Prague that powerful influences had been spreading to this part of Germany. The alchemical and esoteric interests encouraged by Rudolph II had represented a more liberal, Renaissance atmosphere than that which the Reaction wished to impose, and such studies were popular at German courts, particularly those of Hesse and Württemberg. And the traditions of Rudolphine

[1] See my article, 'Paolo Sarpi's *History of the Council of Trent*', *Journal of the Warburg and Courtauld Institutes*, VII (1944), pp. 123–43.

[2] Paolo Sarpi, *Lettere ai Protestanti*, ed. C. Busnelli, 1931.

[3] On Gruter, see Leonard Forster, *Janus Gruter's English Years*, Sir T. Browne Institute, Leiden, 1967.

[4] See below, pp. 31 ff.

Prague were certainly familiar to Christian of Anhalt, the leader of Palatinate policy. Anhalt had been familiar with Count Rožmberk,[1] member of a Bohemian family noted for occult and alchemical interests. That Anhalt shared such interests is strongly suggested by the fact that Oswald Croll, Hermeticist, Cabalist, and Paracelsan alchemist, was his physician.

Into this world, seething with strange excitements, came the Princess Elizabeth, bringing with her influences from the late Renaissance flowering in Jacobean London, and representing a hope of powerful support against the forces of reaction. Heidelberg castle with its magico-scientific marvels, Heidelberg university, centre of Protestant learning, became the symbols of a resistance movement during the years between the wars. Here, for those brief years, people were hoping for a dawn to break, an enlightenment to appear, heralding a new era.

Instead there came unmitigated disaster, with Frederick's total failure in Bohemia and the enemy occupation and devastation of the Palatinate. Eyewitnesses have described the confiscation of the electoral library by the invaders and the destruction of Gruter's papers.[2] A lifetime's collection of books and manuscripts was thrown out into the street and yard where thirty horses were stabled, and were irrevocably fouled and destroyed. This happened to other private libraries in Heidelberg, whilst the great *Bibliotheca Palatina* itself was carried off to Rome,[3] and many of Gruter's own books with it. I have found no description of what happened to the water-organs and singing fountains and other marvels of the castle. Salomon de Caus who had been left in Heidelberg, whence he wrote to the King of Bohemia in 1620 about a musical problem, eventually found new employment at the French court. Gruter wandered unhappily in the neighbourhood of Heidelberg and died in a few years' time. A whole world vanished here, its monuments defaced or destroyed, its books and written records vanished, its population turned into refugees—those who could escape—or were destined to die by violence, plague, or famine in the terrible years to come.

It is this failed Renaissance, or premature Enlightenment, or misunderstood Rosicrucian Dawn, which we are now about to explore. What was the stimulus which had set in motion the movement

---

[1] Peter Wok of Rožmberk; see below, pp. 36–7.

[2] Forster, *Gruter*, pp. 96–100.

[3] H. Trevor-Roper, *The Plunder of the Arts in the Seventeenth Century*, London, 1970, pp. 22–7.

leading to the so-called 'Rosicrucian manifestos' with their strange announcements of the dawn of a new age of knowledge and insight? It is within the sphere of influence of the movements around Frederick of the Palatinate and his bid for the Bohemian crown that one should look for an answer to this question.

CHAPTER III

JOHN DEE AND THE RISE OF 'CHRISTIAN ROSENCREUTZ'

The word 'Rosicrucian' is derived from the name 'Christian Rosen-creutz' or 'Rose Cross'. The so-called 'Rosicrucian manifestos' are two short pamphlets or tracts, first published at Cassel in 1614 and 1615, the long titles of which can be abbreviated as the *Fama* and the *Confessio*.[1] The hero of the manifestos is a certain 'Father C.R.C.' or 'Christian Rosencreutz' who is said to have been the founder of an Order or Fraternity, now revived, and which the manifestos invite others to join. These manifestos aroused immense excitement, and a third publication, in 1616, increased the mystery. This was a strange alchemical romance, the German title of which translates as *The Chemical Wedding of Christian Rosencreutz*. The hero of *The Chemical Wedding* seems also connected with some Order which uses a red cross and red roses as symbols.

The author of *The Chemical Wedding* was certainly Johann Valentin Andreae. The manifestos are undoubtedly related to *The Chemical Wedding*, though they are probably not by Andreae but by some other person or persons unknown.

Who was this 'Christian Rose Cross' who first appears in these publications? Endless are the mystifications and legends which have been woven around this character and his Order. We are going to try to cut a way through to him by quite a new path. But let us begin this chapter with the easier question, 'Who was Johann Valentin Andreae?'

Johann Valentin Andreae, born in 1586, was a native of Württemberg, the Lutheran state which closely adjoined the Palatinate. His grand-father was a distinguished Lutheran theologian sometimes called 'the Luther of Württemberg'. Intense interest in the contemporary religious situation was the main inspiration of his grandson, Johann Valentin, who also became a Lutheran pastor, but with a liberal interest in

[1] For the full titles, see Appendix, below, p. 236.

Calvinism. In spite of endless disasters, Johann Valentin was supported all his life by hopes of some far-reaching solution of the religious situation. All his activities, whether as a devout Lutheran pastor with socialist interests, or as the propagator of 'Rosicrucian' fantasies, were directed towards such a hope. Andreae was a writer of promise, whose imagination was influenced by the travelling English players. Concerning his early life and the influences on him we have authentic information, since he wrote an auto-biography.[1]

From this we learn that in 1601, when he was fifteen, his widowed mother took him to Tübingen so that he might pursue his studies at that famous university of Württemberg. Whilst a student at Tübingen, so he tells us, he made his first juvenile efforts as an author, in about the years 1602 and 1603. These efforts included two comedies on the themes of 'Esther' and 'Hyacinth', which he states that he wrote 'in emulation of the English actors', and a work called *Chemical Wedding*, which he describes deprecatingly as a *ludibrium*, or a fiction, or a jest, of little worth.[2]

Judging by the *Chemical Wedding* by Andreae which is extant, the work published in 1616 with Christian Rosencreutz as its hero, this early version of the subject would have been a work of alchemical symbolism, using the marriage theme as a symbol of alchemical processes. It cannot have been identical with the published *Chemical Wedding* of 1616 which contains references to the Rosicrucian manifestos of 1614 and 1615, to the Elector Palatine and his court at Heidelberg, to his wedding to the daughter of James I. The early version of the *Chemical Wedding*, which is not extant, must have been brought up to date for the publication of 1616. Nevertheless, the lost early version may have provided the core of the work.

We can make a very good guess as to what were the influences and events at Tübingen when Andreae was a student there which inspired these early works.

The reigning Duke of Württemberg was Frederick I, alchemist, occultist, and enthusiastic Anglophil, the ruling passion of whose life had been to establish an alliance with Queen Elizabeth and to obtain the Order of the Garter. He had several times visited England with these

---

[1] Johann Valentin Andreae, *Vita ab ipso conscripta*, ed. F. H. Rheinwald, Berlin, 1849. The first publication of the manuscript of this work was an edition at Winterthur in 1799.

[2] Andreae, *Vita*, p. 10. Andreae's statement that he wrote plays in imitation of the English players is noted by E. K. Chambers, *Elizabethan Stage*, I, p. 344 n.

aims in view and seems to have been a conspicuous figure.[1] The Queen called him 'cousin Mumpellgart', which was his family name, and much discussion has centred round the problem of whether the cryptic references in Shakespeare's *Merry Wives of Windsor* to 'cosen garmombles' and to horses hired at the Garter Inn by retainers of a German duke, might have some reference to Frederick of Württemberg.[2] The Queen allowed his election to the Order of the Garter in 1597 but the actual ceremony of his investiture did not take place until November, 1603, when the Garter was conferred on him in his own capital city of Stuttgart by a special embassy from James I.

Thus James by this act in the very first year of his reign made a gesture towards continuing the Elizabethan alliance with the German Protestant powers, though in after years he was to deny the hopes thus raised. But in Württemberg in 1603 the reign of the new ruler of England seemed opening most auspiciously for German hopes and there was an outpouring of enthusiasm around the embassy come to confer the Garter on the Duke, and on the English actors who accompanied the embassy.

The Garter ceremony at Stuttgart and the festivities which accompanied it are described by E. Cellius in a Latin account published at Stuttgart in 1605, part of which is quoted in English translation by Elias Ashmole in his history of the Order of the Garter.[3]

The processions in which the English Garter officials, bearing the insignia of the Order, took solemn part with the German dignitaries, made a brilliant impression. The Duke's appearance was most splendid, so covered with jewels that they cast forth 'a radiant mixture of divers colours'.[4] One of the English Garter officials was Robert Spenser, who is stated by Cellius to have been a relative of the poet.[5] The interesting point of this remark is that they had heard of Spenser, and perhaps of his *Faerie Queene*, at Stuttgart.

Thus magnificently clad, the Duke entered the church where, to the sound of solemn music, he was invested with the Order. After a sermon,

---

[1] On Frederick of Württemberg and England, see W. B. Rye, *England as seen by Foreigners*, London, 1865, pp. I ff.; Victor von Klarwill, *Queen Elizabeth and Some Foreigners*, London, 1928, pp. 347 ff.

[2] See the introduction by H. C. Hart to *The Merry Wives of Windsor*, Arden edition, 1904, pp. xli–xlvi.

[3] Erhardus Cellius, *Eques auratus Anglo–Wirtembergicus*, Tübingen, 1606; Elias Ashmole *The Institution, Laws and Ceremonies of the most noble Order of the Garter*, London, 1672.

[4] Ashmole, *Garter*, p. 412.

[5] Cellius, *Eques auratus*, p. 119. This point is not included in Ashmole's abbreviated translation from Cellius.

9a   Frederick as a Garterless Pilgrim

9b   The Garterless Frederick doing Menial Tasks

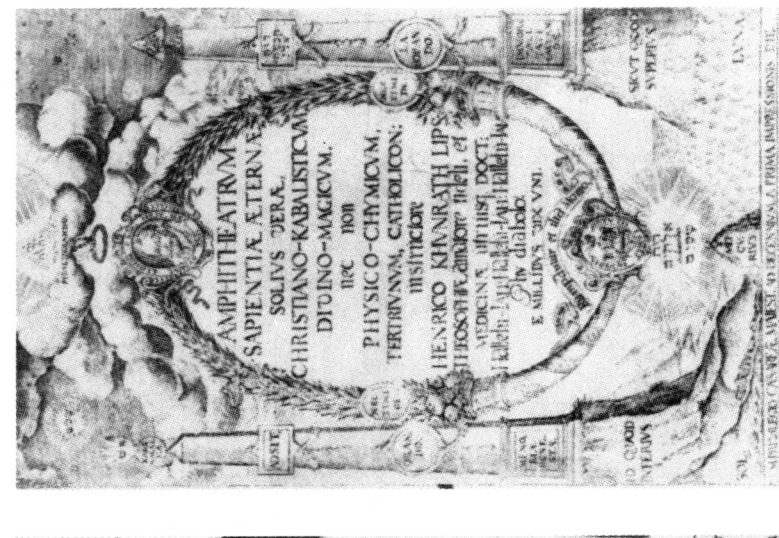

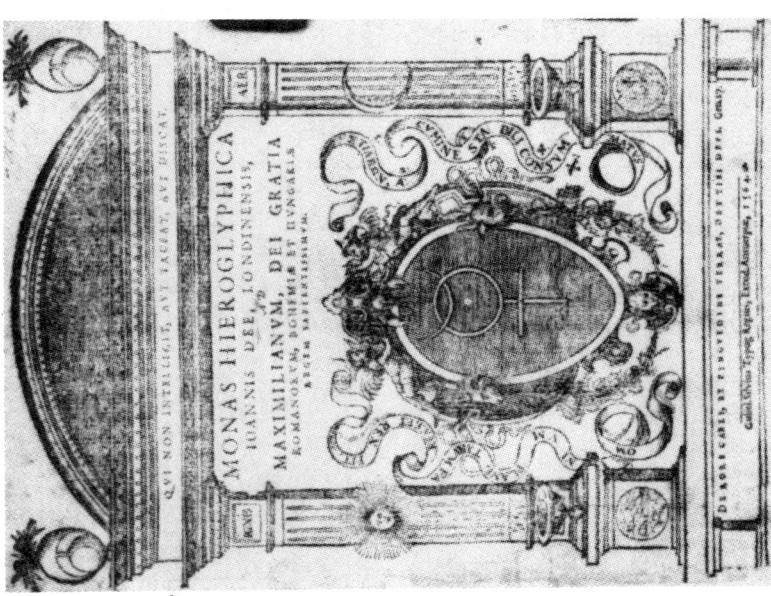

10a John Dee,
*Monas hierogly-
phica*
10b
H. Khunrath,
*Amphitheatrum
Sapientiae Aeternae*

the music was renewed, consisting of 'the Voices of two Youths clad in white garments, with wings like Angels, and standing opposite to one another'.[1]

When the company returned to the hall they partook of the Garter Feast, a banquet which lasted until early the next day. Cellius has some details about the Feast which are not quoted by Ashmole, including mentions of the part in the entertainment provided by 'English musicians, comedians, tragedians, and most skilful actors'. The English musicians gave a combined concert with the Württemberg musicians, and the English actors added to the hilarity of the banquet by presenting dramas. One of these was the 'History of Susanna', which they played 'with such art of histrionic action and with such dexterity' that they were greatly applauded and rewarded.[2]

On later days, the English were conducted to see some of the principal places in the Dukedom, including the University of Tübingen 'where they were entertained with Comedies, Musick and other delights'.

Surely the visit of the Garter embassy and its attendant actors must have been an immensely stimulating and exciting event for the imaginative young student at Tübingen, Johann Valentin Andreae? His *Chemical Wedding* of 1616 is full of brilliant impressions of rich ceremonial and feasts, of some Order, or Orders, and contains fascinating insets of dramatic performances. It becomes more understandable as an artistic product when seen as the result of early English influences on Andreae, both of drama and ceremonial, combining to inspire a new and original imaginative work of art.

The year after the Garter ceremony, in 1604, a very curious work was dedicated to the Duke of Württemberg. This was the *Naometria* by Simon Studion, the unpublished manuscript of which is in the Landesbibliothek at Stuttgart.[3] It is an apocalyptic-prophetic work of immense length, using involved numerology based on Biblical descriptions of the measurements of the Temple of Solomon and involved arguments about significant dates in Biblical and European history, leading up to prophecies about dates of future events. The writer is particularly interested in the dates in the life of Henry of Navarre, and the whole composition seems to reflect a secret alliance between Henry, now King of France, James I of Great Britain, and Frederick, Duke of

---

[1] Ashmole, *Garter*, p. 415.

[2] Cellius, *Eques auratus*, pp. 229–30. On the actors who accompanied the Garter embassy, see E. K. Chambers, *Elizabethan Stage*, II, pp. 270–1.

[3] *Württemberg Landesbibliothek*, Stuttgart; Cod. theol. 4° 23, 34. There is now a microfilm of this manuscript in the Warburg Institute.

Württemberg. This supposed alliance (of which I have not found evidence elsewhere) is very circumstantially described, and the manuscript even includes several pages of music which are to be sung to verses about the eternal friendship of the Lily (the King of France), the Lion (James of Great Britain), and the Nymph (the Duke of Württemberg).

According to the evidence of Simon Studion, it would therefore seem that there was a secret alliance in 1604 between James, Württemberg, and the King of France, perhaps a following up of the *rapprochement* with James through the Garter ceremony of the preceding year. We are still in the early part of James's reign during which he was still continuing the alliances of the previous reign and working in concert with Navarre, now King of France.

The *Naometria* is a curious specimen of that mania for prophecy, based on chronology, which was a characteristic obsession of those times. It contains, however, a very interesting and apparently factual account of something which is said to have taken place in 1586. According to the author of *Naometria*, there was a meeting at Luneburg on 17 July 1586, between 'some evangelical Princes and Electors' and representatives of the King of Navarre, the King of Denmark, and the Queen of England. The object of this meeting is said to have been to form an 'evangelical' league of defence against the Catholic League (then working up in France to prevent the accession of Henry of Navarre to the throne of France). This league was called a 'Confederatio Militiae Evangelicae'.[1]

Now, according to some early students of the Rosicrucian mystery, Simon Studion's *Naometria* and the 'Militia Evangelica' which it describes, is a basic source for the Rosicrucian movement.[2] A. E.

---

[1] The statement about the meeting at Luneburg in 1586 to form the 'Confederatio Militiae Evangelicae' is made on folio 35 of the dedication of *Naometria* to the Duke of Württemberg, with which the manuscript begins. The statement is repeated in almost the same words on folio 122 of the dedication, where it is added that the Duke of Württemberg had a position of no small importance 'among the Confederates'. Cf. A. E. Waite, *Brotherhood of the Rosy Cross*, London, 1924, pp. 639 ff.

It is not impossible that John Dee might have attended this Luneburg meeting; he was in Leipzig in May, 1586, see French, *John Dee*, p. 121.

[2] That Simon Studion's *Naometria* has an important bearing on the Rosicrucian movement is stated by J. G. Buhle, *Ueber den Ursprung ... der Orden der Rosenkreuzer und Freyman*, Göttingen, 1804, p. 119. An earlier statement to the same effect is found in an account of Andreae in *Württembergisches Repertorium der Literatur*, ed. J. W. Petersen, 1782–3, III. De Quincey in his essay 'Rosicrucians and Freemasons', 1824, repeated from Buhle the statement about *Naometria* (T. De Quincey, *Collected Writings*, ed. D. Masson, Edinburgh, 1890, XIII, pp. 399–400). See also A. E. Waite, *Brotherhood of the Rosy Cross*, pp. 36 ff., 639 ff.; Will-Erich Peuckert, *Die Rosenkreutzen*, Jena, 1928, pp. 38–9.

Waite, who had examined the manuscript, believed that a crudely shaped rose design, with a cross in the centre, contained in the *Naometria*, is the first example of Rosicrucian rose and cross symbolism.[1] I cannot say that I am altogether convinced of the importance of this so-called rose, but the idea that the Rosicrucian movement was rooted in some kind of alliance of Protestant sympathizers, formed to counteract the Catholic League, is one which would accord well with the interpretations to be advanced in this book. The date 1586 for the formation of this 'Militia Evangelica' would take one back to the reign of Queen Elizabeth, to the year of Leicester's intervention in the Netherlands, to the year of Philip Sidney's death, to the idea of the formation of a Protestant League which was so dear to Sidney and to John Casimir of the Palatinate.

The problems raised by Simon Studion and his *Naometria* are too complicated to be entered upon in detail here, but I would be inclined to agree that this Stuttgart manuscript certainly is of importance to students of the Rosicrucian mystery. What encourages one in this view is the fact that Johann Valentin Andreae undoubtedly knew the *Naometria* for he mentions it in his work *Turris Babel*,[2] published in 1619. Andreae is here interested, not in any past dates mentioned in the *Naometria*, but in its dates for future events, its prophecies. Simon Studion is very emphatic, in his repetitive way, that the year 1620 (remember that he is writing in 1604) will be highly significant for it will see the end of the reign of Antichrist in the downfall of the Pope and Mahomet. This collapse will be continued in following years and about the year 1623 the millennium will begin. Andreae is very obscure in what he says about the prophecies of *Naometria*, which he links with those of the Abbot Joachim, St Brigid, Lichtenberg, Paracelsus, Postel, and other *illuminati*. It is however possible that prophecies of this type may actually have influenced historical events, may have helped to decide the Elector Palatine and the enthusiasts behind him to make that rash decision to accept the Bohemian crown in the belief that the millennium was at hand.

The obscure movements glimpsed through the study of the Duke of Württemberg and the Garter and the mysteries of *Naometria* belong to the early years of the century when the Protestant Union was being formed in Germany and the Kings of France and England were

---

[1] Waite, *Brotherhood*, p. 641.
[2] Johann Valentin Andreae, *Turris Babel sive Judiciorum de Fraternitate Rosaceae Crucis Chaos*, Strasburg, 1619, pp. 14–15.

hoped for as its supporters. In those earlier years, James I appeared sympathetic to these movements. The assassination of the King of France in 1610, on the eve of making some important intervention in Germany, shattered the hopes of the activists for a while and altered the balance of European affairs. James, however, appeared to be still continuing the old policies. In 1612 he joined the Union of Protestant Princes, the head of which was now the young Elector Palatine; in the same year he engaged his daughter Elizabeth to Frederick, and in 1613 the famous wedding took place, with its apparent promise of support by Great Britain for the head of the German Protestant Union, the Elector Palatine.

Now at the time of the height of the alliance, before James I had begun his backing-out process from it, the energetic Christian of Anhalt began to work towards building up the Elector Palatine as the ideal head of the anti-Hapsburg forces in Europe. Earlier hoped-for leaders had disappeared; Henry of France had been assassinated; Henry, Prince of Wales, had died. The lot fell upon the young Elector Palatine.

Anhalt was generally held responsible for Frederick's unfortunate Bohemian adventure, and it was against Anhalt that propaganda after its disastrous failure was largely addressed.[1] He had many contacts in Bohemia and it would seem that it may have been through his persuasive efforts that the Bohemian rebels were influenced towards offering the crown to Frederick. The figure of Anhalt was an important, a dominating influence, in the years when the Bohemian adventure was working towards its climax and it is therefore essential to take into account the nature of this man's interests, and the nature of his connections in Bohemia.

Theologically speaking, Christian of Anhalt was an enthusiastic Calvinist, but like so many other German Protestant princes at this time he was deeply involved in mystical and Paracelsist movements. He was the patron of Oswald Croll, Cabalist, Paracelsist, and alchemist. And his Bohemian connections were of a similar character. He was a close friend of Peter Wok of Rosenberg,[2] or Rožmberk, a wealthy

---

[1] Papers seized at Heidelberg after the capture of the town in 1622 were published as purporting to show the dangerous character of Anhalt's activities. The publication of these so-called 'Anhalt Chancery' papers was intended to alienate the German Protestants from Frederick; see *Cambridge Modern History*, III, pp. 802–9; David Ogg, *Europe in the Seventeenth Century*, London, 1943 ed., pp. 126 ff.

[2] 'Since 1606 [Anhalt] had remained in continuous contact with Peter Wok of Rosenberg'; Claus-Peter Clasen, *The Palatinate in European History*, p. 23. Clasen thinks it probable that it was Anhalt who suggested to the Bohemians the choice of Frederick as King of Bohemia.

Bohemian noble with vast estates around Trebona in southern Bohemia, a liberal of the old Rudolphine school, and a patron of alchemy and the occult.

Anhalt's Bohemian contacts were of a kind to bring him within the sphere of a very remarkable current of influences from England which arose out of the visit to Bohemia of John Dee, and his associate, Edward Kelley. As is well known, Dee and Kelley were in Prague in 1583, when Dee tried to interest the Emperor Rudolph II in his far-reaching imperialist mysticism and his vast range of studies. The nature of Dee's work is now better known through the recent book by Peter French. Dee, whose influence in England had been so profoundly important, who had been the teacher of Philip Sidney and his friends, had had the opportunity of forming a following in Bohemia, though we have, as yet, little means of studying this. The main centre for the Dee influences in Bohemia would have been Trebona, which he and Kelley had made their headquarters after the first visit to Prague.[1] Dee lived at Trebona, as the guest of Villem Rožmberk, until 1589, when he returned to England. Villem Rožmberk was the elder brother of the Peter who was Anhalt's friend and who inherited the Trebona estates on his brother's death.[2] Given the bent of Anhalt's mind and the nature of his interests, it is certain that the Dee influences would have reached him. Moreover, it is probable that the ideas and outlook originally emanating from Dee, the English and Elizabethan philosopher, were used by Anhalt in building up the Elector Palatine in Bohemia as one having marvellous resources of English influence behind him.

An influence from Dee had been spreading into Germany from Bohemia much earlier. According to the notes about Dee by Elias Ashmole in his *Theatrum Chemicum Britannicum* (1652), Dee's journey through Germany in 1589, on his return from Bohemia to England, was somewhat sensational. He passed near those territories which, twenty-five years later, were to be the scene of the outbreak of the Rosicrucian movement. The Landgrave of Hesse presented his compliments to Dee, who, in return, 'presented him with Twelve Hungarian Horses, that he bought at Prague for his journey'.[3] Dee also made contact at this stage of his journey home with his disciple, Edward Dyer

---

[1] Peter French, *John Dee*, pp. 121 ff.

[2] Valuable new material on the Rožmberk family and their contacts with Dee will be made available in the forthcoming book by Robert Evans on the court of Rudolph II.

[3] Elias Ashmole, *Theatrum Chemicum Britannicum*, London, 1652 (facsimile reprint ed. Allen Debus, Johnson Reprint Corporation, 1967), pp. 482–3.

(who had been Philip Sidney's closest friend) who was going to Denmark as ambassador and who 'the yeare before had been at Trebona, and carried back letters from the Doctor (Dee) to Queen Elizabeth'.[1] Dee must have made a great impression in those parts, both as an immensely learned man and as someone at the centre of great affairs.

Ashmole states that on 27 June 1589, when at Bremen, Dee was visited by 'that famous Hermetique Philosopher, Dr Henricus Khunrath of Hamburgh'.[2] The influence of Dee is in fact apparent in Khunrath's extraordinary work, 'The Amphitheatre of EternalWisdom' (Pl. 10b), published at Hanover in 1609.[3] Dee's 'monas' symbol, the complex sign which he expounded in his *Monas hieroglyphica* (Pl. 10a) (published in 1564 with a dedication to the Emperor Maximilian II) as expressive of his peculiar form of alchemical philosophy, can be seen in one of the illustrations in the 'Amphitheatre', and both Dee's *Monas* and his *Aphorisms* are mentioned in Khunrath's text.[4] Khunrath's 'Amphitheatre' forms a link between a philosophy influenced by Dee and the philosophy of the Rosicrucian manifestos. In Khunrath's work we meet with the characteristic phraseology of the manifestos, the everlasting emphasis on macrocosm and microcosm, the stress on Magia, Cabala, and Alchymia as in some way combining to form a religious philosophy which promises a new dawn for mankind.

The symbolic engravings in 'The Amphitheatre of Eternal Wisdom' are worth pondering over as a visual introduction to the imagery and the philosophy which we shall meet in the Rosicrucian manifestos. Except in the title, the word 'Amphitheatre' does not occur in the work, and one can only suppose that Khunrath may have had in mind in this title some thought of an occult memory system through which he was visually presenting his ideas. One engraving shows a great cave (Pl. 11), with inscriptions on its walls, through which adepts of some spiritual experience are moving towards a light. This may well have suggested imagery in the Rosicrucian *Fama*. And the engraving of a religious alchemist (Pl. 12) is suggestive of the outlook, both of John Dee and of the Rosicrucian manifestos. On the left, a man in an attitude of intense worship kneels before an altar on which are Cabalistic and geometrical symbols. On the right is to be seen a great furnace

---

[1] *Ibid.*, p. 483.

[2] *Ibid.*

[3] H. Khunrath, *Amphitheatrum Sapientiae Aeternae*, Hanover, 1609. This was not the first edition.

[4] *Amphitheatrum*, p. 6.

with all the apparatus of the alchemist's work. In the centre, musical instruments are piled on a table. And the setting of the whole is in a hall drawn with all the expertise of the modern perspectivist, indicating knowledge of those mathematical arts which went with architecture in the Renaissance. This engraving is a visual expression of the kind of outlook which John Dee summed up in his *Monas hieroglyphica*, a combination of Cabalist, alchemical, and mathematical disciplines through which the adept believed that he could achieve both a profound insight into nature and vision of a divine world beyond nature.

It could also serve as a visual expression of the leading themes of the Rosicrucian manifestos, Magia, Cabala, and Alchymia united in an intensely religious outlook which included a religious approach to all the sciences of number.

Should one therefore look for an influence of John Dee in the Rosicrucian manifestos? Yes, one should, and his influence is to be found in them without a shadow of doubt. I give now only a very brief statement about the discoveries which will be worked out more fully in later chapters.

The second Rosicrucian manifesto, the *Confessio* of 1615, has published with it a tract in Latin called 'A Brief Consideration of More Secret Philosophy'.[1] This 'Brief Consideration' is based on John Dee's *Monas hieroglyphica*, much of it being word for word quotation from the *Monas*. This discourse is indissolubly joined to the Rosicrucian manifesto which follows it, the *Confessio*. And the *Confessio* is indissolubly linked with the first manifesto, the *Fama* of 1614, the themes of which it repeats. Thus it becomes evident that the 'more secret philosophy' behind the manifestos was the philosophy of John Dee, as summed up in his *Monas hieroglyphica*.[2]

Further, Johann Valentin Andreae's *Chemical Wedding* of 1616 in which he gave romantic allegorical expression to the themes of the manifestos, has Dee's 'monas' symbol on its title-page, and the symbol is repeated in the text (Pl. 19a), beside the poem with which the allegory opens.[3]

Thus there can be no doubt that we should see the movement behind the three Rosicrucian publications as a movement ultimately stemming from John Dee. The Dee influence could have come into Germany from England with the English connections of the Elector Palatine,

---

[1] See below, Appendix, p. 236, for the Latin title.
[2] See below, pp. 45–7.
[3] See below, p. 61.

and it could have spread from Bohemia where Dee had propagated his stirring mission in earlier years.

Why should these influences have been publicized in this strange way through their dissemination in the Rosicrucian publications? As a tentative answer to this question, about which later chapters will provide more evidence, it is suggested that the Rosicrucian publications belong to the movements around the Elector Palatine, the movements building him up towards the Bohemian adventure. The chief stirring spirit behind these movements was Christian of Anhalt, whose connections in Bohemia belonged right in the circles where the Dee influence would have been known and fostered.

The strangely exciting suggestion is that the Rosicrucian movement in Germany was the delayed result of Dee's mission in Bohemia over twenty years earlier, influences from which became associated with the Elector Palatine. As a Garter Knight, Frederick inherited the cult of English chivalry associated with the movement, and as head of the Protestant Union he represented the alliances which Anhalt was attempting to build up in Germany. From the politico-religious point of view, the Elector Palatine stepped into a situation prepared over previous years, and he had emerged as the politico-religious leader destined to solve the problems of the age. In the years 1614 to 1619— the years of the Rosicrucian furore set off by the manifestos—the Elector Palatine and his wife were reigning at Heidelberg, and Christian of Anhalt was working up towards the Bohemian adventure.

And that adventure was not merely a political anti-Hapsburg effort. It was the expression of a religious movement which had been gathering force for many years, fostered by secret influences moving in Europe, a movement towards solving religious problems along mystical lines suggested by Hermetic and Cabalist influences.

The strange mystical atmosphere in which Frederick and his wife were invested by enthusiasts can be realized from a German print published in 1613 (Pl. 13). Frederick and Elizabeth are suffused in rays descending from the Divine Name above their heads. This print may have been the first of those circulated in Germany on the subject of Frederick and Elizabeth and was to be succeeded by many others. The history of Frederick in the prints affords a major line of evidence concerning his connection with contemporary movements, as will become apparent in the next chapter.

CHAPTER IV

THE ROSICRUCIAN MANIFESTOS

The *Fama* and the *Confessio* (the abridged titles by which we shall continue to refer to the two Rosicrucian manifestos) are printed in an English translation in the appendix to this book,[1] where the reader may study for himself their stirring announcements of a dawn of enlightenment, and the strange romance about 'Christian Rosencreutz' and his Brotherhood in which the announcements are wrapped up. The many problems concerning the manifestos cannot all be dealt with in this chapter but are distributed over this whole book. For example, the problem of why a long extract from an Italian work, translated into German, was printed with the *Fama* will be deferred until the discussion in a later chapter of the slant towards Italian liberals implicit in the German Rosicrucian movement.[2] A simplified bibliography of the manifestos will be found set out in the appendix, with an analysis of what other material was published with the *Fama* and the *Confessio*.[3] This is an important matter, for the readers of early editions of these documents, read with them other material which helped to explain their drift.

Though the earliest known printed edition of the first Rosicrucian manifesto, the *Fama*, did not appear until 1614, the document had been circulating in manuscript before that date, for in 1612 a reply to it by a certain Adam Haselmayer was printed.[4] Haselmayer states that he had seen a manuscript of it in the Tyrol in 1610, and a manuscript of it is said to have been seen in Prague in 1613. Haselmayer's 'reply' is reprinted in the volume containing the first printed edition of the *Fama*. Haselmayer includes himself with the 'Christians of the Evangelical Churches', hails with enthusiasm the illuminated wisdom of

[1] See Appendix, below, pp. 235–60.
[2] See below, pp. 130–9.
[3] See Appendix, below, pp. 235–8.
[4] See Appendix, below, p. 235.

the *Fama*, and makes some strongly anti-Jesuit remarks. He alludes to the widespread expectation of radical changes after the death of the Emperor Rudolph II, who died in 1612. This 'reply' of Haselmayer's at the end of the volume containing the first printed edition of the *Fama* connects with a preface at the beginning of the volume in which it is stated that the Jesuits had seized Haselmayer because of his favourable reply to the appeal of the *Fama* and had caused him to be put into irons on a galley. This preface suggests that the Rosicrucian manifesto is setting forth an alternative to the Jesuit Order, a brotherhood more truly based on the teaching of Jesus. Both the reply of Haselmayer and the preface about him are very obscure, and, as with so much Rosicrucian literature, one is not sure whether they are to be taken literally. However the general intention is clear, an intention of associating the first Rosicrucian manifesto with anti-Jesuit propaganda.

This point is also very clearly made in the full title of the volume containing the *Fama*, which may be translated as follows:[1]

> Universal and General Reformation of the whole wide world; together with the *Fama Fraternitatis* of the Laudable Fraternity of the Rosy Cross, written to all the Learned and Rulers of Europe; also a short reply sent by Herr Haselmayer, for which he was seized by the Jesuits and put in irons on a Galley. Now put forth in print and communicated to all true hearts. Printed at Cassel by Wilhelm Wessel, 1614.

This title covers all the contents of the volume which included an extract from an Italian writer about general reformation (to be discussed in a later chapter); the *Fama*; and Haselmayer's reply. Thus the reader of the first edition of the *Fama* read it in a context which made quite clear the anti-Jesuit trend of the manifesto, which is not so obvious from the *Fama* when studied by itself.

The *Fama* opens with a thrilling call to attention, that trumpet call which was to echo throughout Germany, reverberating thence through Europe. God has revealed to us in these latter days a more perfect knowledge, both of his Son, Jesus Christ, and of Nature. He has raised men endued with great wisdom who might renew all arts and reduce them all to perfection, so that man 'might understand his own nobleness, and why he is called Microcosmus, and how far his knowledge extendeth into Nature'.[2] If the learned were united they might now

---

[1] For the German title, see Appendix, below, p. 236.
[2] See Appendix, below, p. 238.

collect out of the Book of Nature a perfect method of all arts. But the spread of this new light and truth is impeded by those who will not leave their old courses, being tied to the restricting authority of Aristotle and Galen.

After the opening peroration, the reader is introduced to the mysterious Rosencreutz, founder of 'our Fraternity', who laboured long towards such a general reformation. Brother Rosencreutz, an 'illuminated man', had been a great traveller, particularly in the east where wise men are willing to communicate their knowledge. The same should be done in Germany today where there is no dearth of learned men, 'magicians, Cabalists, physicians, and philosophers', who ought to collaborate with one another. The traveller learned the 'Magia and Cabala' of the east, and knew how to use it to enhance his own faith and to enter into 'the harmony of the whole world, wonderfully impressed on all periods of time'.[1]

Brother R. C. next went to Spain in order to reveal there, and to the learned of Europe, what he had learned. He showed how 'the faults of the Church and the whole *Philosophia Moralis*' were to be amended. He prescribed new *axiomata* whereby all things might be restored, but he was laughed at. His hearers feared 'that their great name might be lessened if they should now again begin to learn, and acknowledge their many years' errors'. He was much disappointed, being ready to impart all his knowledge to the learned 'if they would but have undertaken to write the true and infallible *axiomata*, out of all faculties, sciences, arts, and whole nature'. If this were done, a society might be formed in Europe which would enrich rulers with its knowledge and give counsel to all. The world in these days was big with such commotions, and labouring to bring forth men who broke through the darkness. One such was 'Theophrastus' (Paracelsus), who was 'well-grounded in the aforesaid harmonia', though he was not 'of our Fraternity'.[2]

Meanwhile Brother R. C. had returned to Germany, being aware of the alterations to come and the dangerous contentions. (According to the *Confessio*, Brother R. C. was born in 1378 and lived for 106 years; his life and work are therefore supposed to take place in the fourteenth and fifteenth centuries.) He built a house in which he meditated on his philosophy, spent much time in the study of mathematics, and made many instruments. He began to wish still more ardently for reformation and to organize helpers, beginning with three only. 'After this

[1] See Appendix, below, p. 240.
[2] See Appendix, below, pp. 240-2.

manner began the Fraternity of the Rosy Cross, first by four persons only, and by them was made the magical language and writing, with a large dictionary, which we yet daily use to God's praise and glory.'[1]

The writer of the *Fama* then continues to recount the imaginary history of this imaginary Order,[2] which we here abridge, since the full story can be read in the appendix. The Order grew in numbers. They had a building as their centre, the House of the Holy Spirit. Their main business was attendance on the sick, but they also travelled much in order to gain, and to spread, knowledge. They observed six rules, the first of which was to have no other profession save that of healing the sick 'and that gratis'. They were not to wear any distinctive habit, but to follow the custom in dress of any country where they happened to be. They were to meet once a year at their House of the Holy Spirit.

The first of the Fraternity to die, died in England. Many other Brothers have succeeded the original Brothers, and the Fraternity has recently taken on a new significance through the finding of the vault in which Brother Rosencreutz is buried. The door into this vault was miraculously discovered, and it typifies the opening of a door in Europe which is greatly desired by many.

The description of this vault is a central feature of the Rosencreutz legend. The sun never shone in it, but it was lighted by an inner sun. There were geometrical figures on its walls and it contained many treasures, including some of the works of Paracelsus, wonderful bells, lamps, and 'artificial songs'. The Fraternity already possessed its 'Rota' and 'the Book M.'. The tomb of Rosencreutz was under the altar in the vault; inscribed on its walls were the names of Brethren.

The discovery of the vault is the signal for the general reformation; it is the dawn preceding a sunrise. 'We know . . . that there will now be a general reformation, both of divine and human things, according to our desire and the expectation of others; for it is fitting that before the rising of the Sun there should break forth Aurora, or some clearness or divine light, in the sky.'[3] The date at which the vault was discovered is indirectly indicated as 1604.

This very peculiar document, the *Fama Fraternitatis*, thus seems to recount, through the allegory of the vault, the discovery of a new, or rather new-old, philosophy, primarily alchemical and related to medicine and healing, but also concerned with number and geometry

---

[1] See Appendix, below, pp. 242.
[2] See Appendix, below, pp. 242 ff.
[3] See Appendix, below, p. 249.

and with the production of mechanical marvels. It represents, not only an advancement of learning, but above all an illumination of a religious and spiritual nature. This new philosophy is about to be revealed to the world and will bring about a general reformation. The mythical agents of its spread are the R.C. Brothers. These are said to be reformed German Christians, devoutly evangelical. Their religious faith seems closely connected with their alchemical philosophy, which has nothing to do with 'ungodly and accursed gold making', for the riches which Father Rosencreutz offers are spiritual; 'he doth not rejoice that he can make gold but is glad that he seeth the Heavens open, and the angels of God ascending and descending, and his name written in the Book of Life.'[1]

The intense excitement aroused by the *Fama* and its story of the Rosicrucian Order was still further increased in the following year by the publication of the second Rosicrucian manifesto, the *Confessio*, which continued to talk about the R.C. Brothers, their philosophy and their mission, and seemed to be intended as a continuation of the *Fama* to which it constantly referred.[2] It was published at the same place as the *Fama* and printed by the same printer. Unlike the *Fama*, which is in German as are all the other contents of the volume in which it is published, the first edition of the *Confessio* is in Latin, as is also the other discourse published with it. It would seem therefore that the *Confessio* volume was a continuation of the *Fama* volume, but addressed, in Latin, to a more learned audience, and having the intention of giving some interpretation of the romantic allegories of the first manifesto.

The Latin title of the publication which contains the first edition of the *Confessio* may be translated into English as follows:[3]

A Brief Consideration of the more Secret Philosophy written by Philip à Gabella, a student of philosophy, now published for the first time together with the Confession of the R.C. Fraternity. Printed at Cassel by Wilhelm Wessel, printer to the Most Illustrious Prince, 1615.

(on the *verso* of the title-page)

God give thee of the dew of heaven and of the fatness of the land. Genesis. 27.

[1] See Appendix, below, p. 230.
[2] See Appendix, below, pp. 235–60.
[3] For the Latin title, see Appendix, below, p. 236.

Readers were evidently intended to study the *Consideratio brevis* before coming to the *Confessio*, and, as I have already indicated, the *Consideratio brevis* is based on John Dee's *Monas hieroglyphica*. Nothing is known of the identity of 'Philip à Gabella' (could this be a pseudonym referring to 'Cabala'?) but it is certain that he was a close student of Dee.

The clue to his source is given in the quotation on the *verso* of his title-page, which I have given in Biblical English above but which he, of course, gives in Latin: *De rore caeli et pinguedine terrae det tibi Deus*. This text is inscribed on the title-page of Dee's *Monas hieroglyphica* (Pl. 10a), on which the theme of the descending dew (*ros*) uniting heaven and earth is visually illustrated.

The *Consideratio brevis* is not a reproduction of the whole of Dee's *Monas*, but it quotes verbally from the first thirteen theorems of the work, interspersed with other matter. These are the theorems in which Dee expounds the composition of his 'monas' sign, how it includes the symbols of all the planets, how it absorbs into itself the zodiacal sign, Aries, representing fire, and therefore alchemical processes, how the cross below the symbols for sun and moon represents the elements, and how different formations of the four lines of this cross can turn it into a sign for both three and four, both triangle and square, thus solving a great mystery.[1] The diagrams which 'Philip à Gabella' gives, some of which are not in Dee's *Monas*, can actually help to explain a little more clearly how Dee's mind worked on the component parts of his hieroglyph. Clearly it was the 'monas' itself which most interested 'Philip à Gabella', the mysterious sign and its parts, which could include all the heavens and the elements, the sacred figures of triangle, circle, and square, and the cross. Strangely enough, he never uses the word 'monas', and in passages where he is directly quoting from Dee on the 'monas hieroglyphica', he substitutes 'stella' for 'monas'. For 'Philip à Gabella' the monas becomes a star, and the 'monas hieroglyphica' a 'stella hieroglyphica'. This interpretation could, however, have a sanction from Dee's work, on the last page of which a woman holding a star seems to be intended as a figure summing up the whole work.

The *Consideratio brevis* concludes with a Latin prayer couched in a vein of intense piety and aspiration towards the eternal and infinite God, the One strength, the One perfection, in whom all things are

[1] See C. H. Josten, 'A Translation of John Dee's "Monas Hieroglyphica"', *Ambix*, XII (1964), pp. 155–65.

One, who with his Son and the Holy Spirit is Three in One. The prayer is reminiscent of Dee's prayers and its presence at the end of a version of the *Monas* brings the *Consideratio brevis* very much within the Dee atmosphere of ardent piety combined with complex magico-scientific striving.

The prayer is signed 'Philemon R.C.', that is 'Philemon Rose Cross', and it is followed on the opposite page by the preface to the reader, signed 'Frater R.C.', of the second Rosicrucian manifesto, the *Confessio*, which follows immediately.

That is to say, the Dee-inspired *Consideratio brevis*, and its prayer, seems absolutely assimilated to the Rosicrucian manifesto, as an integral part of it, as though explaining that the 'more secret philosophy' behind the Rosicrucian movement was the philosophy of John Dee, as expounded in his *Monas hieroglyphica*.

This may cause one to think again about the old theory, now generally discarded, which argued that the name 'Rosicrucian' was not derived from 'Rose' and 'Cross', but from *Ros* (dew) and *Crux*, having an alchemical meaning connected with dew as a (supposed) solvent of gold and with the cross as the equivalent of light.[1] Without attempting to penetrate these alchemical mysteries, it can be said that the discovery of the close association of Dee's *Monas* and its motto on the 'dew of heaven' with the Rosicrucian manifesto may now give some support to the *Ros* Cross theory.

We now pass on, as the original readers were intended to do, from scrutiny of the *Consideratio brevis*, noting its close dependence on Dee's *Monas hieroglyphica*, to the study of the Rosicrucian manifesto, the *Confessio*.

The address to the reader before the *Confessio* contains the striking statement: 'As we do now altogether freely and securely, and without hurt, call the Pope of Rome Antichrist, the which heretofore was held for a deadly sin, and men in all countries were put to death for it. So we know certainly that the time shall likewise come when that which we yet keep secret, we shall openly, freely, and with a loud voice publish and confess it before all the world.'[2]

The opening phrases of the *Confessio*[3] link it closely with the *Fama*.

---

[1] For an exposition of the theory that 'Rosicrucian' derives from *Ros* (dew) and *Crux*, see the note in James Crossley, *Diary and Correspondence of Dr. John Worthington*, Chetham Society, 1847, I, pp. 239–40 n. The theory is not accepted by R. F. Gould, *History of Freemasonry*, ed. H. Poole, 1951, II, p. 67.

[2] Quoted in Thomas Vaughan's translation. See *Fame and Confession*, ed. Pryce, p. 33.

[3] See Appendix, below, p. 257.

Whatever the reader may have heard concerning the Fraternity by the trumpet sound of the *Fama* is not to be either believed hastily or rejected, says the author of the *Confessio*. Jehova, seeing the world falling into decay, is hastening it again to its beginning. The Brothers have unfolded in their *Fama* the nature of their Order, and it is clear that it cannot be suspected of heresy. Concerning the reform of philosophy, the programme is the same as in the *Fama*. The learned of Europe are again urged to respond to the fraternal invitation of the Order and to co-operate with it in its efforts.

The *Confessio* is enthusiastic about the profound knowledge of Father R.C., whose meditations on all subjects invented since the creation, propagated by human skill, or through the service of angels or spirits, are so all-inclusive that if all other knowledge were lost it would be possible to rebuild from them alone the house of truth. Would it not be desirable to conquer hunger, poverty, disease, old age, to know all countries of the earth and their secrets, to read in one book all that is in all books? 'So to sing and play that instead of stony rocks you could draw pearls, instead of wild beasts, spirits.'

When the Trumpet of the Order shall sound with full voice these things which are now only whispered in enigmas will come forth and fill the world and the tyranny of the Pope will be overthrown. The world has seen many alterations since Father R.C. was born and many more are to come. But before the end, God will allow a great influx of truth, light, and grandeur, such as surrounded Adam in Paradise, to be poured forth on mankind. New stars have appeared in the constellations Serpentarius and Cygnus[1] which are signs of the coming of these things.

The second manifesto repeats the message of the first, though with even greater fervour and intensity. A powerful prophetic and apocalyptic note sounds through it, the end is at hand, new stars foretelling wonders have appeared, the great reformation is to be a millennium, a return to the state of Adam in Paradise.

These announcements aroused at the time a frenzied interest and many were the passionate efforts to reach the R.C. Brothers by

---

[1] The 'new stars' in the constellations Serpentarius and Cygnus which appeared in 1604 were discussed by Johannes Kepler who thought that religious and political changes were heralded by these stars. Kepler's *De Stella nova in pede Serpentarii*; *De Stella incognita Cygni* was printed at Prague in 1606 (reprinted Kepler, *Gesammelte Werke*, ed. M. Caspar, 1938, I, pp. 146 ff.).

John Donne was also deeply interested in these new stars; see C. M. Coffin, *John Donne and the New Philosophy*, Columbia University Press, 1937, pp. 123 ff.

11 The Cave of the Illuminati. From H. Khunrath, *Amphitheatrum Sapientiae Aeternae*

12 The Cabalist-Alchemist. From H. Khunrath, *Amphitheatrum Sapientiae Aeternae*

letters, printed appeals, pamphlets.[1] A river of printed works takes its rise from these manifestos, responding to their invitation to get into touch with the writers and to co-operate in the work of the Order. But appeals would seem to have remained unanswered. The Brothers, if they existed, seemed invisible and impervious to entreaties to make themselves known. This mystery did not diminish interest in the fabulous Brothers, but, on the contrary, intensified it.

Of the various schools of thought about the Rosicrucian mystery, we can surely, today, dismiss the fundamentalists, the people who believe in the literal truth of the story of Christian Rosencreutz and his Brotherhood. Then there are the scoffers, the people who think that the whole thing was a hoax. The invisibility of the Brothers, their apparent refusal to give any sign of their existence to their disciples, naturally encourages this view.

The meditative reader of the manifestos is struck by the contrast between the serious tone of their religious and philosophical message and the fantastic character of the framework in which the message is presented. A religious movement using alchemy to intensify its evangelical piety, and including a large programme of research and reform in the sciences, is surely an interesting phenomenon. That the sciences are thought of in Renaissance Hermetic-Cabalist terms, as related to 'Magia' and 'Cabala', is natural for the period, and even the millenarianism—that the new dawn is thought of as a period of light and advance preceding the end of the world—is not inconsistent with advanced thinking at that time. Francis Bacon's Great Instauration of the sciences has a millenarian tinge, as Paolo Rossi has shown.[2] The story of Christian Rosencreutz and his R.C. Brothers and of the opening of the magic vault containing his tomb was not intended to be taken as literally true by the framers of the manifestos who were obviously drawing on legends of buried treasure, miraculously rediscovered, such as were particularly prevalent in the alchemical tradition. There is ample evidence in the texts themselves that the story was an allegory or fiction. The opening of the door of the vault symbolizes the opening of a door in Europe. The vault is lighted by an inner sun, suggesting that entry into it might represent an inner experience, like the cave through which the light shines in Khunrath's *Amphitheatrum Sapientiae* (Pl. 11).

Yet many gullible readers at the time and since have taken the story

---

[1] See below, pp. 91 ff.
[2] Paolo Rossi, *Francis Bacon, From Magic to Science*, London, 1968, pp. 128 ff.

literally. The most recent critical scholarship on the Rosicrucian mystery has emphasized that Johann Valentin Andreae himself described it as fictitious, or a comedy, or a 'joke'. Andreae was certainly behind the scenes of the whole movement to which he frequently refers in his numerous works (works other than his *Chemical Wedding* which ranks almost as a third Rosicrucian manifesto). The Latin word which Andreae uses most frequently when mentioning the Rosicrucian movement is *ludibrium*. Of the manifestos he uses expressions like 'the *ludibrium* of the vain *Fama*', or 'the *ludibrium* of the fictitious Rosicrucian Fraternity'. Paul Arnold translated *ludibrium* into French as 'une farce' and decided that Andreae himself has told us that the whole thing was a joke.[1] Charles Webster thinks that the phrases about the *ludibrium* are 'derisive terms'.[2]

It is true that by these terms Andreae was trying to disassociate himself from the Rosicrucian mystery, which, by the time he thus wrote of it, had become dangerous, yet I do not think that this is the whole explanation of his use of the term *ludibrium*. A *ludibrium* could be a play, a comic fiction, and—as will be discussed more fully in a later chapter—Andreae thought highly of the theatre as a moral and educative influence.[3] The theatricality of the Rosicrucian movement, as revealed in Andreae's comments and allusions, is one of the most fascinating aspects of the whole affair. I mention this here in advance in order to suggest that the *Fama* and the *Confessio* as a *ludibrium*, whatever that may mean (and we must keep our minds open about this until it has been more fully discussed) encourages the thought that, though the framers of the manifestos did not intend the story of Christian Rosencreutz to be taken as literally true, it might yet have been true in some other sense, might have been a divine comedy, or some allegorical presentation of a complex religious and philosophical movement having a direct bearing upon the times.

We are in a stronger position than earlier enquirers for having some inkling of what the Rosicrucian manifestos might be about, for we know that a major influence on them was John Dee's *Monas hieroglyphica*. This was the 'more secret philosophy' behind them. The allegory of the opening of the vault and the revelation of the marvels it contained, would represent the release of a new influx of influences

---

[1] Paul Arnold, *Histoire des Rose-Croix*, Paris, 1935, p. 50.
[2] Charles Webster, 'Macaria: Samuel Hartlib and the Great Reformation', *Acta Comeniana*, 26 (1970), p. 149.
[3] See below, pp. 140 ff.

ultimately stemming mainly, though not entirely, from the influence of Dee—who had conducted a mission in the fifteen-eighties in a milieu known to Christian of Anhalt, who was the organizer of the movement for making Frederick, Elector Palatine, King of Bohemia. The manifestos represent, I believe, the mystical background behind this movement, an intensely religious, Hermetic, magical, alchemical reforming movement such as Dee had propagated in Bohemia. One must not over-emphasize this aspect of the background of the manifestos, in which many other influences would also have played a part, but it is of paramount importance to take into account the Frederickian movement contemporary with the manifestos, and the fact that the Dee influence on them (of which there can be no doubt) fits in with the suggestion that they could belong in the atmosphere of that movement.

These hypotheses can be strikingly confirmed from other evidence. The enemies of the movement can supply us with most valuable information, and it is to the enemies that we now turn for guidance.

One of these enemies was Andreas Libavius, a well-known name in the history of early chemistry. Libavius was one of those 'chymists' who was influenced up to a point by the new teachings of Paracelsus in that he accepted the use of the new chemical remedies in medicine, advocated by Paracelsus, whilst adhering theoretically to the traditional Aristotelian and Galenist teachings and rejecting the Paracelsist mysticism.[1] Aristotle and Galen appear, honourably placed, on the title-page of Libavius's main work, the *Alchymia*, published at Frankfurt in 1596. The Rosicrucian manifestos attack Aristotle and Galen as characteristic of out-of-date rigidity of mind. Whether Libavius had felt himself personally indicated in this attack by enthusiastic Paracelsists on traditional teaching one cannot say, but certainly Libavius's critique of the Rosicrucian manifestos turns on antagonism to those 'chymists' who, like impious Paracelsus, differ little from magicians. He accuses the authors of the manifestos of not understanding serious, scientific alchemy, for which they substitute wild theorizing, and he intends his 'well-meaning observations' as instructions through which they are to realize their errors through being given a grounding in true scientific alchemy.

Libavius criticized the Rosicrucian *Fama* and *Confessio* in several works, the most important of which is called 'Well-meaning

---

[1] See J. R. Partington, *History of Chemistry*, London, 1961, II, pp. 244 ff. Libavius did not reject alchemy itself; see John Read, *Prelude to Chemistry*, London, 1936, pp. 213–21.

Observations on the *Fama* and *Confessio* of the Brotherhood of the Rosicrucians', published at Frankfurt in 1616.[1] Basing himself on the texts of the two manifestos, Libavius raises serious objections to them on scientific, political, and religious grounds. Libavius is strongly against theories of macro-microcosmic harmony, against 'Magia and Cabala', against Hermes Trismegistus (from whose supposed writings he makes many quotations), against Agrippa and Trithemius—in short he is against the Renaissance tradition as transmitted to the authors of the R.C. manifestos and in the spirit of which they interpret Paracelsus. Libavius regards all this as subversive of Aristotelian and Galenic tradition, as indeed it was, and he strongly criticizes the manifestos for departing from orthodoxy.

It is significant that in a work published years before, in 1594, Libavius had attacked Dee's *Monas hieroglyphica*, pointing out the Cabalist elements in it of which he disapproved.[2] He would thus certainly have been able to recognize the influence of Dee's *Monas* in the Rosicrucian manifestos, which would confirm him in his disapproval of them.

And it is also significant that Libavius frequently mentions Oswald Croll in his tracts against the Rosicrucians and seems to associate their doctrines with those of Croll, towards whom he is equally unfavourable. He quotes with disapproval Croll's preface to his *Basilica* near the beginning of his 'well-meaning observations'.

Oswald Croll, or Crollius, was a Paracelsist physician who, unlike Libavius, adopted, not only Paracelsist chemical remedies but also the whole background of Paracelsus's thought, like him rejecting Aristotle and Galen, and adhering enthusiastically to the mysticism, magic, and harmonic theories of Paracelsist teaching as a whole. Croll's *Basilica Chymica*, published at Frankfurt in 1609, constantly cites Hermes Trismegistus and Hermetic texts with reverence, and is imbued with respect for the great Renaissance Neoplatonists, such as Pico della Mirandola. Its theme is the magical harmonies of macrocosm and microcosm and its whole atmosphere is such as would have been

---

[1] A. Libavius, *Wohlmeinendes Bedencken der Fama und Confession der Bruderschaft des Rosencreutzes*, Frankfurt, 1616. Other works, in Latin, by Libavius against the Rosicrucian manifestos are printed in *Appendix necessaria syntagmatis arcanorum chymicorum*, Frankfurt, 1615, reprinted Frankfurt, 1661 with a slightly different title. See Ian Macphail, *Alchemy and the Occult, A Catalogue of Books and Manuscripts from the Collection of Paul and Mary Mellon*, Yale, 1968, I, p. 71.

[2] A. Libavius, *Tractatus duo de physici*, Frankfurt, 1594, pp. 46, 71; cf. F. Secret, *Les Kabbalistes Chrétiens de la Renaissance*, Paris, 1964, p. 138.

highly congenial to the authors of the Rosicrucian manifestos. Another of Croll's works, published at Prague in 1608, expounds the Paracelsist correlation of great and little worlds through the doctrine of astral 'signatures'.[1]

In Libavius and Croll we thus have representatives of the 'chemist', or alchemist, who is traditionally Aristotelian and Galenist in his theory, contrasted with the extreme, mystical, Paracelsist alchemist. Libavius classes the Rosicrucian manifestos as belonging, with Croll, to an unorthodox school of alchemical thought.

Now, as I have mentioned before,[2] Oswald Croll was in touch with Christian of Anhalt as his physician. His *Basilica* is dedicated to Anhalt, with a privilege from the Emperor Rudolph II. And his *De signatura rerum* is dedicated to Peter Wok of Rožmberk, the Bohemian nobleman who was Anhalt's close ally and confederate and whose brother had been the Bohemian patron of John Dee. By associating the teachings of the Rosicrucian manifestos with those of Croll, Libavius might therefore be suggesting that the manifestos belonged in an atmosphere congenial to Anhalt, an atmosphere in which influences from John Dee mingled with those of Croll.

And Anhalt was, of course, the moving spirit behind the 'activist' tradition in German Protestantism, the tradition which had been looking for leaders throughout the early part of the century and which by now (by the time the Rosicrucian manifestos were actually printed) had fixed on Frederick V, Elector Palatine, as the leader destined to head the movement and to lead it to victory.

In addition to his criticisms of the thought of the Rosicrucian manifestos, Libavius also expresses disapproval of their politics, particularly when commenting on the passage in the *Fama* in which the authors say that they acknowledge the authority of the Empire but are expecting alterations in it which they will support with secret aid.[3]

> In *Politia* we acknowledge the Roman Empire and *Quartam Monarchiam* for our Christian head, albeit we know what alterations be at hand, and would fain impart the same with all our hearts to other godly learned men . . . we shall help with secret aid this so good a cause, as God shall permit or hinder us . . .

[1] Oswald Croll, *De signaturis internis rerum*, Prague, 1608.
[2] See above, p. 28.
[3] See Appendix, below, p. 249.

Libavius sees in this passage an allusion to some 'Paracelsist Lion' who will ally himself with the Turk and seek to overthrow the 'Romische Reich' and substitute for it a world government based on magic spells.[1] He is, in fact, conflating this passage in the *Fama* with the prognostications of changes in the Empire in Haselmayer's 'reply', which was published with the *Fama* and in which the anti-Jesuit trend of the Paracelsist politics is made quite explicit.

By the time the manifestos were published, a Lion leader of the movements fostered by Anhalt had materialized, Frederick V, of the Palatinate, whose heraldic emblem, as all the world knew, was a lion.

Time and place agree that it is not only possible but probable that the Rosicrucian movement, by the time that it emerged into print, was connected with the Elector Palatine. It spreads during the years in which Frederick was reigning in the Palatinate and working up to his great Bohemian adventure. Its moving spirit, Andreae, is situated in Württemberg; the manifestos are published at Cassel. Württemberg and Hesse-Cassel were the two Protestant principalities neighbouring the Palatinate and deeply interested in what was going on there. The emotional and imaginative centre to which they were looking in these years was Heidelberg—Heidelberg with its magic gardens and its Lion prince.

There are other enemies, more bitter and ferocious than Libavius, who can now be brought forward to support this interpretation.

The satirical prints against Frederick which were circulated after his defeat show a great deal of knowledge of his movement, which they use to caricature it.[2] These caricatures evidently emanated from one source and were a carefully planned propaganda campaign, designed to discredit and ridicule the defeated ex-King of Bohemia. Samples of these caricatures have already been reproduced in this book, one of Frederick and Elizabeth in a garden leading to Hell (Pl. 7b), others showing Frederick with one garterless leg (Pl. 9), playing on the theme of his loss of a Garter. Other caricatures use animal themes, following

---

[1] Libavius, *Wohlmeinendes Bedencken*, pp. 194–5, 205. Libavius associates the 'Paracelsist Lion' with the Turk through what he supposes to be the Mohammedan teachings imbibed by 'Christian Rosencreutz' at Damascus. The accusation of being allied with the Turk was made against Frederick and Anhalt; one of their allies was Bethlen Gabor, a converted Mohammedan.

[2] Publications containing reproductions of the caricatures are E. A. Beller, *Caricatures of the 'Winter King' of Bohemia*, Oxford, 1928; E. A. Beller, *Propaganda in Germany during the Thirty Years War*, Princeton, 1940; H. Wascher, *Das deutsche illustrierte Flugblatt*, Dresden, 1955; Mirjam Bohatcova, *Irrgarten der Schicksale: Emblematdrucke vom Anfang des Dreissig-Jährigen Krieges*, Prague, 1966.

a medieval tradition of political animal-imagery, and dwelling on the fortunes of the Hapsburg Eagle and the Palatine Lion, for example, a wheel with the triumphant Hapsburg Eagle at the top and the defeated Palatine Lion at the bottom, the wheel representing the 'Romisches Reich' which has turned to reinstate the Hapsburg Eagle and to drive the Palatine Lion out of Bohemia (Pl. 14a). In his introduction to his collection of reproductions of some of these satires, E. A. Beller emphasizes that the Eagle is always the Emperor Ferdinand and the Lion, Frederick of the Palatinate, the moral being always the failure of the latter's impious attempt to interfere with the Empire. Some of these satires reply, in a very instructive way, to themes in the Rosicrucian manifestos.

The *Fama*, the manifesto which foretells great changes in the Empire, ends with the words 'under the shadow of thy wings, Jehova'. The words are quoted in Latin at the end of the German text—*sub umbra alarum tuarum, Jehova*.[1] It is a quotation of the prayer for protection which occurs several times in this form in the Psalms. 'Keep me as the apple of the eye, hide me under the shadow of thy wings' (17, viii). Or, 'Be merciful unto me, O God, be merciful unto me; for my soul trusteth in thee; yea, in the shadow of thy wings will I make my refuge until these calamities be overpast' (57, i). Coming at the end of the *Fama*, the Latin words of this prayerful ejaculation emphasize the religious character of the theme of the manifestos. The words are like a seal at the end of the document.

This motto from the *Fama* can be seen expressed visually in some Rosicrucian publications, for example on the title-page of the *Speculum Sophicum Rhodo-Stauroticum* of 1613, at the top of which are the wings, enclosing the Name of God in Hebrew, surrounded by rays, and above, a scroll with the motto *sub umbra alarum tuarum* (Pl. 15b).

The Rosicrucian motto is replied to in one of the satirical prints against Frederick the theme of which is the Triumphant Eagle ('Triumphirender Adler') (Pl. 15a). Triumphantly perched on the top of a column, the Hapsburg Eagle spreads wide its wings, whilst a discomfited Lion lies prostrate on the ground. The Eagle has taken the place of Jehova, for the Name of God appears above it and pours divine rays upon it. A modification of the words of the Rosicrucian motto drives home the lesson of this fierce propaganda: SUB UMBRA ALARUM MEARUM FLOREBIT REGNUM BOHEMIAE 'Under the shadow of my wings the kingdom of Bohemia will flourish'.

[1] See Appendix, below, p. 251.

On the left are terrified and discomfited supporters of Frederick, amongst whom is 'Anhalt', gazing through a telescope at the Triumphant Eagle.

This print can be used as evidence that the Rosicrucian manifesto called the *Fama* carried with it politico-religious allusions to the aims of Frederick and his supporters, particularly Anhalt, and that the Rosicrucian manifestos and movement belonged in the context of the Frederickian movement to transfer Bohemia from the Hapsburg Eagle to the Palatinate Lion. The sharp eyes of the Eagle had seen in the *Fama* the allusion which Libavius had also detected, years before.

In another of these anti-Frederick satires (Pl. 14b), the Hapsburg Eagle is triumphing over the prostrate figure of Frederick and removing from his head the crown of Bohemia. Supporters are putting new feathers into the Eagle's wings, which are labelled with the names of Palatinate towns, Oppenheim and so on. This scene may be a reply to the words in the *Confessio*, the second Rosicrucian manifesto, about 'some eagle's feathers' being 'yet in our way' and 'hindering our purpose'.[1] Here, instead of the Eagle losing feathers through the action of Frederick, feathers taken from the vanquished Palatinate are being added to its wings.

Still more important as evidence that his enemies regarded Frederick as being associated with the Rosicrucian movement is the strange print which shows Frederick standing on a capital Y (Pl. 16), the allusions in which are explained in the verses below it. The Y stands for the Pythagorean Y, emblematic of choice between two ways, one, the vicious way, leading to ruin, the other representing virtuous choice. Frederick, argues this satire, chose the wrong way which led him to disaster. Inset in the background are pictures of battles which Frederick lost, beginning, on the left, with the Battle of the White Mountain, outside Prague. The Y rests on a Z which rests on a round ball precariously held in position by three of Frederick's supporters, one of these being Christian of Brunswick, shown with only one arm (he had recently lost an arm in battle). Brunswick was noted for his chivalrous attachment to Elizabeth Stuart, ex-Queen of Bohemia, and was a tremendous fighter on Frederick's side. On the right stands Saturn, with scythe and hour-glass.

The text below tells the whole story of Frederick's attempt to wrest the Bohemian crown from Ferdinand and its failure. Towards the end,

[1] See Appendix, below, p. 257.

13   The Marriage of the Elector Palatine and the Princess Elizabeth

14a   The Hapsburg Eagle and the Palatine Lion on the turning
wheel of Fortune

14b   The Hapsburg Eagle triumphing over the fallen Frederick

15a Under the wings of the Triumphant Hapsburg Eagle 15b Under Jehova's Wings. From Theophilus Schweighardt, *Speculum Sophicum Rhodo-Stauroticum*

16 Frederick on the Pythagorean Y

these verses speak of a 'high society of the Rosicrucians' which they associate with Frederick's enterprise. These words are led up to by an account of a world reformation which the Bohemians had associated with the Elector Palatine. The relevant passage is as follows in E. A. Beller's English translation of the text:[1]

> The round wooden ball (the ball under the Y) represents the world
> To which the Bohemians married the Palatine,
> They expected to teach the world,
> And to reform all schools, churches, and law courts,
> And to bring everything to the state
> In which Adam found it,
> And even to my state, Saturn's,
> And this was called the golden time.
> To that end the high society of the Rosicrucians
> Wish to turn all the mountains into gold for their own good.

Here is the general reformation of the world announced in the Rosicrucian manifestos described as a world reformation which the Bohemians expected to achieve through the Elector Palatine. Whilst involving definite reforms in education, church, and law, this general reformation has millenarian overtones; it will bring the world back to the state in which Adam found it, which was also Saturn's golden age. So, in the *Confessio*, the second Rosicrucian manifesto, the general reformation is said to presage 'a great influx of truth and light' such as surrounded Adam in Paradise, and which God will allow before the end of the world. And, in the verses of the print, this millennium, this return to the golden age of Adam and Saturn, is said to be assisted by 'the high society of the Rosicrucians' who wish to turn all the mountains into gold. The satire here associates the whole movement with a 'Rosicrucian' type of alchemy, for the gold referred to is not the material gold of alchemical transmutation but the spiritual gold of a golden age and a return to Adamic innocence.

The enemies who composed this satirical print and its accompanying verses have given invaluable evidence as to the politico-religious aspect of the message contained in the Rosicrucian manifestos. It was an apocalyptic message of universal reformation leading to a millennium and associated with movements around the Elector Palatine which were eventually to lead to the Bohemian enterprise. The Bohemians who 'married the Palatine' to the world, expected world reformation to be

[1] Beller, *Caricatures*, p. 62.

the result. The verses speak later, with contemptuous satire, of the wild aims of 'the Palatine's politics':[1]

> When a mouse gives birth to an elephant,
> And a cuckoo to a pheasant,
> When a gnat draws off the whole sea,
> And the Rhine runs from Cologne to Strasburg,
> Then the Palatine's politics
> Will bring concord to the Empire,
> And union to the Church
> And will strengthen all religion.

From the enemy satire we learn of the vast scope of the 'Palatine's politics' as a religious movement for reforming church and empire. His short-lived attempt to challenge the Hapsburg domination in Bohemia had wide historical and European perspectives behind it. The framers of these caricatures were extremely well informed as to the ideas behind the Frederickian movement; they knew of its connection with the Rosicrucian movement; and they also doubtless knew of the connection of the latter with the ideas of John Dee. The *Monas hieroglyphica*, the influence of which we have traced behind the Rosicrucian manifestos, opens with a diagram of the Pythagorean Y, and applies this to two possible ways which a ruler may take, one the broad way of 'tyrants', the other the straight and narrow way of the 'adepti' or inspired mystics. Was this perhaps a reason for showing the defeated Frederick on a Y, to underline the failure of a movement emanating from Dee's influence in Bohemia?

The satirical and contemptuous account of Frederick's movement and its aims given by this caricature-print disseminated by his enemies, if divested of the satirical tone and read in a positive sense, gives an impression of Frederick as a religious and reforming leader which fits in well with the visionary and reforming tone of the Rosicrucian manifestos.

[1] *Ibid.*

CHAPTER V

THE CHEMICAL WEDDING OF
CHRISTIAN ROSENCREUTZ

In the years before the war, Heidelberg castle, the abode of the Palatine Lion and his royal mate, must have been an object of intense romantic sentiment and religious excitement, or of intense hatred and disapproval. Whatever the point of view, Heidelberg could not be ignored. The improvements made by De Caus in the enlargement and modernizing of the building, the marvels of his mechanical statues, water-organs, and other wonders of modern magico-science, were in themselves enough to excite amazement. And the occupants of the castle were remarkable. Elizabeth Stuart had a powerful and noticeable personality (her grandmother, let us not forget, was Mary Queen of Scots). Observers seem to have been struck by the affectionate relations between her and her husband. It was a very different court from the other courts of Germany, and the life lived in it may have seemed as romantically novel as the fantastic décor in which it was framed. Gazing at Merian's engraving of Heidelberg castle and gardens, one wonders again what can have been the influence in Germany of the marriage of the Thames and the Rhine, of that royal wedding which had been celebrated with so much splendour at the Jacobean court.

Other views of Heidelberg can be seen in emblems, here reproduced for the first time. They come from a little book of 'Ethico-Political' Emblems by Julius Gulielmus Zincgreff (Pl. 17), published by Johann Theodore De Bry with engravings by Matthieu Merian in 1619,[1] and dedicated to the Elector Palatine. We shall return later to examine more fully this book of emblems. Here we are looking only at the views of Heidelberg castle in them, which are authentic since they are engraved by Matthieu Merian who was the engraver of the great

---

[1] 'A Hundred Ethico-Political Emblems by Julius Gulielmus Zincgreff, engraved by Matthieu Merian', 1619, published by Johann Theodore De Bry (*Emblematum Ethico-Politicorum Centuria Iulii Gulielmi Zincgrefii, Caelo Matth. Meriani, MDCXIX, Apud Iohann Theodor de Bry*). On this book of emblems, see further, below, p. 71.

panorama of the castle and gardens in the *Hortus Palatinus*, and so was very familiar with this subject.

The first emblem in the book (Pl. 18a) shows a view of Heidelberg castle; on the left is the town, with the spire of the Church of the Holy Spirit. In the foreground is a lion, 'watching while he sleeps' as the French verses under the emblem explain. He is the Prince (the Elector Palatine) watching over the safety of his subjects. Other emblems (Pl. 18b) show warlike Palatine lions with the castle in the background; these views give a very good idea of the 'English wing' with its many windows. Another more distant view of castle and town has in the foreground a lion holding a book, with the motto *Semper Apertus* (Pl. 18c).

It will soon become apparent why these views of Heidelberg castle with its Lion owner are a useful introduction to this chapter.

The Chemical Wedding of Christian Rosencreutz is the English translation of the title of the remarkable German romance, or novel, or fantasy, published at Strasburg in 1616.[1] It is the third item in the series which launched the Rosicrucian furore. The series came out annually for three years, the *Fama* in 1614, the *Confessio* in 1615, the *Wedding* in 1616, each adding to the mounting excitement about the Rosicrucian mystery. And the historical clue which we have found to the *Fama* and the *Confessio* can also help towards the unravelling of the *Wedding*, which is a romance about a husband and wife who dwell in a wondrous castle full of marvels and of images of Lions, but is at the same time an allegory of alchemical processes interpreted symbolically as an experience of the mystic marriage of the soul—an experience which is undergone by Christian Rosencreutz through the visions conveyed to him in the castle, through theatrical performances, through ceremonies of initiation into orders of chivalry, through the society of the court in the castle.

The narrative is divided into Seven Days, like the Book of Genesis. The First Day opens with the author preparing himself on Easter Eve for his Easter Communion. Sitting at a table, he conversed with his Creator

---

[1] *Chymische Hochzeit Christiani Rosencreutz. Anno 1459*, Strasburg, 1616 (Lazarus Zetzner). There is no name of author in the book which is supposed to be by 'Christian Rosencreutz' himself. The German text was republished at Berlin, 1913, edited by F. Maack. An English translation by Ezechiel Foxcroft was published in 1690, with the title: *The Hermetic Romance, or The Chymical Wedding, written in High Dutch by C.R.*, translated E. Foxcroft, London, 1690. Foxcroft's translation is reprinted in A. E. Waite, *The Real History of the Rosicrucians*, London, 1887, pp. 99 ff; and in *A Christian Rosenkreutz Anthology*, ed. Paul M. Allen, Rudolf Steiner Publications, New York, 1968, pp. 67 ff.

in humble prayer and considered many great mysteries 'whereof the Father of Lights had shown me not a few'. Suddenly a fearful tempest arose, and in the midst of it appeared a glorious vision whose garments were sky-coloured, bespangled with stars. In her right hand she bore a golden trumpet whereon a Name was engraved which the narrator (Christian Rosencreutz) could read but dared not reveal. In her left hand she had a bundle of letters in all languages which she was to carry into all countries. Her large wings were covered with eyes, and as she mounted aloft she gave a mighty blast on her trumpet.

This figure has attributes of the conventional allegorical figure of Fame, with a trumpet and with wings covered with eyes.[1] She thus connects with the trumpet sounds of the first Rosicrucian manifesto, the *Fama*.

When Rosencreutz opened the letter which the vision with the trumpet had given him, he found that it contained verses beginning:

> This day, this day, this, this,
> The Royal Wedding is.
> Art thou thereto by birth inclined,
> And unto joy of God design'd?
> Then may'st thou to the mountain tend
> Whereon three stately Temples stand,
> And there see all from end to end.

In the margin beside the poem there is a symbol (Pl. 19a); below it are the words 'Sponsus' and 'Sponsa', the bridegroom and the bride. The same symbol, reversed, also appears on the title-page of the book.

This symbol is a roughly drawn version of John Dee's 'monas hieroglyphica', as C. H. Josten has noticed.[2] Its appearance here brings the *Chemical Wedding* into line with the second Rosicrucian manifesto, the *Confessio*, which had appeared the year before preceded by a work based on the *Monas hieroglyphica*. That the *Wedding* begins with Dee's sign in the margin is yet another, very strong indication that the 'more secret philosophy' underlying the Rosicrucian publications was that of John Dee.

Christian Rosencreutz hastened to accept the invitation to the Royal Wedding. He put on a white linen coat, bound a blood-red ribbon

---

[1] See Cesare Ripa, *Iconologia*, ed. Rome, 1603, pp. 142 ff.

[2] See C. H. Josten, 'A Translation of John Dee's "Monas Hieroglyphica" with an introduction', *Ambix*, XII (1964), p. 98. In Foxcroft's English translation of the *Wedding*, a representation of Dee's sign is shown in the margin beside the poem (Pl. 19b).

crossways over his shoulder, and 'in my hat I stuck four red roses'. These were his wedding garments; and the white and red livery, with the red roses in the hat, are the distinguishing marks of Christian Rosencreutz throughout the story.

The Second Day sees the hero journeying towards the Wedding, amid the rejoicings of nature. Arrived at a royal portal on a hill, the porter demanded his Letter of Invitation which, fortunately, he had not forgotten to bring with him, and asked who he was. He replied that he was 'a brother of the Red Rosy Cross'. At the next gate, a roaring Lion was chained, but the porter drove him back and the hero passed in. Bells began to ring in the castle; the porter urged him to hurry or he would be too late. Anxiously he hurried, following a lamp-lighting Virgin, and only just got inside the gate before it clapped shut.

The castle was most splendid, with many rooms and staircases, and seemed full of people. Some of the other guests were rather tiresome boasters. One said that he had heard the movements of the spheres; another could see Plato's Ideas; a third could count the atoms of Democritus. Their behaviour was rowdy but it was stilled when excellent and stately music began in the hall. 'There were all stringed instruments sounding together in such harmony that I forgot myself.' When the music ceased, trumpets began to sound, and a Virgin entered who announced that the Bride and Bridegroom were not far away.

On the Third Day, the sun dawned bright and glorious, trumpets sounded for the assembling of the guests, and again the Virgin appeared. Scales were brought in and everyone was weighed, including several Emperors who were present. Some people came off very badly in this weighing. But when Christian Rosencreutz was weighed, who held himself very humbly and seemed less important than the others, one of the pages cried 'That is he!' The Virgin saw the roses in his hat and asked to have them.

At a stately banquet on this day, Rosencreutz was given a high place, sitting at a table covered with red velvet and spread with costly gold and silver drinking cups. Pages presented the guests with 'the Golden Fleece' and a 'Flying Lion' which they were requested to wear. These emblems represented the Order which the Bridegroom was bestowing on them 'and would ratify with suitable ceremonies'.

Afterwards, time was spent in examining the rarities in the castle, the Lion fountain in the gardens, the many pictures, the noble library, the costly clockwork showing the motions of the heavens, the great globe with all the parts of the world. At the end of the day, the Virgin brought them to a room where there was nothing costly, only some curious little prayer books. The Queen was there and they all knelt down and prayed that this Wedding might tend to the honour of God and their own benefit.

On the Fourth Day, Rosencreutz went out early to refresh himself at the fountain in the garden, where he found that the Lion, instead of his sword, had a tablet beside him with an inscription beginning HERMES PRINCEPS. The main event of this day was a theatrical performance, given before the King and Queen and attended by all the guests and household.

This 'merry comedy' was presented by 'artists and students', on a 'richly furnished scaffold'; some of the audience were allotted 'a peculiar standing at the top of all', but the rest stood below 'between the columns'. The plot of the play was unfolded in seven acts. On a sea-shore, an old king found an infant in a chest washed up by the waves; an accompanying letter explained that the king of the Moors had seized the child's country. In following acts the Moor appeared and captured the infant, now grown into a young woman; she was rescued by the old king's son and betrothed to him, but fell again into the Moor's power. She was finally rescued again, but 'a very wicked priest' had to be got out of the way. When his power was broken the wedding could take place; bride and bridegroom appeared in great splendour and all the people cried 'vivat sponsus, vivat sponsa', by this comedy congratulating 'our King and Queen'. At the end all joined in a Song of Love:

> This time full of love
> Does our joy much approve

which prophesied that thousands would arise from this union.

The extremely simple plot of the comedy was punctuated by a display of Biblical emblems, 'the four beasts of Daniel', or 'Nebuchadnezzar's image' were brought in, suggesting that the audience was expected to see in it allusions to prophecy.

Afterwards, all returned to the castle where, later, a strange episode took place, described in impressive detail. Amidst silence and deep mourning, six coffins were brought in. Six persons were beheaded and put into the coffins. Later, on the following day, the corpses were resuscitated.

On the Fifth Day, the narrator was exploring the underground parts of the castle, when he came to a door on which was a mysterious inscription. When it opened, a vault was disclosed, into which the light of the sun could not penetrate; it was lighted by huge carbuncles. In the midst of it was a sepulchre adorned with many strange images and inscriptions.

The Sixth Day was occupied by hard work with furnaces and other alchemical apparatus. The alchemists succeeded in creating life, in the form of the alchemical Bird. Processes in connection with the creation and tending of this Bird are described in a humorous and sprightly manner.

On the Seven and Last Day, the party gathered upon the shore preparing to leave in their twelve ships which flew flags showing the signs of the zodiac. The Virgin informed them that they were 'Knights of the Golden Stone'. In the sumptuous processions which followed, Christian Rosencreutz rode with the King, 'each of us bearing a snow-white ensign with a Red Cross'. Rosencreutz again had his tokens, the roses, in his hat. A page read out from a book the rules of the Order of the Golden Stone, which were:

I.   You, my Lords and Knights shall swear that you will at no time ascribe your order either unto any Devil or Spirit, but only to God, your Creator, and his hand-maid Nature.

II. That you will abominate all whoredom, incontinency, and uncleanness, and not defile your order with such vices.

III. That you, through your talents, will be ready to assist all that are worthy and have need of them.

IV. That you desire not to employ this honour to worldly pride and high authority.

V.   That you shall not be willing to live longer than God will have you.

Afterwards they were 'with the usual ceremonies, installed Knights' which was ratified in a little chapel. And there the hero hung up his golden fleece and his hat (with the roses in it) and left them for an eternal memorial, writing there as his motto and name:

Summa Scientia nihil Scire
Fr. CHRISTIANUS ROSENCREUTZ

The Chemical Wedding is too long to print in an appendix and the above brief résumé must suffice to give an impression of the work.

Basically, it is an alchemical fantasia, using the fundamental image of elemental fusion, the marriage, the uniting of the *sponsus* and the *sponsa*, touching also on the theme of death, the *nigredo* through which the elements must pass in the process of transmutation. Contemporary alchemical emblems of the school of Michael Maier[1] can provide visual illustrations of the alchemical wedding (Pl. 26a), the alchemical death, of the lions and virgins who typify, or conceal, the operations of the 'chymists'. The alchemical basis of the story is underlined by the fact that one Day is devoted to alchemical work.

The allegory is of course also a spiritual one, typifying processes of regeneration and change within the soul. Alchemy had always carried such double meanings, but in this case the theme of spiritual alchemy being introduced by Dee's 'monas' figure is of a particularly subtle kind. In the almost mathematical precision of the movements of the figures, there may even be quite close echoes of the theory of the *Monas hieroglyphica* which further study might be able to elicit.

And it will be realized, after our examination of the manifestos in the previous chapter, that the *Wedding* is but another version of the allegories of the *Fama* and the *Confessio*. In the manifestos, Christian Rosencreutz was associated with an order of benevolent brethren; in the wedding, he is associated with an order of chivalry. The R.C. Brothers were spiritual alchemists; so are the Knights of the Golden Stone. The activities of the R.C. Brothers were symbolized through the treasures in their vault; similar activities are symbolized through the treasures in the castle. In fact, the theme of a vault containing a tomb actually occurs in the *Wedding*, surely an allusion to the famous vault of the *Fama*: and the *Wedding* opens with a personification of Fame, sounding her trumpet call.

Though *Fama* and *Confessio* may not be written by the same hand as the *Wedding*, the plan of the allegories in all three works bears the stamp of minds working in concert, bent on sending out into the world their myth of Christian Rosencreutz, a benevolent figure, centre of brotherhoods and orders.

But what was the origin of the name? Why 'Christian Rosencreutz'? Many are the suggestions which have been made about this. The rose is an alchemical symbol; many alchemical treatises have the title *Rosarium*, or rose garden. It is a symbol of the Virgin, and more generally a mystical religious symbol, whether in Dante's vision or in Jean de Meung's *Roman de la rose*. More immediate and personal sources have been explored. Luther used a rose in his emblem; Johann Valentin Andreae's arms were a St Andrew's cross with roses.[2]

[1] See below, pp. 82 ff.
[2] For all these suggestions, see Waite, *Real History of the Rosicrucians*, pp. 7 ff.

Symbols are ambivalent by their very nature and all these suggestions can be taken into account and left in the picture. But let us think back to the time when Johann Valentin Andreae was a young student at Tübingen, when he wrote the first version of his *Chemical Wedding* under the thrilling influence of the investiture of the Duke of Württemberg with the Order of the Garter, and of the visit of the English players. Was that vision of Württemberg, occultist and alchemist, resplendent in the Garter robes, the origin of Christian Rosencreutz, the noble German who belongs to an Order of which the symbols are a red cross and roses, symbols of St George of England and of the Order of the Garter?

The *Chemical Wedding* of 1616 contains the elements of what may have been the early impressions under which Andreae wrote his first version of the work; it dwells on splendid ceremonial feasts and initiations into orders of chivalry, combined with a theatrical display. Under the influence of the English players, says Andreae, he wrote plays at about the same time as he wrote a *Chemical Wedding*. Dramatic influences and influences from Garter ceremonial absorbed in that early period have gone, I suggest, into the making of the *Chemical Wedding* of 1616. Christian Rosencreutz is not only a knight of the Golden Fleece and of the Golden Stone;[1] he is also a Red Cross knight. Allusions to the Garter are behind the composite allusions to chivalrous feasts and ceremonies of initiation in Andreae's work; the Red Cross of the Order of the Garter, the Red Cross of St George of England have been absorbed into the German world, to reappear as 'Christian Rosencreutz', with his red roses and his Red Cross ensign.

There is one writer on the Rosicrucian problems who, I think, came near to the truth about the name, though he knew nothing of the evidence collected here. Paul Arnold in his *Histoire des Rose-Croix* suggested as a parallel to the *Chemical Wedding* the episode of the Red Cross Knight in Spenser's *Faerie Queene*.[2] Arnold thought that the allegories built by Spenser around the Red Cross Knight and those concerning the Rosy Cross Brother in the *Chemical Wedding* were similar. Beyond the fact that both works weave an allegory around a Red, or Rosy, Cross Knight there is not much detailed similarity

[1] The knight of the Golden Fleece would transfer very easily into a knight of the Golden Stone (the Philosopher's Stone). It was usual to interpret the Golden Fleece of the Jason legend as having alchemical reference to the Philosopher's Stone; see Natalis Comes, *Mythologiae*, VI, 8. The alchemical interpretation of the Golden Fleece is enormously expanded by Michael Maier, *Arcana arcanissima*, 1614, pp. 61 ff.

[2] Paul Arnold, *Histoire des Rose-Croix*, Paris, 1955. pp. 184 ff.

between the two fictions. Yet by this indirect route Arnold had hit on something. For Spenser's Red Cross Knight is inspired by the Order of the Garter.

When Frederick of the Palatinate came forward as a leader, his propaganda emphasized that he was a Garter Knight. We have seen that this was brought out in fireworks at the time of his wedding, that it appeared in the festivals at Heidelberg castle after his arrival there with his bride (during which the Elector entered on a triumphal chariot bearing emblems of both the Order of the Golden Fleece and the Order of the Garter), that the enemy propaganda after his defeat dwelt maliciously on his loss of the Garter—that Garter which represented the supposed support of his royal father-in-law. Thus, in accordance with the general trend through which Frederick of the Palatinate stepped into positions prepared earlier, he would also step into the Garter propaganda.

Thus when Johann Valentin Andreae re-wrote his youthful version of the *Chemical Wedding* he would bring it up to date by allusions to the present notable German representative of the Order of the Garter, the prince whom we have already found implied in the Rosicrucian movement, Frederick of the Palatinate. It seems to me that we can now easily locate the castle in which the scenes of this strange romance are supposed to take place. It was Heidelberg castle owned by the Palatine Lion, that Lion whom we see guarding the castle in those 'Ethico-Political Emblems' with which we began this chapter. The *Chemical Wedding* introduces us into a vast castle, full of wonders, and with a marvellous garden—Heidelberg castle and gardens full of the wondrous works of Salomon de Caus. There is a Lion at the gate and a very prominent Lion fountain in the gardens, emphasizing that we are in the domains of the Palatine Lion. Castle and gardens are full of movement, they are inhabited by members of a wealthy court whose life centres on a married pair, a King and Queen, a *sponsus* and *sponsa*, who are both emblems of marriage as a mystical experience, and of the alchemical *sponsus* and *sponsa* spiritually interpreted, and also have a real basis in history as the Elector Palatine and his wife Elizabeth Stuart.

Elizabeth may even be recognizable among the mazes of the *Chemical Wedding*, particularly on the Third Day when the guests came to a room containing curious little prayer books, where they all knelt down and prayed that the wedding might tend to the glory of God. This might refer to Elizabeth's plain, Puritan oratory, to her English prayer books, and to the divine significance of her wedding—that wedding which had been celebrated with such pomp and circumstance in London as a wedding 'for religion'.

It is not easy for us to recapture the spirit in which Renaissance princes planned and furnished their palaces and grounds, as a kind of living memory system, through which in elaborate arrangements of places and images, all knowledge, the whole encyclopaedia, could be stored in memory. The wonder-rooms of the Emperor Rudolph at Prague had been planned on some such lines, and it may even have been in preparation for a Hermetic imperial destiny that Frederick had lavished such care on his Heidelberg. We cannot reconstruct the vanished glories of Heidelberg, but the *Chemical Wedding* may give us some idea of what their aim may have been, to present the encyclopaedia in symbolic form, and also, perhaps, to induce an atmosphere through which occult relationships might be perceived, and the hidden harmonies of the universe might be heard.

The Elector Palatine and his wife are surrounded by theatrical influences at all stages of their career, from their wedding in London onwards. In the Palatinate these theatrical traditions were continued and it is in keeping that the activities described in the *Chemical Wedding* should include a play. The company seems to have made its way towards the place where this play was presented through the gardens, where was a building called 'the House of the Sun'. In Merian's engraving of the Heidelberg gardens (Pl. 5) a curious building, or complex of buildings, is shown; two round, amphitheatre-like constructions are connected by covered ways with a central hall. Is it possible that what we see here, in the engraving, may represent the setting for pageantries or theatrical displays of some kind?

The main events described in the *Wedding* evidently reflect or in some way refer to ceremonies and rituals connected with orders of chivalry. This may refer, not only to the original scenes at Stuttgart, but also to more recent displays at Heidelberg. The culmination of the whole story, at the end of the Seventh Day, was the reception of the guests into the Order of the Golden Stone, after which they sailed away in their ships. This is a point at which the topography of the *Chemical Wedding* does not appear to agree with that of Heidelberg castle, which is not on the sea-shore. But pageant cars in the form of ships were used at Heidelberg; it is in the illustration of one of these pageant ships that we can see the Palatine as Jason, sailing with the Fleece and Garter on the ship's rigging (Pl. 3a).

Thus many details concur to suggest that brilliant impressions of the

Heidelberg court may have stimulated Andreae's imagination as he wrote this memorable work, the climax of the Rosencreutz myth. Yet it is above all a work of creative imagination, the artistic first fruits of a movement which was to be cut short when only just begun. And it is the work of a deeply religious genius, transcending all political and sectarian labels to become an allegory of progressive spiritual experience comparable in its intensity to Bunyan's *Pilgrim's Progress*.

What then of the origins of 'Rose Cross'? The reader has been given a choice of possibilities, including old ideas about this and some new ones. In this chapter, I have suggested a chivalrous origin, that it referred to the red cross of St George of the Order of the Garter, and the roses of England. In the preceding chapter I took up again the old hypothesis of an alchemical origin, from *Ros*, dew, and *Crux*, light, with a reference to the mysteries of alchemy. The possibility that there was truth in that theory was indicated by the fact that Dee's *Monas*, with its text about *ros*, or dew, on the title-page, its discussion of the 'monas' as an alchemical form of the cross, is closely linked with the Rosicrucian *Confessio*. Whilst avoiding being too positive about these elusive questions, I would think that both these suggestions might stand together, that there was both an exoteric chivalrous application of 'Rose Cross', and an esoteric alchemical meaning, *Ros Crux*. On this theory, Dee's *Monas* would be the origin of 'Rosicrucianism' in the alchemical sense, and the name would have had chivalrous overtones as 'Red Cross'. Both origins would be English, English chivalry and English alchemy combining to influence a German movement in which the name translates as 'Rosencreutz' and takes on new shades of meaning in the new environment.

CHAPTER VI

THE PALATINATE PUBLISHER:
Johann Theodore De Bry and the publication
of the works of Robert Fludd and
Michael Maier

Apart from Andreae and the unknown persons who may have co-operated with him in spreading the Rosicrucian myth, there are two writers who are generally recognized as the chief exponents of Rosicrucian philosophy. These are Robert Fludd and Michael Maier. Though both Fludd and Maier denied that they were Rosicrucians, they both spoke with interest and approval of the Rosicrucian manifestos, and their philosophies are, roughly speaking, in line with the attitudes expressed in the manifestos. But the modes of thought which are veiled in the fictions of *Fama*, *Confessio*, and *Wedding* are developed by Fludd and Maier into whole libraries of weighty books which were published in the years following the appearance of those three exciting works. Fludd gives most full expression to the philosophy of macrocosm and microcosm; Maier gives brilliant expression to the themes of spiritual alchemy. The solid support of Fludd and Maier imparts reality to the Rosicrucian myth, which now begins to look like a movement with a body of serious literature behind it.

It is thus with a sense of satisfaction, as of a confirmation from another quarter of the correctness of the historical line of approach followed in the preceding chapters, that one notes that the major works of Fludd and Maier were published in the Palatinate during the reign of Frederick V. The huge tomes of Robert Fludd's 'History of the Macrocosm and the Microcosm' were published by Johann Theodore De Bry at Oppenheim in 1617, 1618, 1619. Michael Maier's *Atalanta fugiens*, a book of emblems in which spiritual alchemy reached a high point of artistic expression, was published by Johann Theodore De Bry at Oppenheim in 1618. Oppenheim was the first Palatinate town entered by Elizabeth in 1613 on her arrival in her new country where she was welcomed with triumphal arches. One of these has been reproduced earlier (Pl. 2); it was covered with roses and engraved by Johann Theodore De Bry.

Johann Theodore was the son of Theodore De Bry; the family was originally of Liège.[1] Being Protestants, they became refugees when Liège fell under Catholic domination, and settled in Frankfurt. Theodore De Bry had a prosperous engraving and publishing business in Frankfurt in the later sixteenth century, and had many connections with England through his publication of the great series of volumes on voyages of discovery which used English materials. He was often in England where he was in demand as an engraver in the Elizabethan age. Theodore died in 1598 and was succeeded in the business by his son, Johann Theodore. One of Johann Theodore's daughters married the Swiss artist and engraver, Matthieu Merian, a useful strengthening of the staff of the firm. Another daughter married an Englishman, William Fitzer.

Johann Theodore moved his business from Frankfurt to Oppenheim for religious reasons, so it used to be said, without specifying what these religious reasons were. Since he was apparently there by 1613, ready to engrave the decorations for the arrival of Elizabeth, it is likely that he was attracted by the religious outlook of the regime in the Palatinate and shared the hopes raised by the Elector's marriage to the daughter of James I. And indeed there is ample evidence that De Bry sympathized with the Palatinate movement. The book of Emblems by Zincgreff (Pl. 17), containing the emblems of Heidelberg castle and its Lion owner referred to in the last chapter, was published by De Bry at Oppenheim in 1619, with a dedication by Zincgreff to the Elector Palatine thanking him for the help and protection he has afforded. The emblems are engraved by De Bry's son-in-law, Merian, and amongst the prefatory verses in the volume there are Latin lines addressed to Merian by Janus Gruter. Gruter was librarian of the Palatine library at Heidelberg; and there are other verses in the volume said to be by an official of the Heidelberg court. These indications show that the De Bry firm was closely associated with the Heidelberg court. And it was De Bry who, in 1620, published the *Hortus Palatinus* (Pl. 6a), with its view of the gardens, engraved by Merian (Pl. 5). De Bry was thus associated with recording the splendours of Heidelberg, just before their destruction in the wars; and he had been associated with the beginning, recording the hopeful entry into Oppenheim in 1613.

When disaster broke, with the invasion of the Palatinate by Spinola's

---

[1] On the De Brys, see 'William Fitzer, the publisher of Harvey's *De motu cordis,* 1628', *Transactions of the Bibliographical Society,* New Series, XXIV (1944), p. 143. Fitzer, the publisher of Harvey's book on the circulation of the blood, was Johann Theodore De Bry's son-in-law.

armies in 1620, De Bry moved his business back to Frankfurt. Spinola entered Oppenheim in September 1620; when Frederick revisited it in 1632 he wrote to Elizabeth that she would not be able to recognize it as the town she had once known; half of it was burnt and the rest in ruins.[1] The De Bry firm may have got out in time with most of its equipment, since it started publishing again in Frankfurt fairly soon, but its Oppenheim period must have come to a sudden end shortly before the publication of the *Hortus Palatinus* in 1620, which was published at Frankfurt, not at Oppenheim. And the volume in the series of Fludd's works published by De Bry in 1621, was published at Frankfurt. The change in the place of publication of the Fludd series from Oppenheim to Frankfurt, which one used to dismiss as merely a bibliographical detail, now stands out as fraught with tragedy.

Zincgreff's 'ethico-political' emblems of 1619 are a statement of moral and political support for the Elector Palatine. One emblem shows the Israelites moving on their journey to the promised land, bearing the ark of the covenant (Pl. 18d), surely an allusion to the journey to Prague in 1619 to assume the Bohemian crown. That all these emblems were closely associated with Frederick can be proved (though there is not space to do this in detail here) from the satires against Frederick after his fall, which pick up objects in these emblems, particularly the spider's web and the bee-hive, and associate these sarcastically with Frederick in their caricatures.[2] The De Bry firm, which published these emblems, and Merian, their engraver, would certainly have been marked down as dangerous by the invading armies.

Thus, when in the years up to 1619 De Bry was so energetically pouring from his press at Oppenheim the brilliantly illustrated volumes by the Rosicrucian philosophers, Fludd and Maier, he was supporting a cause in which he believed, and on account of which he had moved his firm into Palatinate territory.

Printers and publishers were frequently centres for obscure religious movements in those days. We know that the great Antwerp printer, Christopher Plantin, was secretly a member of the Family of Love,[3] a

---

[1] Green, *Elizabeth of Bohemia*, p. 296.

[2] Compare for example the Zincgreff emblems on the spider's web as a symbol of a prudent monarch (emblems XXV, XXVII) and on the bee-hive as symbol of a beneficent monarch (emblem C), with the caricatures showing Frederick as a lion destroyed by a spider (Spinola) and Frederick in a bee-hive (Beller, *Caricatures of the 'Winter King'*, Pls III, IV.)

[3] H. De la Fontaine Vervey, 'Trois heresiarques dans les Pays-Bas du XVIe siècle', *Bibliothèque d'humanisme et Renaissance*, XVI (1954), pp. 312–30; B. Rekers, *Benito Arias Montano*, 1960, J. A. Van Dorsten, *The Radical Arts*, Leiden, 1970, pp. 26 ff.

NON TIBI SVM STRATVS

EMBLEMATVM
ETHICO-POLITICORVM
CENTVRIA
IVLII GVILIELMI
ZINCGREFII.
Caelo
Matth. Meriani.
MDCXIX.

AD SPIRANTE DEO.

Prostat
Apud Iohann.
Theodor de Bry

VBERTATE
MORAM REPENDET

17   Julius Guglielmus Zincgreff, *Emblematum Ethico-Politicorum Centuria*

18a, 18b, 18c   The Palatine Lion guarding Heidelberg Castle
18d   The Pillar of Cloud leading the Israelites. From Zincgreff,
Emblematum Ethico-Politicorum Centuria

(6)

Devi. Whereupon I tenderly opened the Letter, and within it, in an *Azure* Field, in *Golden* Letters, found the following Verses written.

This day, this day, this, this
The Royal Wedding is.
Art thou thereto by Birth inclin'd,
And unto joy of God design'd,
Then mayst thou to the Mountain tend,
Whereon three stately Temples stand,
And thereafter all from end to end.
    Keep watch, and ward,
    Thyself regard;
Unless with diligence thou bathe,
The Wedding can't thee harmless save;
He'l damnnage bear that here delays;
Let him beware, too light that weighs.

Underneath stood *Sponsus* and *Sponsa*.

De Sponso

As soon as I had read this Letter, I was presently like to have fainted away, all my Hair stood an end, and a cold Sweat trickled down my whole Body. For although I well perceived that this was the appointed *Wedding*, whereof seven Years before I was acquainted in a *bodily Vision*, and which now so long time I had with great caruck-

---

Christiani Rosencreutz.

Sigillum.

befahle ich ein klein Sigill / damit es vermacht / mit der Inscription: *In hoc signo ✠ Vinces.* So bald ich nun des Zeichens beschawen ward / hab ich dieses Engell dem Teuffel mit welchem mit ehemals viel seiniger gewandschafft per s. Wacht derowegen der Brieffschafft halt auf: Darinnen befand ich im blawen Feld mit Güldenen Buchstaben / nachfolgende Vers geschriben.

Dont / Dont / Dont /
Ist des Königs-Hochzeit /
Bistu hierzu gebohren /
Von Gott zu Frewd erkohren /
Magst auff den Berg gehen /
Darauff drey Tempel stehen /
Daselbst die Sach sihst du besehen.
Halt Wacht /
Dich selbst betracht /
Wirst dich nicht fleissig baden /
Die Hochzeit kan dir schaden.
Schad har wer sich versäumet /
Hüt sich wer ist zu leicht /

Unten an stund: *Sponsus & Sponsa.*

Da ich nun die sen Brieff gelesen / entfiele mir zu mir gantz geschwinden / aus Haar giengen mir zu Berg / enzo lieff mir der kalte Schweiß über den gantzen Leib herab. dann ob wol ich merckte / das dißdie angesetzte Hochzeit wehre / deren mit eben sieben Jahren in einem leiblichen Gesicht geoffenbaret worden

x iii

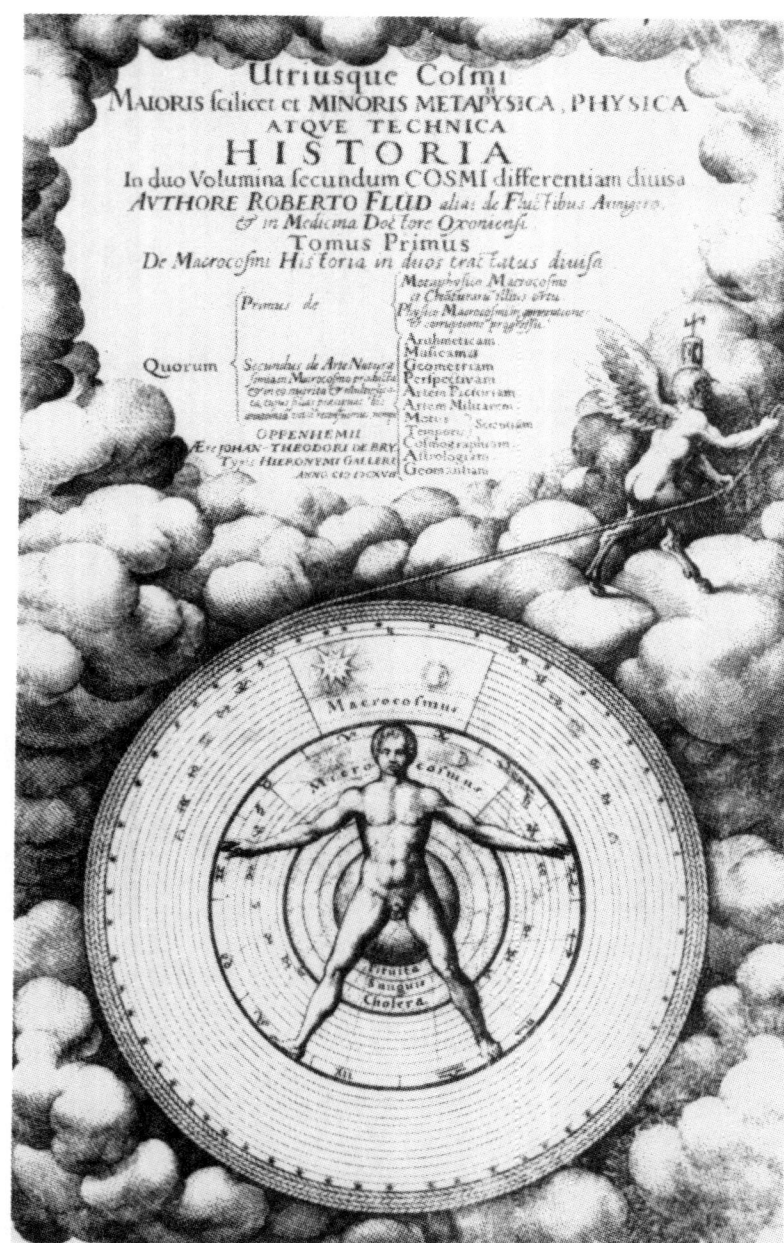

20 Robert Fludd, *Utriusque Cosmi Historia*

sect which believed in avoiding doctrinal statements and in concentrating on mystical and allegorical interpretations of Biblical texts. The printer Wechel at Frankfurt had been resorted to by Philip Sidney and his friends after the Massacre of St Bartholomew in 1572.[1] Another Frankfurt printer, also called Wechel, had harboured Giordano Bruno and in 1590-1 had printed Bruno's long Latin poems,[2] also reprinting in 1591 John Dee's *Monas hieroglyphica*.[3] Through his long family association with printing in Frankfurt it is likely that Johann Theodore De Bry would have had a good deal of knowledge of deep European currents of thought moving and mingling in that great international centre of the book trade.

The De Bry firm's Oppenheim period of publishing coincides with the time when the Palatinate policies were rising to a climax, when the brilliant alliances which seemed to strengthen the position of the Elector Palatine—above all, his marriage—seemed to promise a hopeful outcome to the whole Palatinate anti-Hapsburg movement, which attracted the support of liberal European elements of many kinds.

The Rosicrucian authors published by De Bry represent two countries towards which Palatinate policy was directed, England and Bohemia. Robert Fludd was an Englishman, a Paracelsist physician practising in London, and his philosophy was in line of descent from Renaissance Magia and Cabala,[4] with the addition of Paracelsist alchemy and strong influences from John Dee.[5] Whilst Michael Maier, also a Paracelsist physician, represented the atmosphere of the court of Rudolph II at Prague, Maier had been physician to Rudolph and had been in his confidence.[6] Maier's outlook was one which would have been natural in the court of Rudolph II in Prague, with its magico-scientific trends, its Cabalism, its Paracelsism—all contributing to a more liberal religious attitude than that imposed on Prague by his successors. The fact that Maier was a Lutheran, and that this did not disqualify him for attendance on the Catholic emperor, is in itself an

---

[1] Howell, *Sir Philip Sidney*, p. 142.

[2] Yates, *Giordano Bruno and the Hermetic Tradition*, pp. 318, 320, 325.

[3] Josten, 'Translation of Dee's "Monas"', *Ambix*, XII (1964), p. 96.

[4] I have given some account of Fludd's philosophy in relation to the Renaissance tradition of Magia and Cabala in my *Giordano Bruno*, illustrating this with Fludd's diagrams.

[5] On Dee and Fludd on the mathematical or 'Vitruvian' subjects, see my *Theatre of the World*, 1969, pp. 20-59, on Fludd and Paracelsus, see Allen Debus, *The English Paracelsians*, London, 1965, *passim*, and numerous articles.

[6] On the life of Michael Maier, see J. B. Craven, *Count Michael Maier*, Kirkwall, 1910.

indication of Rudolph's liberal outlook. Robert Fludd's philosophy could represent a line of appeal emanating from England, whilst Michael Maier was continuing the traditions of Rudolphine Prague, which would have been understandable in Bohemia. These were the two strands which Christian of Anhalt strove to weave together through the marriage of the Elector Palatine to an English princess and through presenting him in Bohemia as acceptable as King of Bohemia.

The very large amount of material included in Fludd's tomes on the 'History of the Macrocosm and the Microcosm' must represent a good deal of earlier work, now brought together and published simultaneously. The same applies to the many works by Michael Maier brought out in rapid succession during these years, either by De Bry at Oppenheim or by the firm of Luca Jennis at Strasburg which was closely associated with the De Bry firm.[1] These could not all have been written so rapidly and some must represent earlier work, perhaps written while Rudolph was still alive and Maier was at his court. These publishers were bent on publishing quickly a large amount of material by these two authors and this must have been a definite policy—to publish quickly material congenial to the Palatinate movement. Considerable sums of money must have been available to subsidize these publications, which are illustrated on a lavish scale.

The normal way of trying to get in touch with the R.C. Brothers, after reading the manifestos, was to publish something addressed to them, or expressing admiration for them. These appeals were not answered; the R.C. Brothers did not reply either to their admirers or to their critics. The Rosicrucian 'silence after noise', the withdrawal into invisibility after the loud trumpeting of the manifestos, is the theme of Michael Maier's *Silentium post clamores*.

Robert Fludd began his Rosicrucian career in the usual way, that is to say he published two works expressing admiration for the R.C. Brothers and their aims as expressed in their manifestos. The two little books, both in Latin, which Fludd published in his early efforts to get into touch with the R.C. Brothers were, first, the 'Compendious Apology for the Fraternity of the Rosy Cross, washing away as in a Flood (a pun on his name) the spots of suspicion and infamy with which it has been aspersed',[2] henceforth referred to as the *Apologia*; and second,

---

[1] Luca Jennis's mother married J. Israel De Bry, brother of Johann Theodore, as her second husband; see W. K. Zülch, *Frankfurter Künstler*, Frankfurt, 1935, 'Jennis, Luca'.

[2] R. De Fluctibus (i.e. Robert Fludd), *Apologia Compendiaria Fraternitatem de Rosea Cruce suspicionis & infamia maculis aspersam, veritatis quasi Fluctibus abluens & abstergens*, Leiden (Godfrey Basson), 1616.

'The Apologetic Tractatus for the Society of the Rosy Cross',[1] henceforth referred to as the *Tractatus*. They were published by Godfrey Basson at Leiden in 1616 and 1617.

Godfrey Basson was the son of Thomas Basson, an Englishman settled at Leiden as printer and publisher.[2] Thomas, who had been a protégé of the Earl of Leicester, was interested in the occult. He it was who published in 1597 the *Thamus* of Alexander Dicson, the disciple of Giordano Bruno, which is a magic art of memory imitated from Bruno.[3]

Fludd's *Apologia* opens in a vein of invocation of the traditions of ancient wisdom, of the *prisci theologi*, particularly of 'Mercurius Trismegistus'[4] who is stated to be a most important authority for this wisdom, both in his 'Sermons' (that is, the *Corpus Hermeticum*) and in the *Emerald Table*, that brief statement of Hermetic philosophy which was so greatly revered by the alchemists. It is thus as an adherent of the 'Egyptian' philosophy, the Hermetic philosophy of the supposed Egyptian priest, Hermes Trismegistus, that Fludd approaches the R.C. Brothers.

Next he tells how the fame of the *Fama* of the Society of the Rosy Cross went through all Europe and reached his ears.[5] Fludd has not only seen the two manifestos, the *Fama* and the *Confessio*; he has also seen the attack on them by Libavius. Libavius, he says, has bitterly attacked the Brothers R.C. and in one place has accused them of political insubordination or sedition: 'Nam uno loco fratres in seditionis suspicionem adduxit.'[6] I take this to refer to Libavius's analysis of the passages on Empire in the manifestos in which he sees rebellious designs. Fludd rejects Libavius's criticisms and approves the manifestos. The Brothers, he maintains, are true Christians. They are not wickedly magical or seditious. They would not have trumpeted their message aloud had they been wicked people. Like Lutherans and Calvinists they are against the Pope but are not therefore heretical. Perhaps these Brothers are truly illuminated by God. Fludd earnestly entreats them to receive him into their company.

The *Tractatus* of the following year opens with the same preface as

---

[1] R. de Fluctibus, *Tractatus Apologeticus Integritatem Societatis de Rosea Cruce*, Leiden (Godfrey Basson), 1617.

[2] See J. A. Van Dorsten, *Thomas Basson*, Leiden, 1961.

[3] See Yates, *The Art of Memory*, p. 285.

[4] *Apologia*, pp. 1 ff.

[5] *Ibid.*, p. 6.

[6] *Ibid.*, p. 7.

the *Apologia*, but takes further the defence of 'good magic'. There are good and bad kinds of magic, but if the good kind is excluded or condemned 'we take away all natural philosophy'.[1] The Magi are expert in mathematics, says Fludd, and here he gives the usual list of magico-mechanical marvels, beginning with the wooden dove of Archytas and continuing with the marvellous feats of Roger Bacon, Albertus Magnus and others[2] (compare the lists of such marvels given by Agrippa, Dee, and indeed practically all writers on mechanics at the magical stage[3]). The Brothers R.C., continues Fludd, use only good kinds of magic, mathematical and mechanical, and the magic of the Cabala which teaches how to invoke the sacred names of angels. Magia, Cabala, and Astrologia as studied by the Brothers R.C. are both scientific and holy.

Fludd then passes to a review of the arts and sciences, urging that these are in need of improvement. Natural philosophy, alchemy, medicine, all are defective, says Fludd, and the all-important mathematical sciences are also defective. According to Fludd, the Rosicrucian *Fama* has urged their improvement. He seems to have read this meaning into the mysterious geometrical cave and other weird apparatus of the *Fama*; these represent, he thinks, the mathematical sciences, the improvement of which the *Fama* is urging in its reform programme.[4]

Fludd lists the mathematical arts as geometry, music, military art, arithmetic, algebra, optics; all are in need of improvement and reform. We are here within range of John Dee's Preface to Euclid, with its survey of the mathematical arts listed by Vitruvius, and of which architecture is the chief. I have elsewhere examined the influence of Dee's Preface on Fludd.[5] In the *Tractatus*, Fludd seems to assume that such a programme of reform of the mathematical arts is what the R.C. Brothers desire and are urging in their manifestos; which is tantamount to saying that the R.C. manifestos are influenced by Dee, that their magical movement is of the mathematical and scientific type which Dee had taught. In view of the facts which have been discovered about the influence of Dee's *Monas hieroglyphica* on the manifestos and on the *Chemical Wedding*, Fludd's suppositions seem likely to be correct. Continuing his survey of subjects in need of reform, Fludd

---

[1] *Ibid.*, p. 22. For a useful discussion of the thought of the *Tractatus*, see Allen Debus, 'Mathematics and Nature in the Chemical Texts of the Renaissance', *Ambix*, XV (1968).

[2] *Tractatus*, p. 24.

[3] See my *Giordano Bruno*, pp. 147-9; *Theatre of the World*, p. 30.

[4] *Tractatus*, pp. 102 ff.

[5] *Theatre of the World*, pp. 42 ff.

next lists ethics, economics, politics, jurisprudence, theology, which must all come into the reform scheme. After which he turns to prophecy and the invocation of the Holy Spirit and of angels,[1] as most necessary for the movement, and ends with allusions to the wonderful occult powers of music.

Finally, as in the tract of the previous year, Fludd addresses the Brothers R.C. and begs to be allowed to participate in their work.

Fludd's plea for the reform of the sciences has a Baconian ring and may in part be influenced by *The Advancement of Learning*. But its emphasis on mathematics and the invocation of angels is more like Dee, and it would seem that it was the Dee type of intellectual programme that Fludd recognized in the Rosicrucian manifestos.

Some years later, when defending himself from attacks by enemies in England who have accused him of being a 'Rosicrucian' because of his apology for those 'learned and famous Theosophists and Philosophers' who call themselves the 'Fraternity of the Rosy Cross', Fludd says that he received no reply from the R.C. Brothers, though he thinks that their 'Pansophia or universal knowledge in Nature' must be like his own philosophy.[2] This was always the usual line about enquiries aroused by the Rosicrucian manifestos, that no reply was ever received, that there was always silence after the trumpet sounds. Though Fludd seems to believe here that the R.C. Brothers really exist, he admits that he has never seen one.

In Fludd's case, it would seem that something after all did happen in reply to his *Apologia* and *Tractatus*. He must have been invited to publish his work in the Palatinate with the De Bry firm. This may mean that his defence of the R.C. Brothers against Libavius had been recognized as proof of his support of Palatinate policies.

When later defending himself from the charge made against him in England that he had had his books printed 'beyond the seas' because the magic in them forbade their publication in England, Fludd quotes a letter from a German scholar stating that the printer (that is De Bry) had shown his volume before printing to learned men, including some Jesuits, who had all admired it and recommended publication, though the Jesuits disapproved of his sections on geomancy and wished them omitted.[3] They were, however, evidently not omitted. Fludd is

---

[1] *Tractatus*, p. 146.

[2] See C. H. Josten, 'Robert Fludd's *Philosophical Key* and his Alchemical Experiment n Wheat', *Ambix*, XII (1963), p. 12; cf. *Theatre of the World*, p. 68.

[3] 'A Philosophical Key', quoted *Theatre of the World*, p. 67.

convinced that his volumes are not distasteful to the Calvinists, amongst whom his printer lives, nor to the Lutherans 'which are his bordering neighbours', nor even to the Papists, who have approved them, but he ignores the fact that, according to himself, the Jesuits had not wholly approved.

The first of Fludd's Oppenheim volumes, the 'History of the Macrocosm' of 1617, is dedicated to James I, a most impressive dedication in which James is saluted as 'Ter Maximus', the epithet sacred to Hermes Trismegistus, and as the most potent and wise prince in the world. The significance of this dedication stands out now that we more fully understand the significance of the publication of Fludd's books at Oppenheim. Fludd and his Palatinate publisher were assuming the interest of James in a work published in his son-in-law's dominions. They were drawing this most potent prince into their philosophy, assigning to him a Hermetic role. If this book circulated much in Germany, or in Bohemia, it would have confirmed the impression, or illusion, that thought movements in the Palatinate had the approval of King James.

We can also now begin to see the situation more clearly from James's point of view. His son-in-law, and that son-in-law's advisers and friends, were not only trying to involve James in a political line of action of which he disapproved—the activist policy which was leading towards the Bohemian enterprise. They were also trying to involve him in a philosophy of which he disapproved. James was desperately afraid of anything savouring of magic; this was his most deep-seated neurosis. He had disapproved of Dee, would not receive him,[1] and relegated him to a kind of banishment. And now, in his son-in-law's domains, there is published an immense work on the Dee type of Hermetic philosophy, dedicated to him, and attempting by that dedication to draw him into that point of view, or to give the impression that he is favourable to it. No wonder that the second volume of the 'History of the Macrocosm and the Microcosm' was not dedicated to James, and that Fludd seems to have encountered obscure difficulties in England about the publication of his works.[2]

When replying to accusations that he had had his books published beyond the seas because they contained forbidden magic, Fludd said that his reason for publishing abroad was because the De Bry firm gave him far better illustrations than would have been possible in

---

[1] French, *John Dee*, p. 10.
[2] See my *Art of Memory*, pp. 323–4; *Theatre of the World*, pp. 65–72.

England.[1] The illustrations present in visual form the complex 'hiero-glyphs' of Fludd's philosophy. The engravers followed his instructions precisely, as anyone who studies carefully Fludd's text in relation to the illustrations will discover. The constant going and coming of messengers between London and the Palatinate, keeping in touch with the English princess at Heidelberg, must have greatly facilitated the work of a Palatinate publisher in publishing manuscript materials from England.

Fludd's *Utriusque Cosmi Historia*,[2] or History of the Two Worlds—the Great World of the Macrocosm and the Little World of Man, the Microcosm—is an attempt to cover, and to present with some lucidity, the philosophy based on the harmonious design of the cosmos and the corresponding harmonies in man. The engraved illustrations help a great deal in presenting these cosmic schemes. Basically, Fludd's scheme is the same as that laid down in the early Renaissance when Pico della Mirandola added the revival of Hebrew Cabala to the revival of Hermetic philosophy encouraged by Ficino's use of the newly recovered Hermetic texts. Fludd's volumes are full of quotations from the Hermetic texts in Ficino's Latin translation, and 'Mercurius Trismegistus', the supposed Egyptian author of those texts, is Fludd's most revered authority, which he reconciles with Biblical authority through Cabalistic interpretation of *Genesis*. The resulting cosmic scheme is one in which Jehovah, presented in the form of the Name of God in Hebrew in a glory, reigns over the schemes of concentric circles consisting of angels, stars, elements, with man at the centre. Astral connections run through all, and the close analogies between macrocosmic and microcosmic harmonies are made even closer then they were in the time of Pico and Ficino through the influence of Paracelsus who had made these correspondences more precise through his medico-astral theories.

Fludd's second volume, on the microcosm, includes an important section on what he calls 'technical history', or the survey of the arts and sciences used by man. These are based on nature which is itself based on number. As I have shown in my *Theatre of the World*, Fludd's section on technology is closely following Dee's mathematical preface to Euclid in which Dee had urged the prosecution of the mathematical sciences,

---

[1] *Dr. Fludd's Answer unto M. Foster*, 1631, p. 11; cf. *The Art of Memory*, p. 324.

[2] Robert Fludd, *Utriusque Cosmi. Historia, Tomus Primus, De Macrocosmi Historia*, Oppenheim (Johann Theodore De Bry), 1517, 1618; *Tomus Secundus, De Microcosmi Historia*, Oppenheim (Johann Theodore De Bry), 1619.

grouping these, as Vitruvius did in his treatise on architecture, under architecture as the queen of the mathematical sciences.

Fludd's 'History of the Two Worlds' is, in general, a presentation of Renaissance Magia and Cabala, with the addition of Alchymia as developed by Paracelsus and of the developments introduced by John Dee into these traditions. If the Rosicrucian manifestos are interpreted as a fiction through which is set forth a plea for reformation based on new developments of Magia, Cabala, and Alchymia introduced by Paracelsus and John Dee, then it can be seen that Fludd's philosophy was indeed a 'Rosicrucian' philosophy, a Renaissance philosophy brought up to date, and was rightly welcomed as such by its publication in the Palatinate.

The study of Palatinate culture under Frederick V must include as one of its most important representatives, Salomon de Caus, the designer of the *Hortus Palatinus*, the ingenious architect and mechanic who provided those magico-mechanical wonders which helped to impart an aura of mystery to Heidelberg castle. De Caus worked within the harmonious world-view, as is shown by his intense interest in music and organs combined with the intense Vitruvianism out of which his mechanics are evolved in his *Les raisons des forces mouvantes*. Except for the *Hortus Palatinus*, De Caus's works were not published by the Palatinate publisher, but the exception is an important one for through the *Hortus Palatinus*, published by De Bry with engravings by Merian, De Caus does enter the circle. As a practising technologist and Vitruvian garden-architect, De Caus provided the harmonious setting for Palatinate culture in his work for the Heidelberg court.

Michael Maier was born at Rindsberg in Holstein in 1566. He graduated as a doctor of medicine and lived at Rostock, and then at Prague, where he was physician to the Emperor Rudolph II, as already mentioned. Some time after the death of Rudolph, in 1612, Maier visited England where he was almost certainly in contact with Robert Fludd, though exactly when or under what circumstances is not known. His first publication, the *Arcana arcanissima* (1614), was dedicated to the English physician Sir William Paddy, who was a friend of Fludd's. From mentions in his later works it appears that he also knew other Englishmen, for example Francis Anthony, the alchemist, and Sir Thomas Smith.

Maier was slightly older than Fludd, who was born in 1574, and the earlier part of his life, passed in the atmosphere of Prague in the time of Rudolph II, would seem to have little connection with that of the

21   Michael Maier, *Viatorum, hoc est de montibus planetarum*

22   Michael Maier, *Atalanta fugiens*

Englishman, Fludd, born in the quiet Kentish village of Bearstead and buried there in 1637. What could there have been in common between the German imperialist, immersed in the confusing currents of the court of Rudolph II, and overtaken at the end of his life by the Thirty Years War (Maier disappeared at Magdeburg in 1622 when that city was in the hands of the troops), and the English philosophical physician? Yet there were undoubtedly close connections between the two, and Fludd and Maier belong together as 'Rosicrucian' philosophers, writers who published works in defence of the R.C. Brothers, though both maintain that they did not themselves belong to the Brotherhood, which was of course the usual attitude of writers on the Rosicrucian mystification.

The obvious points of contact between the two are that they were both Paracelsist physicians and both published with Johann Theodore De Bry at Oppenheim. It used to be thought that it was Maier who introduced Fludd to the Rosicrucian world; more recently the theory has been advanced that it was the other way round, that it was Fludd who influenced Maier. All such theories in the past have not, of course, taken into account the historical situation in the Palatinate as a factor in the problem. If Maier knew Fludd and came rather frequently to England, might not this have been because, like many others, he hoped great things from the marriage of the Palatinate ruler with the daughter of James I, and was in the secret of some connection between Rosicrucian propaganda and the affairs of the 'Palatinate Lion'?

After the death of Rudolph, Maier became physician to Maurice, Landgrave of Hesse. He was thus connected with a German prince who was closely in the circle of the Elector Palatine, who had strong sympathies with England, who was influenced by alchemical mysticism, and at whose town of Cassel the Rosicrucian manifestos were first published. Maier's position with the Landgrave of Hesse did not prevent him from doing a good deal of travelling. In 1618, he says in one of his prefaces that he is in Frankfurt on his way from London to Prague. As one who knew both London and Prague, Maier might have been usefully employed by Christian of Anhalt in preparing the way for the great Bohemian adventure.

And in fact, indubitable evidence of connection between Maier and Anhalt does exist. In 1618 there was published by De Bry at Oppenheim a book by Maier which is dedicated to Christian, Prince of Anhalt. This is the *Viatorum, hoc est de Montibus Planetarum Septem*. On the engraved title-page (Pl. 21) we see the mild and dreamy face of

Michael Maier, accompanied by seven figures representing the planets. The book is a characteristic statement of Maier's alchemical mysticism which he loves to present in mythological guise, hidden in the fables of the poets. The theme of the book, thus disguised, is the search for the *materia philosophica*, the truth hidden in the arcana of nature, by holding fast, like Theseus, to the Ariadne's thread which will lead through the labyrinth. One should begin the study of Maier with the *Viatorum*, the dedication of which to Anhalt immediately places him and his spiritual alchemy within the circle of the most important of the advisers of the Elector Palatine.

In the same year, 1618, another book by Maier was published at Oppenheim by the De Bry firm, again with a splendid engraved title-page. This was the *Atalanta fugiens*, a book much sought after for the beautiful illustrations to its enigmatic text. The engraver was almost certainly Matthieu Merian, though the engravings are not signed.

The *Atalanta fugiens* is a book of emblems with philosophical commentaries. Atalanta, on the title-page (Pl. 22), tempted aside from the race for spiritual, moral, and scientific truth, presents a lesson in perseverance and purity of intention to the spiritual alchemist. Maier teaches a very subtle religious, alchemical, philosophy through the emblems of the book, each of which has a musical, as well as the pictorial, mode of expression.[1]

One of the most striking of the emblems shows a philosopher with his lantern carefully following the footprints left by Nature (Pl. 23). This is somewhat reminiscent of the preface dedicated by Giordano Bruno to Rudolph II when in Prague in 1588, reiterating his favourite theme, that one must study the vestiges or footprints left by Nature, avoiding the strife of religious sects and turning to Nature who is crying out everywhere to be heard.[2] Maier, though a devout Lutheran Christian (Fludd was a devout Anglican), may have had some such idea in mind when in these years of fierce religious controversy, just before the outbreak of the Thirty Years War, he teaches his religious and philosophical attitudes through alchemical symbolism.

Another emblem in the *Atalanta fugiens* shows a philosopher pointing to a geometrical figure (Pl. 24a). The commentary on this emblem is

---

[1] On the music of the *Atalanta fugiens*, see John Read, *Prelude to Chemistry*, London, 1936, pp. 213–54, 281–89.

[2] G. Bruno, *Articuli adversus mathematicos*, Prague, 1588, preface; cf. *Giordano Bruno and the Hermetic Tradition*, pp. 314–15.

entitled *'Monas* or the One'. This has been compared by a recent editor of Maier's book[1] to John Dee's *Monas hieroglyphica.* Thus once again we find Dee's *Monas* at the heart of Rosicrucian mystery, enshrined among the emblems of Maier. Maier would have met the Dee influence in Bohemia.

There can be no doubt that the kind of alchemy of which Maier's emblems are the abstruse pictorial expression is the kind of which Libavius disapproved, the alchemy of the Rosicrucian manifestos and of Dee's *Monas.* If one gazes at such an emblem as the one in which the philosopher is about to attack an egg with a sword (Pl. 24b), one can begin to recognize in it the egg which symbolizes the universe[2] in the *Monas hieroglyphica* (Pl. 10a), and the fire, symbolized by the Aries sign in the *Monas,* and expressive of alchemical processes. Looking again now at Khunrath's 'Alchemist', which is expressive of the Dee kind of alchemy, we can see that the perspective in the Maier emblem, stretching out behind the egg, is comparable to the perspective in the Khunrath picture. The perspective symbolizes, I believe, architecture and its allied mathematical subjects. When one remembers that music is supplied by Maier to accompany the 'egg' emblem, one realizes that it contains all the elements summed up in the *Monas hieroglyphica.* I am entirely unable to understand all this, nor how it would be possible to work out a mathemetical problem in terms of this kind of alchemy. But I believe that implications of this kind are present in the Maier emblems, and that Maier may have been the deepest of the 'Rosicrucians'.

Though Maier expresses himself mainly through alchemical emblems, whilst Fludd aims at building a complete philosophical statement, their philosophies have the Dee influence in common and an intense Hermetic basis. Maier's cult of Hermes Trismegistus and of 'Egyptian' Hermetic truth is as enthusiastic as that of Fludd. Whatever else they may represent, Fludd and Maier are most certainly Hermetic philosophers, representing indeed a kind of Hermetic Renaissance at a time when the original Hermetic impulses of the earlier Renaissance were waning in some quarters. Isaac Casaubon had already dated the

[1] See H. M. E. De Jong, *'Atalanta Fugiens': Sources of an Alchemical Book of Emblems,* Leiden, 1969.

[2] The 'monas' sign is enclosed within the outline of an egg on the title-page of *Monas hierglyphica* (Pl. 10a), and an egg-shaped diagram of the universe is also shown in the text. The 'cutting' of the Monas with knives is mysteriously described in the 'Testament of John Dee' published in Elias Ashmole, *Theatrum Chemicum Britannicum,* p. 334. See below, p. 197.

Hermetic writings as post-Christian,[1] and therefore not the work of the very ancient Egyptian priest, Hermes Trismegistus. The work in which Casaubon dated the *Hermetica* was actually dedicated to James I in 1614, a dedication which would seem to put James into the anti-Hermetic camp, and in a very different world from the intensive pseudo-Egyptianism of Fludd and Maier.

It is impossible to discuss adequately, or even to mention here, all the works of Michael Maier published between 1614 and 1620. The following remarks represent only a few points drawn from this vast and rich material.

Maier's *Lusus serius* was published at Oppenheim by Luca Jennis in 1616, who republished it also at Oppenheim in 1618. It is in the preface to this book that Maier states that he is at Frankfurt, on his way from London to Prague. The three dedicatees of the book are Francis Anthony, described as an Englishman of London (a well-known English Paracelsist physician),[2] Jacob Mosanus, said to be a dignitary in the household of the Landgrave of Hesse, and Christian Rumphius, said to be physician to the Elector Palatine of the Rhine. These dedicatees are indicative of the circles in which Maier was moving, Paracelsist medical circles in London and in Germany at the courts of the Landgrave of Hesse and of the Elector Palatine.

The *Lusus serius*, or serious game, is perhaps what Andreae might have called a *ludibrium*. It is a simple little allegory in which a cow, a sheep, and other creatures set out their claims to importance, but supreme importance is awarded to Hermes Trismegistus after his speech in which he describes his role of peacemaker and reconciler and the usefulness of the activities over which he presides, which include medicine and mechanics. This story is perfectly silly on the face of it. One can only suppose that it had some secret meaning in the circles in which Maier was moving. There is another Hermetic joke by Maier called the *Jocus Severus*, an allegory about birds of night which was first published much earlier in 1597, under the auspices of the elder De Bry at Frankfurt, and republished at Frankfurt in 1616 with a preface addressed 'to all the Chemists of Germany' and containing allusions to the Rosicrucian manifestos. This pretty clearly connects the Maier type of 'joking' with that of the manifestos.

In the *Symbola aurea*, published at Frankfurt by Luca Jennis in 1617, Maier extols the sublimity of 'chymia', the all-wisdom of Hermes,

---

[1] See *Giordano Bruno and the Hermetic Tradition*, pp. 398–403.
[2] See Debus, *The English Paracelsians*, pp. 142–5.

King of Egypt, and the sacredness of the 'Virgin', or 'Queen Chemia', and ends with an Hermetic hymn of regeneration. We have here the expression of an intense Hermetic mysticism, reminding one very much of Giordano Bruno's use of Hermetic religious themes, though with more use of alchemical imagery than in Bruno. In the *Symbola*, Maier refers to the R.C. Fraternity at some length, but too vaguely to be informative.

Maier may have been influenced by a Bruno tradition as well as by the Dee tradition. We know that Bruno claimed to have founded a sect of 'Giordanisti' among the Lutherans.[1] Maier was a Lutheran; his intensively Hermetic religious movement might therefore have included some Bruno influence, might be an attempt at the Hermetic reform of religion, the infusion of greater life into religion through Hermetic influences, such as Bruno had so passionately advocated. On the other hand the strongly alchemical aspect of Maier's movement points to Dee as the major influence. Perhaps in the Palatinate type of Hermetic reform, currents descending from the Dee type of Hermetic tradition mingle with a Bruno type.

Maier's *Silentium post clamores* and *Themis aurea*, both published by Luca Jennis at Frankfurt in 1617 and 1618 respectively, reflect the excitement aroused by the Rosicrucian manifestos of the preceding years. In mentioning the R.C. Brothers and their affairs in these books, Maier is touching on the theme which was arousing most eager curiosity. He seems in these books to be both giving and withholding information. In both works he maintains that the R.C. Fraternity actually exists, and is not a mere mystification, as some have said. On the other hand, he states that he is not a member and is too humble a person to have access to such exalted beings.

In the *Silentium post clamores* Maier is defending the R.C. Brethren from calumnies and purporting to explain why they do not reply to the many persons who have tried to get in touch with them. He says that the writers of the *Fama* and the *Confessio* have done their duty by publishing those tracts, and that they prefer to exhaust calumny by silence rather than by writing further. He hurries on to add that he does not think that the Rosicrucian Society needs his insignificant patronage. The members of it are upright and pious, their purposes are good, they are sufficient unto themselves. He states that the Rosicrucian Society, as well as its pious and philanthropic purposes, is concerned with the investigation of nature. Nature is yet but half revealed, he says; what is

[1] See *Giordano Bruno and the Hermetic Tradition*, pp. 312–13.

wanted is chiefly experiment and tentative enquiry.[1] This suggestion of a Baconian influence, perhaps an influence of *The Advancement of Learning* itself, is important. A Baconian influence could have come into Germany in the wake of the Elector Palatine's marriage, and of the contacts with England such as Maier's movements suggest.

In the *Themis aurea* (an English translation of which was published in 1652, dedicated to Elias Ashmole), Maier purports to reveal the structure of the Rosicrucian Society and its laws. Unfortunately these laws are merely a digest of what was told to the public about the R.C. Brethren in the *Fama*, that they were to heal the sick, to meet once a year, and so on. Once again Maier teasingly reveals and yet does not reveal at the same time. Yet he is positive that some such society really existed, and people who knew what his connections were, in what circles he was moving, might have been able to guess at his allusions. In the following he seems to be intending to reveal the meeting place of the R.C. Brethren:[2]

> I have sometimes observed Olympick Houses not far from a river, and known a city which we think is called S. Spiritus—I mean Helicon, or Parnassus, in which Pegasus opened a spring of overflowing water, wherein Diana wash'd herselfe, to whom Venus was handmaid, and Saturne gentleman usher. This will sufficiently instruct an intelligent reader, but more confound the ignorant.

Parnassus, Pegasus, are indeed safely classical allusions, most indistinct, and a city called Sanctus Spiritus near a river might be anything. On the other hand, Heidelberg is near a river, its church was the church of the Holy Spirit, its gardens contained a wondrous Parnassus fountain. In reading Maier after close study of the Heidelberg milieu and of Andreae's *Chemical Wedding*, one has the impression that Maier, like Andreae, may be making allusions to Heidelberg, that some of his emblematic pictures might reflect symbolic constructions which could be seen in the Hortus Palatinus. Compare, for example, the grotto which De Caus constructed at Heidelberg containing a fountain decorated with coral (Pl. 25a) with Maier's delightful emblem of a man fishing for coral (Pl. 25b). The commentary to the emblem explains that coral represents the Philosopher's Stone.

---

[1] *Silentium post clamores*, pp. 11 ff.; cf. Waite, *Brotherhood of the Rosy Cross*, p. 321.

[2] *Themis aurea, hoc est de legibus Fraternitatis R.C.*, Frankfurt, 1618, p. 143; cf. Waite, *ibid.*, p. 328.

An important point in the *Themis aurea*, and one which tends to confirm some earlier arguments in this book, is its discussion of the R.C. Fraternity as an Order of Chivalry, comparing its 'R.C.' emblem with the insignia of other Orders, the double cross of the Knights of Malta, the Fleece of the Order of the Golden Fleece, or the Garter of the Order of the Garter. The passage should be compared with the allusions to Orders of Chivalry in the *Chemical Wedding*. Maier goes on to say, after comparing the R.C. Order with other Orders, that its emblem is neither a double cross, a Fleece, nor a Garter, but the words R.C. Of these words he gives the peculiar interpretation that R. signifies 'Pegasus', and C. 'Iulius' (no explanation as to why), adding 'Is not this a claw of a rosy lion?'[1] I am glad to leave this in the form of a question!

In his *Verum inventum* published at Frankfurt by Luca Jennis in 1619 and dedicated to the Landgrave of Hesse, Maier seems to be in a patriotic vein, discusses the history of the Empire in its relation to Germany, extols the riches of German learning, for example the great number of manuscripts stored in libraries such as the one at Heidelberg, praises Martin Luther and his stand against the Roman tyrant, desires a return to the primitive church, and highly exalts Paracelsus 'who is followed by many thousands of doctors in all countries'.[2]

Finally we come to 1620. In that year Luca Jennis published at Frankfurt Maier's *Septimana philosophica* which describes a conversation between Solomon, the Queen of Sheba, and Hiram, King of Tyre, and includes mystical conferences on various themes, including one on the Rose.[3]

The strange publications of Michael Maier follow a distinct time graph. They begin in 1614, the year after the wedding of Frederick and Elizabeth; they end in 1620 (though there is one later one), the year of the brief reign of Frederick and Elizabeth in Bohemia. They are throughout characterized by Hermetic mysticism expressed in terms of Hermetic or 'Egyptian' interpretation of fable and myth, as containing hidden alchemic and 'Egyptian' meanings, combined with an idiosyncratic use of alchemical symbolism. The *Atalanta fugiens* is the finest product of this outlook, and suggestive of a highly educated and sophisticated background in which alchemy is being used as a symbol of

---

[1] *Themis aurea*, p. 159.
[2] *Verum inventum*, dedication.
[3] *Septimana philosophica*, pp. 118–21. These remarks seem deliberately unrevealing.

a religious and intellectual movement of uncommon importance and interest.

It seems now obvious that the time graph of the religious and intellectual movement which Maier represents is the time of the Frederick-Elizabeth movement, working up from the wedding to the fatal year in Bohemia, and that Maier is expressing the religious and intellectual sides of that movement in his Hermetic symbolism. His definite contact with Anhalt in a dedication suggests strongly that he was working with Anhalt in forming links between England, Germany, and Bohemia, preparatory to the establishment of Frederick and Elizabeth as King and Queen of Bohemia.

Maier is activated by a very strong religious Hermetic impulse, as strong, in its way, as that which had moved Giordano Bruno in the late sixteenth century, though combined in Maier with Lutheran piety— the sort of combination one might expect if Bruno's influence took root in Lutheran circles in Germany.

The strength of this impulse was not extinguished in Maier even by the disasters of 1620. His last work seems to have been the *Cantilenae intellectuales de Phoenice redivivo*,[1] with a dedication to Frederick, Prince of Norway, dated at Rostock, 23 August 1622. In this, his swan song, or rather his phoenix song, Maier prophesies the rebirth of the Phoenix, the Hermetic and Egyptian bird whose supremacy over all other birds he had celebrated in one of his earlier 'jokes'. In the dedication of his phoenix song to the Norwegian prince, Maier speaks of his life as having been spent—not, curiously enough, in the framing of complex works of Hermetic symbolism, which he does not mention— but in the study of mathematics.

A young Bohemian alchemist, a refugee from the horrors taking place in his country after 1620, revered the memory of Michael Maier and kept it green by republishing his works, using the same plates as had been used in the original publications. The young Bohemian was Daniel Stolck, or Stolcius, a medical graduate of the university of Prague who, in 1621, had reached Marburg, where he matriculated, and then went on to Frankfurt, where he called on Luca Jennis. Jennis showed him the plates of a number of recently published alchemical works, chiefly those of Maier, and Stolcius agreed to edit a new collected publication of them.[2] This came out as the *Viridarium*

---

[1] See Craven, *Michael Maier*, p. 146.
[2] See John Read, *Prelude to Chemistry*, pp. 254–77. Stolcius's use of plates from works by Maier and Mylius is analysed by Read.

chemicum, published by Luca Jennis at Frankfurt in 1624,[1] with a preface by Stolcius dated 1623 at Oxford. England was the haven which the Bohemian refugee had now reached, like many others from his country in later years. In this preface, Stolcius tells of his unhappiness which he has tried to alleviate by dwelling in imagination in 'the pleasure garden of Chymistry', and he wishes to offer this solace also to his distressed countrymen. He evidently hopes that the 'pleasure garden' will circulate in oppressed Bohemia. In his journey abroad he is, he says, most grieved by the disasters of his country, and interrupted by the tumults of war. The only refuge is in the pleasure garden of chemistry:[2]

> Therefore kind reader, use and take pleasure in these (emblems) as seems best to thee, and take a pleasant stroll in my garden. Thank the cherished memory of the very famous and learned Herr Michael Maier, the most celebrated Doctor of Physic and Medicine, for part of the illustrations; Master John Mylius, that industrious Chymist, for the rest.

Many of Maier's emblems are republished in this book, from the original plates which Jennis had preserved, together with many of the emblems of Mylius, originally published in 1622. Mylius was a disciple of Maier and evidently sympathized strongly with the 'cause', for he speaks in a preface of the year 1620 as 'that ominous year which weeps so that the skies fall'.[3]

Stolcius provides a link between the alchemical emblem movement around Maier and the Bohemian side of the movement which came to so disastrous an end in 1620. The refugee hastens to Luca Jennis, as to a sympathizer, and sadly and reverently puts together a reprint of Maier's emblems. The *Viridarium chemicum* opens with a series of emblems on the uniting of the *sponsus* and the *sponsa* as the image of elemental fusion in alchemical processes. In the first of these 'chemical weddings' (Pl. 26a), which is the first picture in the book,[4] the alchemical *sponsus* and *sponsa* have a curious resemblance to Frederick and Elizabeth as they appear in the 'Four Lions' print (Pl. 8), published at Prague at the time of their coronation.

---

[1] A German edition was published by Jennis, also in 1624; this edition is accessible in a reprint; see Stoltzius von Stoltzenberg, *Chymisches Lustgärtlein*, ed. F. Weinhandl, Darmstadt, 1964.

[2] Quoted Read, *Prelude*, p. 257.

[3] Johann Daniel Mylius, *Philosophia Reformata*, Frankfurt (Luca Jennis), 1622, Preface, quoted Read, p. 260.

[4] It was first published in Maier's *Tripus Aureus*, Frankfurt (Luca Jennis), 1618, p. 27.

This study of Fludd and Maier has attempted to show that both these 'Rosicrucian' philosophers belonged to the orbit of the Frederickian movement in the Palatinate. They were both published by the Palatinate publisher, De Bry, though Maier was also published by the allied firm of Jennis. The importance of printers and publishers in the movement has come out. And we have seen that Hermetic philosophies from England, represented by Fludd, are being propagated in the Palatinate area, together with the alchemical symbolist movement, propagated by Maier, probably as part of a mission of developing links with Bohemia, and especially with Prague, the chief European centre of alchemy. There was then, it would seem, in the Palatinate, an effort towards encouraging lines of thought through which the English alliance could be integrated with expansion into Bohemia. The Bohemian adventure of the Elector Palatine was clearly not such a matter of surface politics or misguided ambition as used to be supposed. There were currents of very serious purpose running within this movement.

A culture was forming in the Palatinate which came straight out of the Renaissance but with more recent trends added, a culture which may be defined by the adjective 'Rosicrucian'. The prince around whom these deep currents were swirling was Frederick, Elector Palatine, and their exponents were hoping for a politico-religious expression of their aims in the movement towards the Bohemian adventure. As I begin to see it, all the mysterious movements of former years around such figures as Philip Sidney, John Dee, Giordano Bruno, were gathered to a head in the Anhalt propaganda for Frederick. The Frederickian movement was not the cause of these deep currents, and it was far from being the only expression of them. But it was an attempt to give those currents politico-religious expression, to realize the ideal of Hermetic reform centred on a real prince. The movement tried to unite many hidden rivers in one stream, the Dee philosophy and the mystical chivalry from England were to join with German mystical currents. The new alchemy was to unite religious differences, and found a symbol in the 'chemical wedding' with its overtones of allusion to the 'marriage of the Thames and the Rhine'. We know that this movement was to fail disastrously, was to rush over a precipice into the abyss of the Thirty Years War. But in the meantime it had created a culture, a 'Rosicrucian' state with its court centred on Heidelberg, its philosophic literature published within the state, having artistic manifestations in the alchemical emblem movement around Maier, and in the work of Salomon De Caus.

CHAPTER VII

THE ROSICRUCIAN FURORE IN GERMANY

The 'Rosicrucian furore' which arose in response to the stirring announcements of the manifestos soon became inextricably confused through the large numbers who tried to join in without inside knowledge of what it was all about, being merely attracted by the exciting possibility of getting into touch with mysterious personages possessing superior knowledge or powers, or angered and alarmed by the imagined spread of dangerous magicians or agitators. Maier thought of the manifestos as an appeal to all the 'chymists' of Germany;[1] perhaps he meant by this an appeal to all mystical Paracelsists or seekers after some way of illumination. Those responsible for the original manifestos may well have been surprised and alarmed by the effect of their words, by the wild excitement which broke out in response to the appeal of the supposed R.C. Brothers for the support of their movement.

The response was chiefly in reply to the *Fama* and the *Confessio*, the authors of which, though obviously belonging to the school of Rosencreutz mythology propagated by Andreae in the *Chemical Wedding*, may have been other than Andreae himself. I do not put forward any theories about the identities of the writers who may have co-operated with Andreae over the Rosencreutz propaganda. There have been many suggestions made about this, some obviously wide of the mark, some which ought to be considered. Amongst the latter is Joachim Jungius, the noted mathematician admired by Leibniz. The candidacy of Jungius as author of the Rosicrucian manifestos was put forward in 1698 by a writer who said that he was informed of this by a member of the court of Heidelberg in exile.[2] This source may possibly now

---

[1] Maier, *Jocus Severus*, dedicatory epistle.

[2] J. A. Fabricius stated that Joachim Jungius was the author of the *Fama* and that he had been told this by 'a secretary of Heidelberg'; see *Acta eruditorum*, 1698, p. 172; cf. Arnold, *Histoire des Rose-Croix*, p. 85. Partington (*History of Chemistry*, II, p. 415) quotes the *Acta eruditorum* reference but says that there is no truth in the statement that Jungius wrote the *Fama*, though he did belong to Andreae's circle.

strengthen the candidacy of Jungius. The fact that we now know that the Rosencreutz myth was a kind of 'magic parable' which, as in the case of John Dee's *Monas hieroglyphica*, might include very serious scientific work, particularly in mathematics, raises the possibility that figures as important as Jungius might have been behind the manifestos. However no definite statements can be made on the problems of the background of the manifestos until more work has been done on the historical background. The destruction of books and papers at Heidelberg when the town fell into the hands of the enemies may mean that much of the evidence was irrevocably destroyed. It is possible that Janus Gruter, the librarian of the *Bibliotheca Palatina* and the centre of a large international correspondence, is someone who might be watched for clues.

The duration of the Rosicrucian furore, of the spate of literature aroused by the manifestos, supports the argument that the manifestos were connected with the movement around the Elector Palatine, for the furore comes to rather a sudden end after 1620, or at a time coinciding with the collapse of the Bohemian venture, the invasion of the Palatinate, and the suppression of the court of Heidelberg.

What is badly needed for the elucidation of the tangled maze of the literature of the Rosicrucian furore is a clearing of the ground by the skills of the bibliographical specialist, an assessment of dates, places of publication, printers' marks, paper, and so on, through which a more accurate conspectus of the movement could be arrived at, and the many problems of anonymity and use of pseudonyms by the writers might be cleared up.[1] The whole field is really virgin soil, as yet untilled by serious modern research, because hitherto dismissed as unworthy of serious study. In the present chapter, I do not aim at digging in the field to any great depth, but only at giving a brief impression of the literature of the furore (apart from the works of Fludd and Maier, which the last chapter attempted to survey).

---

[1] At present, the only work purporting to be a Rosicrucian Bibliography is F. Leigh Gardner, *A Catalogue Raisonné of works on the Occult Sciences: Rosicrucian Books*, privately printed, 1923. This is very unsatisfactory, though it can help as an introduction to the material. Some information can be found by going through J. Ferguson, *Bibliotheca Chemica*, Glasgow, 1906.

The best available accounts of what I have called 'the Rosicrucian furore' are to be found in the following books: A. E. Waite, *The Real History of the Rosicrucians*, London, 1887, pp. 246 ff.; A. E. Waite, *The Brotherhood of the Rosy Cross*, London, 1923, pp. 213 ff; Paul Arnold, *Histoire des Rose-Croix*, Paris, 1955, pp. 137 ff.; Will-Erich Peuckert, *Die Rosenkreutzer*, Jena, 1928, pp. 116 ff. Peuckert's book is valuable, particularly for the German background.

There are the many simple souls, frequently referring to themselves only by initial letters, who print appeals to the R.C. Brothers expressing admiration and asking to join their movement. Others publish longer works, dedicated to the R.C. Brothers, hoping to gain their attention. Then we have the antagonists, the disapprovers, who attack the impiety, magical practices, or subversiveness of the R.C. Brothers. We have already considered one critic, Libavius. The pseudonyms 'Menapius' and 'Irenaeus Agnostus'[1] hide severe critics.

The most interesting of the publications are those which emanate from people who seem well-informed about the movement, or were possibly themselves involved in it from the inside. They are mysterious people, who use pseudonyms. In what follows I concentrate on this type of Rosicrucian publication, selecting those which seem to me most important, in the endeavour to learn more, if possible, about the movement from the inside, and disregarding the flood of publications from outsiders who obviously know nothing save what they have read in the manifestos.

Theophilus Schweighardt[2] published in 1618, with no name of place of publication or printer, a work with the following title: *Speculum sophicum Rhodo-Stauroticum, Das ist: Weilauffige Entdeckung des Collegii und axiomatum von sondern erleuchten Fraternitet Christi-Rosen Creutz*. This is a typical example of a Rosicrucian title, with its mixture of Latin and German. In this work Theophilus Schweighardt, who may be one Daniel Mögling, or may be the same as 'Florentinus de Valentia', who may be Andreae himself, is enthusiastic about the 'Pansophia' of the Brotherhood and their threefold activities, which he classifies as (1) divinely magical (2) physical or 'chymical', and (3) 'Tertriune' or religious and Catholic. They believe in 'divine Elias' (an allusion to Paracelsus's prophecy of the coming of Elias). They possess colleges with large libraries, and they read with particular enthusiasm the works of Thomas à Kempis, finding here, in Christian mystical piety, the true 'magnalia', the final explanation of the macro-microcosmical mystery.[3]

This work is fairly typical of such publications, with its 'Pansophic' philosophy of macrocosm and microcosm, infused with Magia,

---

[1] The person who signed himself thus began by collaborating with the movement but afterwards attacked it; see Arnold, pp. 114–15. 'Menapius' parodied the R. C. Brothers in 1619; he is thought by Waite (*Real History*, p. 258) to be the same person as 'Irenaeus Agnostus'.

[2] Waite, *Brotherhood of the Rosy Cross*, p. 259; Arnold, p. 113.

[3] Schweighardt, *Speculum*, p. 12.

Cabala, and Alchymia, with its hint of earnest pursuit of learning and scientific activities, its prophetic side, its strong pietistic vein.

Bound with the British Museum copy of the *Speculum* there is a very interesting collection of prints and drawings. One of these refers closely to the Rosicrucian *Fama*. I know of another copy of this print[1] which was apparently circulating by itself, independently of the *Speculum*.

This print (frontispiece) shows a peculiar building above which is an inscription containing the words *Collegium Fraternitatis* and *Fama*, and is dated 1618. On the building, on either side of its door, there is a rose and a cross. We are therefore presumably now beholding a representation of the Invisible College of the R.C. Brothers. Another main Rosicrucian emblem is alluded to in the wings with Jehova's Name, expressive of the words which seal the conclusion of the *Fama*, 'Under the shadow of thy wings, Jehova'. In the sky, to left and right of the central Name and wings, are a Serpent and a Swan, bearing stars and alluding to the 'new stars' in Serpentarius and Cygnus mentioned in the *Confessio*[2] as prophetic of a new dispensation.

A hand proceeding from a cloud around the Name holds the building, as on a thread, and the building itself is winged, and on wheels. Does this mean that the winged, moveable, College of the Fraternity of the Rosy Cross is Nowhere, like Utopia, invisible, because non-existent in a literal sense? The Rose Cross College is defended by three figures on its battlements who bear shields on which are engraved the Name, and brandish what appear to be feathers. Are they angelic presences defending those dwelling under the Shadow of the Wings?

From one side of the building projects a trumpet, and the initials 'C.R.F.', perhaps 'Christian Rosencreutz Frater', announced by the trumpeting of the manifestos. On the other side, a hand holding a sword projects, labelled 'Jul. de Campi', alluding to the character called 'Julianus de Campis' who appears in the *Speculum* and whose defence of the R.C. Brotherhood was printed with the 1616 (Cassel) edition of the manifestos.[3] Perhaps this is why he brandishes a defensive sword in the print. Near the projecting arm, the words 'Jesus nobis omnia' are written on the building, a motto which also occurs in the

---

[1] British Museum, Print Room, Foreign History, 1618, number 1871.12.9.4766. Ben Jonson, who describes this print (see below, p. 143), had evidently seen it in a copy of Schweighardt's *Speculum*.

[2] See Appendix, p. 256 and above, p. 48.

[3] See Appendix, below, p. 237.

Fama and is expressive of the point already quoted from the *Speculum*, that the true approach to the macro-microcosmical mystery is in the imitation of Christ as defined by Thomas à Kempis. Other little pairs of wings have inscriptions, one is 'T.S.', perhaps Theophilus Schweighardt, the supposed author of the *Speculum*.

A figure kneeling on the ground on the right directs most earnest prayers straight upwards to the Name. Seen within the windows of the angel-protected College of the Rose Cross Fraternity are figures of people who appear to be engaged in studies. A man is working at something at one window, at the other there appear to be scientific instruments of some kind. The prayerful attitude of the kneeling figure might be expressive of an approach to scientific, angelic, and divine studies rather like that of John Dee.

I leave the reader to puzzle further over the mysteries of this print which is undoubtedly showing us in emblematic form the message of the Rosicrucian *Fama*. We are here near the centre of the 'joke', the *ludibrium*, in the minds of the strange people who framed the Rosicrucian manifestos.

'Joseph Stellatus' wrote in Latin, without German admixture, his work called 'The Pegasus of the Firmament or a brief introduction to the Ancient Wisdom, formerly taught in the Magia of the Egyptians and Persians and now rightly called the Pansophia of the Venerable Society of the Rosy Cross.'[1] It was published in 1618, with no name of place or printer, and with a privilege from 'Apollo'. The author knows and quotes from the *Fama* and the *Confessio*, and also the *Chemical Wedding*. He is an ardent Lutheran, but deeply imbued with 'Ancient Wisdom', Hermetic and Cabalist (he quotes Reuchlin). He proclaims that it is deeply pious to read in the Book of Nature. Amongst the first interpreters of Nature he places Hermes Trismegistus, whom he dates as contemporary with Moses; and another most important interpreter of Nature is Paracelsus. He knows some of the works of Maier, and quotes from them, and in what he says of the mystery of the 'utriusque Mundi majoris et minoris Harmonica comparatione' he is obviously alluding to Fludd's work.

'Stellatus' gives one of the clearest definitions of the Rosicrucian movement as inspired by 'Ancient Theology' which encourages enquiry into Nature. He is strongly anti-Aristotelian and in favour of

---

[1] Joseph Stellatus, *Pegasus Firmamenti sive Introductio brevis in veterum sapientiam, quae olim ab Aegyptiis & Persis Magia, hodie vero a Venerabili Fraternitate Roseae Crucis Pansophia recte vocatur*, 1618.

animistic interpretation of Nature. He may make personal allusions, but these are extremely obscure. At one point he seems to have the Landgrave of Hesse in mind, and I am inclined to think that 'Pegasus' may have been one of the epithets for the Elector Palatine.

Among other mysterious supporters of the R.C. Brothers was 'Julianus de Campis', already mentioned, and Julius Sperber, the latter the author of the *Echo der von Gott Hocherleuchten Fraternitet des löblichen Ordens R.C.*, published at Dantzig in 1615. Julius Sperber was the real name of a real person,[1] who is said to have held an official position at Anhalt-Dessau, so he may possibly have been connected with Christian of Anhalt. In his *Echo*, Sperber seems to write with some authority about the Brothers R.C., and shows himself deeply imbued with Magia and Cabala, with the works of Henry Cornelius Agrippa and Johannes Reuchlin; he also knows the *Harmonia Mundi* of Francesco Giorgi, and the works of 'Marsilius Ficinus Theologus'. He is interested in the views of Copernicus, and strongly recommends as a work of piety reading the hieroglyphs and characters in the Book of Nature. Sperber would seem a typical example of the turning towards investigation of nature arising out of the Rosicrucian current.

The 'Judgment of Some Celebrated Doctors about the position and religion of the Famous Fraternity of the Rosy Cross',[2] published at Frankfurt in 1616, is, as its title suggests, a collection of opinions by various people. The first essay is a eulogy of the motto 'Jhesus mihi omnia' of the Rosicrucian Order and is by 'Christianus Philadelphus,' a lover of Pansophia, who emphasizes the profoundly Christian character of the Order. Another contribution urges all the pious of Europe to throw off the 'Pseudo-Ethnic' (that is, the Aristotelian) philosophy and to turn to the 'Divine Macro-Microcosmic Theosophy'.

One of the most interesting of all these tracts is the *Rosa Florescens*[3], published in 1617 and 1618 with no name of place or printer, and said to be by 'Florentinus de Valentia'. It is a reply to a criticism of the R.C. Fraternity by 'Menapius'. The author of the *Rosa Florescens* shows perhaps the widest knowledge and reading of any of the group. He is interested in architecture, mechanics (Archimedes), arithmetic, algebra, musical harmony, geometry, navigation, the fine arts (Dürer). He thinks that the sciences are imperfect and calls for their improve-

---

[1] *Bibliotheca Chemica*, II, pp. 391–2; cf. Waite, *Real History*, p. 253; Arnold, p. 133.

[2] *Iudicia Clarissimorum aliquot ac doctissimorum virorum . . . de Statu & Religione Fraternitatis celebratissimae de Rosea Cruce*, Frankfurt (J. Bringeren), 1616.

[3] Florentinus de Valentia, *Rosa Florescens contra F. G. Menapius*, 1617, 1618. See *Bibliotheca Chemica*, I, pp. 281–2.

23 Following the Foot-prints of Nature.
From *Atalanta fugiens*

24a   Alchemy and Geometry

24b   The Philosopher's Egg. From *Atalanta fugiens*

ment. Astronomy is in the highest imperfection; Astrology is un-certain. Is not 'Physica' lacking in experiment? Does not 'Ethica' need re-examination? What is medicine but conjecture?[1]

These passages have an almost Baconian ring, and there may indeed have been an influence of *The Advancement of Learning* on the group, coming in from England, along with other English influences, through the marriage of the Elector Palatine. Nevertheless, the chief interests of the author of *Rosa Florescens* seem to be in the sciences based on number, in the 'Vitruvian' subjects which John Dee had wished to see improved in his preface to Euclid. Fludd in his *Tractatus* of 1616, in which he praised the Rosicrucian movement and repeated Dee's arguments for the improvement of the mathematical sciences, may have been the influence on the *Rosa Florescens*. But whatever the influences on him may have been, the writer of this work is making a strong, independent plea for the advancement of all branches of learning. We may take it that such an outlook as this was behind the plea of the Rosicrucian *Fama* for co-operative effort for the spread of enlightenment.

For the author of the *Rosa Florescens* the impulse towards the in-vestigation of Nature is profoundly religious in its motive. God has imprinted his signs and characters in the Book of Nature. In con-templating that Book we contemplate God Himself. The spirit of God is at the centre of Nature; it is the ground of Nature and of the know-ledge of all things. The reader is adjured to study with the R.C. Brothers the Book of Nature, the Book of the World, and to return to the Paradise which Adam lost. (Bacon, too, hoped to restore to man the knowledge which Adam had before the Fall.) The writer assures the critical 'Menapius' that the R.C. Brothers love God and their neighbour; they seek knowledge of Nature for the glory of Christ and have nothing to do with the Devil and his works. The writer believes firmly in the Father, the Son, and the Holy Ghost, and fer-vently desires to dwell 'under Jehova's wings'.

It has been suggested that this passionate tract may be by Johann Valentin Andreae himself.[2] It is certainly a striking work and worthy of the author of the *Chemical Wedding*.

The criticism of the R.C. Brothers by 'Menapius', 'Irenaeus Agnos-tus', Libavius, and others rests mainly on the following points. It is

[1] *Rosa Florescens, passim.*

[2] This suggestion was made by Gottfried Arnold, *Unpartheyische Kirchen-und Ketzer-Historien*, 1699, p.624. Cf. *Bibliotheca Chemica, loc. cit.*

suspected that their activities may be subversive of established governments; Libavius is the most direct about this charge. There is a frequently made general accusation of magical practices.[1] Finally—and this is one of the most important points—their enemies complain that the religious position of the R.C. Brothers is not clear. Some call them Lutherans, others Calvinists, and some, Socinians[2] or Deists. They are even suspected by some of being Jesuits.[3]

This is suggestive of what may have been one of the most important aspects of the Rosicrucian movement, that it could include different religious denominations. As we have seen, Fludd claimed that his work found favour with truly religious persons of all denominations. Fludd was a devout Anglican, friend of Anglican bishops; so was Elizabeth Stuart, the wife of the Elector Palatine. The Elector was a devout Calvinist, as was Christian of Anhalt, his chief adviser. Maier was a devout Lutheran, as was also Andreae and many of the other Rosicrucian writers. The common denominator which would weld them all together would be the macro-microcosmic musical philosophy, the mystical alchemy, of which Fludd and Maier were the two chief exponents, though the minor writings which we have been examining in this chapter all reflect a similar outlook.

By the diffusion of a philosophy, or a theosophy, or a Pansophia, which they hoped might be accepted by all religious parties, the members of this movement perhaps hoped to establish a non-sectarian basis for a kind of freemasonry—I use this word here only for its general meaning and without necessarily implying a secret society— which would allow persons of differing religious views to live together peaceably. The common basis would be a common Christianity, interpreted mystically, and a philosophy of Nature which sought the divine meaning of the hieroglyphic characters written by God in the universe, and interpreted macrocosm

[1] Defenders maintain that their magic is good and godly.

[2] On the suggestion of Socinian influence, see Henricus Neuhusius, *Pia et utilissima admonitio de Fratribus Rosae Crucis*, Dantzig, 1618. Neuhusius maintains that the Rosicrucians are Socinians. Though Socinians may have been attracted by the liberalism of the movement, the characteristic religious affiliation of the manifestos and of the furore which they aroused seems to me to have been primarily an evangelical and mystical type of Christianity.

[3] This impression may have been encouraged by the 'Adam Haselmayer' material published with the *Fama* (see above, pp. 41–2, and Appendix, below, p. 235). Though Haselmayer is said to have been persecuted by the Jesuits he seems also to have given the impression that the 'Rosicrucian Order', with its attachment to Jesus, was a kind of Jesuit Order, though with very different aims. Some Jesuit enemies of the Rosicrucians seemed also to want to give the impression that the two Orders were the same; see below, p. 101.

and microcosm through mathematical-magical systems of universal harmony.

And here we may remind ourselves that John Dee entertained wide aspirations for the mitigation of religious differences, the establishment of a universal reign of mystic and philosophic harmony, as in the angelic realms. Here too, then, influences from Dee's mission in Bohemia may have percolated to the German Rosicrucian movement.

Yet this chapter has also brought out the strongly German side of the movement, and the influences upon it of German mystical traditions. In reading these German Rosicrucian authors one is frequently reminded of Jacob Boehme, famous German mystical philosopher. Boehme was beginning to write just before the issue of the first printed edition of the Rosicrucian *Fama*. His earliest work was an 'Aurora', promising a new dawn of insight, like that manifesto.[1] Boehme aimed at refreshing with Paracelsus-inspired alchemical philosophy the deadness and dryness of contemporary Lutheran piety, which is an aim of the Rosicrucian writers. Boehme's native town was near Gorlitz, in Lusatia and on the borders of Bohemia. Living where he did and when he did Boehme cannot have failed to know of the Rosicrucian furore and of the movement around the Elector Palatine and its crashing failure in 1620. One of the few dates known in Boehme's obscure biography is that he was in Prague in 1620.[2] Though there is no proof of any connection between Boehme and the Rosicrucian movement, one could say that he was the kind of native German 'chymist' whom the authors of the manifestos might have hoped to attract.

After examining the works mentioned in this chapter, I came no nearer to the solution of the problem of whether or not there was an organized secret society behind this movement. The normal practice of Rosicrucian writers is to say that they are not themselves Rosicrucians, nor have they ever seen one. Invisibility seems to have been an essential feature of the legend of the R.C. Brothers. The best light

---

[1] Boehme wrote his 'Aurora' (*Die Morgenroete im Aufgang*) in 1612, but it was not published until later. See A. Koyré, *La philosophie de Jacob Boehme*, Paris, 1929, p. 34. Koyré (*ibid.*, p. 42 n.) compares Boehme's hope of universal reformation with the outlook of the Rosicrucian *Fama*.

It is interesting to note that one of Boehme's best friends, Balthasar Walter, was a physician who was in touch with a Prince Anhalt (Koyré, p. 48 n.). A new approach to Boehme could be opened up through the new historical approach to the Rosicrucian movement.

[2] Koyré, *Boehme*, p. 51.

arrived at on this problem in this chapter is the print of the winged and moveable College of the Rosy Cross Fraternity, with its militia of angel, or spirit, defenders. If such were the R.C. Brothers, it would always be true to say that one had never seen one, and could not claim to belong to such an exalted society, though it might be true that one belonged to a group of human beings pledged to dwell 'under Jehova's wings'.

Writers on the Rosicrucian literature have noted that it seems to come to a sudden stop in Germany in about 1620 to 1621, and they have wondered why. Semler, in the late eighteenth century, sought an explanation for the abrupt disappearance of the R.C. literature in about 1620.[1] Arnold states that, after the publication of the manifestos, many others joined in and created complete confusion until the whole thing collapsed around 1620.[2] Waite speaks of the year 1620 as closing the gates on the past,[3] meaning the past of the Rosicrucian movement. All these writers, and all other writers on the Rosicrucian movement, have known nothing of the historical events in the Palatinate and in Bohemia, or at least have shown no knowledge of their connection with the Rosicrucian movement. To us, who have examined these connections, the answer to this mystery is clear. The R.C. movement collapsed when the Palatinate movement collapsed, when those inspiring vistas opened up behind the Elector Palatine and his brilliant alliances failed utterly with the flight of the King and Queen of Bohemia from Prague after the Battle of the White Mountain, when it was realized that neither the King of Great Britain nor their German Protestant allies would help them, when the Hapsburg troops moved into the Palatinate and the Thirty Years War began its dreadful course.

In 1621 there was published at Heidelberg a 'Warning against the Rosicrucian Vermin'.[4] In 1621 Heidelberg was under the heel of the invading Austro-Spanish armies. Such a publication would be a counterpart to the physical stamping out and obliteration of a movement associated with the former rulers.

Also in 1621 there was published at Ingolstadt, the great Jesuit centre in the heart of Catholic territory, a work called *Palma Triumphalis*, or 'the Miracles of the Catholic Church', by Fredericus

---

[1] J. S. Semler, *Unparteiische Sammlung zur Historie der Rosenkreuzer*, Leipzig, 1786–88; quoted Arnold, p. 190.

[2] Arnold, p. 101.

[3] Waite, *Brotherhood of the Rosy Cross*, p. 353.

[4] Philip Geiger, *Warnung für die Rosenkreutzen Ungeziefer*, Heidelberg, 1621; cf. Waite, *Brotherhood of the Rosy Cross*, p. 342.

Fornerus.[1] I have not myself actually examined this work (nor the one just mentioned against the Vermin) but according to Waite, the author, a bishop, derides the R.C. Fraternity because it gives itself glorious titles, claims to be divinely inspired for the reformation of the world, and that it can restore all sciences, transmute metals, and prolong human life. This would be a garbled version of the manifestos, and the triumphant attitude would correspond to the spirit of those propaganda caricatures of the ex-King of Bohemia and his policies which were disseminated after his defeat.

Another development is to be observed. In accordance with their usual missionary policies, the Jesuits evidently planned to capture the Rosicrucian symbolism and to present it in their own way in their work of re-Catholicizing the conquered areas and establishing in them the Counter Reformation. A certain J.P.D. a S. published at Brussels in 1619 a work which was reprinted in Prague in 1620 (obviously after the Catholic triumph) entitled *Rosa Jesuitica, oder Jesuitische Rotgesellen*[2] which adapts rose symbolism to Catholic uses (where of course it naturally belonged, as a symbol of the Virgin) and enquires whether the two Orders, namely that of the Jesuits and that of the Rosicrucians, were not in reality one and the same body, the one having been driven into concealment to emerge later as the other. Confusing the issues in this way would have facilitated the acceptance by the conquered populations of the Counter Reformation propaganda.

Conquered Bohemia would thus gradually lose touch with the movement which had promised it liberty. There were few individuals who were able, like Daniel Stolcius, to escape to a German Rosicrucian printer and thence to England. And in Germany, as must also have been the case in Bohemia, the Rosicrucian movement was discredited by the disastrous failure of the Palatinate-Bohemian movement, which had ended, for its supporters, in disillusion and despair.

Amongst the disillusioned ones was Robert Fludd. In a book published in 1633 Fludd said: 'those who were formerly called Brothers of the Rosy Cross are today called the Wise, the name (of Rose Cross) being so odious to contemporaries that it is already buried away from

---

[1] Fredericus Fornerus, *Palma Triumphalis Miraculorum Ecclesiae Catholicae*, Ingolstadt, 1621, dedicated to the Emperor Ferdinand II: cf. Waite, *Brotherhood*, p. 353.

[2] J.P.D. a S., *Rosa Jesuitica, oder Jesuitische Rotgesellen. Das ist eine Frag ob die zween Orden der gennanten Ritter von der Heerscheren Jesu und die Rosen Creutzer ein einziger Orden sey*, Brussels, 1618; Prague, 1620.

the memory of man.'[1] Yet Fludd had probably collaborated with Joachim Frizius in the book called *Summum bonum*, or 'the true magic, cabala, and alchemy of the true Fraternity of the Rose Cross', published in 1629 in Frankfurt. The title-page of this book shows the Rose, with the Cross indicated on its stem, and with the emblems of the spider's web and the bee-hive which the Zincgreff emblems had associated with the Elector Palatine, to which the satirical caricatures of that unfortunate man had replied by showing him many times involved with spiders' webs and bee-hives.

Such allusions would only have been understood by those who remembered the emblems and the replies to them in the caricatures, and most of the people who could have remembered were probably dead by 1629. The atmosphere of the Thirty Years War did not encourage delicacy of expression, and, in the caricatures against Frederick and all that he stood for, the subtleties of the 'chemical wedding' or of Maier's emblematics are obliterated under a witch-craft scare. And it was in that form that rumours of the Rosicrucian movement in Germany spread abroad, to France.

[1] Robert Fludd, *Clavis philosophiae et alchymiae*, Frankfurt, 1633, p. 50; cf. Arnold, p. 193.

CHAPTER VIII

THE ROSICRUCIAN SCARE IN FRANCE

In the year 1623 placards are said to have appeared in Paris announcing the presence in the town of the Brethren of the Rose Cross.[1]

> We, being deputies of the principle College of the Brothers of the Rose Cross, are making a visible and invisible stay in this city through the Grace of the Most High, towards whom turn the hearts of the Just. We show and teach without books or marks how to speak all languages of the countries where we wish to be, and to draw men from error and death.

This announcement is thus quoted by Gabriel Naudé in his 'Instruction to France about the truth of the Rose Cross Brothers', published in 1623. Naudé thinks that some people had the idea of putting up such placards because there was not much news about, and the kingdom tranquil, so some excitement was needed. These people certainly succeeded if their aim was to create excitement about the R.C. Brothers. Naudé speaks of a 'hurricane' of rumour now blowing through France at the news that the mysterious Fraternity, spread recently in Germany, had now reached France. It is difficult to decide whether these placards were really put up, or whether the excitement about them was generated by sensational books published in this year. Naudé should probably be believed about their reality and he is certainly right in thinking that these rumours were deliberately spread with the intention of creating a sensation or a scare.

Another version of the supposed manifestos on the placards is given in an anonymous work, published in 1623, with the taking title, 'Horrible Pacts made between the Devil and the Pretended Invisible Ones'.[2]

---

[1] Gabriel Naudé, *Instruction à la France sur la vérité de l'histoire des Frères de la Rose-Croix,* Paris, 1623, p. 27.

[2] *Effroyables pactions faites entre le Diable et les prétendus Invisibles,* Paris, 1623; cited Arnold, *Histoire des Rose-Croix,* pp. 7–8.

We deputies of the College of the Rose Cross, give notice to all
those who wish to enter our Society and Congregation, that we
will teach them the most perfect knowledge of the Most High, in
the name of whom we are today holding an assembly, and we
will make them from visible, invisible, and from invisible,
visible . . .

There are said to be thirty-six of these Invisible Ones, dispersed through
the world in groups of six. On 23 June last they held an assembly at
Lyons at which it was decided to install six deputies in the capital. This
meeting was held two hours before the Grand Sabbath at which one
of the princes of the infernal cohorts appeared, luminous and splendid.
The adepts prostrated themselves before him, and swore to abjure
Christianity and all the rites and sacraments of the Church. In return
they were promised the power to transport themselves wherever they
wished, to have purses always full of money, to dwell in any country,
attired in the dress of that country so that they were taken for native
inhabitants, to have the gift of eloquence so that they could draw all
men to them, to be admired by the learned and sought out by the
curious and recognized as wiser than the ancient prophets.

This great scare presupposes some knowledge of the Rosicrucian
manifestos in its readers. The pious organization of the R.C. Brothers
is turned into an organization of devil worshippers; their secrecy
becomes a diabolical secret; their rule that they are to wear the costume
of the country in which they find themselves becomes an alarming
scheme of infiltration. Their interest in the advancement of learning
and natural philosophy becomes a wicked bait to lure the learned and
the curious to them. Nothing, naturally, is said here of the Christian
motto of the manifestos, 'Jesus mihi omnia', of their philanthropic aim
of healing the sick. An attempt is being made to start a witch-craze
with the frighteningly 'invisible' Rosicrucians as the objects of the hunt.

Such a movement was not funny, not a *ludibrium* or a joke, in the
early seventeenth century. It could have terrible consequences of the
kind which the noted French Jesuit, François Garasse, seems to have
in mind in his book *La doctrine curieuse des beaux esprits de ce temps*,
published in this same year, 1623. The Rosicrucians, says Garasse, are a
secret sect in Germany;[1] Michael Maier is its secretary. In Germany,
the inn-keepers hang roses in the taverns to indicate that what is said

---

[1] François Garasse, *La doctrine curieuse des beaux esprits de ce temps*, Paris, 1623, pp. 83 ff.
on the Rosicrucians.

there should not be repeated but kept secret. The Rosicrucians are drinkers and secret people, hence the meaning of the rose in connection with them (rather an interesting suggestion). Garasse has read the *Fama* and states that the author's learning came from Turkey and is therefore heathen. He says that some Rosicrucians have recently been condemned as sorcerers at Malines, and gives it as his very firm opinion that they all deserve to be broken on the wheel or hanged on the gallows. In spite of some appearance of piety they are really wicked sorcerers, dangerous to religion and the state.

The traditional witch is a woman, able to transport herself magically to the Sabbath. In this attempted start of a witch-craze against Rosicrucians in France there is no mention of women; the sex of the Invisibles as devil-worshippers and attendants at Sabbaths is not mentioned. The traditional witchlore, such as the invisibility and the command of magical means of transport, is transferred to the R.C. Brothers. The Invisible Rosicrucians are becoming objects of a witch hunt, and some of their characteristics, particularly their deep learning through which they attract the 'curious', do not fit with those of the general run of witches, who were usually poor ignorant women. Nevertheless, it seems that the author of the 'Horrible Pacts', and Garasse, are really working up a witch-craze against the 'invisible' Rosicrucians, using the manifestos as their material and reading diabolical meanings into the supposed movements and activities of the R.C. Brothers. The scare creates 'the Rosicrucians' as real witch-like characters, belonging to a diabolical secret society.

Witch-crazes, which were so terrible a feature of the social scene in Europe in the sixteenth and early seventeenth centuries, were not peculiar to either side in the great religious division of Europe. Some of the worst witch-crazes were generated in Lutheran circles in Germany. Nevertheless, 'the worst of all witch persecutions, the climax of the European craze', were the persecutions which broke out in central Europe in the sixteen-twenties 'with the destruction of Protestantism in Bohemia and the Palatinate'[1] and the Catholic reconquest of Germany. 'All over Europe ... the witch-trials multiplied with the Catholic reconquest.'

It is thus clear that the author of the 'Horrible Pacts', and the Jesuit, Garasse, were quite in the fashion of the sixteen-twenties in working up a witch-craze. We have seen how the Rosicrucian literature in Germany came to a sudden end in Germany in 1620, and was

[1] H. R. Trevor-Roper, *Religion, the Reformation and Social Change*, London, 1967, p. 156.

stamped out after the overthrow of the Elector Palatine as King of Bohemia, and the Catholic conquests in Bohemia and the Palatinate. Was the witch-craze in those parts of the world and at that time a part of the effort to stamp out the Palatinate-Bohemian movement with its connections with the Rosicrucian manifestos? We have seen with what pertinacity the enemies of the Elector Palatine circulated those caricature-satires against him after his defeat. We have seen how one at least of those satires definitely associates him with Rosicrucianism. There is a general tendency in the satires to suggest magic in connection with Frederick. If the literature of the German witch-craze of the 1620s and after were to be examined with the possibility in mind that it might be associated with a Rosicrucian scare, as it evidently is in these works published in 1623 in France, more evidence might be found that the great concentration of Renaissance studies with esoteric tendencies, which found expression in the Rosicrucian manifestos, might actually have helped to intensify the witch-craze which broke out after the Catholic victories.

It is important to note the date, 1623, at which the witch-craze plus Rosicrucian scare spreads to France. In 1623, the suppression of Bohemia and the Palatinate was complete, and the destruction of the ideas behind the Bohemian adventure had been made as complete as possible by the suppression of 'Rosicrucian' publications. News of the events of the first years of the Thirty Years War had spread throughout Europe, and in the wake of those events some news had percolated about the Rosicrucian movement. Hence the spread to France of the repressive techniques, in the form of a witch-craze against the Invisible Ones and their pompous manifestos.

From Gabriel Naudé's 'Instruction to France' more can be learned than from the hysteria of the 'Horrible Pacts' and other productions of that type, for Naudé is better informed. He quotes at length from the *Fama*, of which he has a printed copy by him, after which he says: 'Behold, gentlemen, the huntress Diana whom Actaeon presents to you naked.'[1] This may be intended to be satirical, but it shows knowledge of a favourite mythological wrapping for the pursuit of natural science. He speaks of the enormous influence of the *Fama* and the *Confessio* and knows of some of Maier's works. According to Naudé, the *Fama* had been making a great impression in France, arousing hopes of some impending new advance in knowledge. He says that it is being rumoured everywhere that after all the 'novelties' which

[1] Naudé, *Instruction*, p. 38.

surprised 'our parents'—the discovery of new worlds, the invention of cannon, compasses, clocks, novelties in religion, in medicine, in astrology—another age of discoveries is at hand. The new movements are culminating, so runs the rumour, in the Brothers R.C. and the hopes which they raise.[1] Tycho Brahe is making new discoveries; Galileo has invented his 'spectacles' (the telescope), and now comes the company of the R.C. Brothers announcing the imminent 'instauration' or renewal of knowledge promised by the Scriptures[2] (which sounds like an echo of Bacon). Naudé's remarks give evidence that the Rosicrucian manifestos were widely read outside Germany and were being taken as prophecy of a coming new enlightenment, a still further advance after the age of the Renaissance.

Naudé evidently has to be careful because of the scare. He clearly thinks that the supposed Rosicrucian manifesto on the placards was invented by 'some people' to cause excitement. But he mentions Garasse's book with approval and speaks slightingly of the many German books about the R.C. Brothers. In dealing with their reputation for magic he mentions Fludd, and later gives a list of authors who represent, he thinks, the kind of teachings of which the R.C. Brothers approve. This list includes the following:[3]

> John Dee, *Monas hieroglyphica*
> Trithemius, *Steganographia*
> Francesco Giorgi, *Harmonia mundi*
> François de Candale, *Pimandre*
> 'Thyart sa Musique'
> 'Brunus les umbres de ses idees'
> Ramon Lull 'sa Dialectique'
> Paracelsus 'son commentaire de Magie'

Here we have the interests of the R.C. Brothers firmly placed in the Hermetic tradition, with the mention of François de Candale's French translation of the *Hermetica*[4] and of Giorgi's Hermetic-Cabalist 'Harmony of the World'[5] (much used by Fludd). Trithemius's

[1] *Ibid.*, pp. 22 ff.
[2] *Ibid.*, p. 24. Bacon's *Novum Organum* had been published in 1620, which made his views on advancement of learning available in Latin. And the Latin translation of *The Advancement of Learning* was published in 1523.
[3] *Ibid.*, pp. 15–16.
[4] François de Foix de Candale, *Le Pimandre de Mercure Trismegiste*, Bordeaux, 1579; Cf. D. P. Walker, 'The Prisca Theologia in France', *Journal of the Warburg and Courtauld Institutes*, XVII (1954), p. 209; Yates, *Giordano Bruno and the Hermetic Tradition*, p. 173.
[5] Francesco Giorgi, *De harmonia mundi*, Venice, 1525.

Steganographia associates the R.C. Brothers with angel-magic,[1] and it is particularly important that Naudé mentions Dee's *Monas* and a work by Bruno (*De umbris idearum*),[2] a welcome confirmation of the influence of Dee and Bruno on the movement. Pontus de Tyard's 'Musique'[3] brings in the musical philosophy behind the French Pléiade, of which Tyard was a member. Naudé, the Frenchman, is able to assimilate the Rosicrucian philosophy to a French Hermetic tradition, through using François de Candale on the *Hermetica* and giving Tyard as a French example of musical philosophy.

The authors mentioned by Naudé are all profoundly representative of the Renaissance Hermetic tradition, and he regards the new developments promised by the R.C. Brothers as issuing out of this.

Among other interesting points in Naudé's comments is his mention of 'Hentisberus' and 'Suisset Calculator'[4] as congenial to the Rosicrucians. This is an allusion to two mathematicians of medieval Oxford,[5] members of the Merton school of mathematics, whose works, revived and printed, influenced important lines of early seventeenth-century mathematical studies. Naudé may here be showing some inside knowledge of mathematical studies of the 'Rosicrucians' not revealed in their 'misleading and useless' publications.

Still in a slighting tone, he goes on to speak of the fables of the poets, the chimera of magicians and charlatans, the Abbaye of Thélème of Rabelais, and Thomas More's Utopia as all belonging to the R.C. 'labyrinth'.

He concludes on a note of orthodox disapproval of the R.C. Brothers, stating that he heartily concurs with Jesuit opinion of their perniciousness. Moreover, he adds, they have been excellently refuted by the arguments of Libavius.[6] So Naudé knew about Libavius, too. He was really

---

[1] Trithemius's *Steganographia* (first published in 1606 but long known in manuscript before that) was a main Renaissance manual of practical Cabala or angel-conjuring; see *Giordano Bruno and the Hermetic Tradition*, p. 145. On its use by Dee for his angel-magic, see French, *John Dee*, pp. 111 ff.

[2] G. Bruno, *De umbris idearum*, Paris, 1582; see *Giordano Bruno and the Hermetic Tradition*, pp. 192 ff.; *The Art of Memory*, pp. 200 ff.

[3] This could refer to any of Tyard's philosophical dialogues, which are all based on assumptions of universal harmony, but alludes more particularly to his *Solitaire second, ou Discours de la Musique*, Lyons, 1555; see my *The French Academies of the Sixteenth Century*, Warburg Institute, 1947, reprinted Kraus, 1968, pp. 77 ff.

[4] Naudé, *Instruction*, p. 16.

[5] John Hentisbury and Richard Swineshead; see Thorndike, III, pp. 370–85; R. T. Gunther, *Early Science at Oxford*, Oxford, 1923, II, pp. 42 ff.

[6] Naudé, *Instruction*, p. 90.

very well informed and obviously deeply interested, though in the year 1623 when the scare was sweeping through France, counteracting the rumours of the *Fama*, and when it looked as though a witch-hunt was getting up, it behoved a scholar to be very careful.

Two years later, in 1625, Naudé showed more courage by publishing his famous work, 'Apology for Great Men Suspected of Magic',[1] in which he states that there are four kinds of magic, divine magic, theurgy which is religious magic, freeing the soul from the contamination of the body, goetia which is witchcraft, and natural magic which is natural science. Only the third, goetia, is wicked, and of this the great men have been innocent. Amongst great men whom he defends as free from evil magic are Zoroaster, Orpheus, Pythagoras, Socrates, Plotinus, Porphyry, Iamblichus, Ramon Lull, Paracelsus, Henry Cornelius Agrippa (who has a whole chapter to himself), Pico della Mirandola—in short the Neoplatonists and the Renaissance tradition decended from them, particularly Agrippa, the main representative of Renaissance magic. He urges greater care in prosecutions for magic, lest good people should be confused with evil magicians.

He does not mention the R.C. Brothers in the 'Apology' but since the writers whom, two years previously, he had listed as congenial to Rosicrucians all belong to the tradition which he now defends, it is reasonable to assume that he was also thinking in the 'Apology' of the Rosicrucians, the scare against whom was still in full force. It is therefore interesting to note that Naudé gives two main reasons as to how people can become falsely accused of bad magic.

One reason is that students of mathematics tend to be accused of magic, because an aura of magic has always been attached to such studies, and the wonderful works which a knowledge of mathematics and mechanics can produce seem magical to the ignorant.[2] This was John Dee's complaint in his Preface to Euclid, that he is falsely accused of being a 'conjuror' because of his mathematical skill and ability to produce mechanical marvels.[3] And Naudé brings Dee into his argument about mathematicians being accused of being magicians, citing, not Dee's Preface to Euclid, but his Preface to his *Aphorisms* in

---

[1] Gabriel Naudé, *Apologie pur les grands hommes soupçonnés de Magie*, Paris, 1625; page references are to the edition of Amsterdam, 1712.

[2] *Apologie*, pp. 49 ff.

[3] *Giordano Bruno and the Hermetic Tradition*, p. 149; *Theatre of the World*, pp. 30–1; French, *John Dee*, p. 8.

which Dee says that he is writing a defence of Roger Bacon[1] to show that the marvels he performed were not done by 'conjuring' but by mathematical skill. Naudé regrets that this defence by Dee of Roger Bacon is not extant. The following is a translation of what Naudé says about it:[2]

> If we had the book which John Dee, citizen of London and a very learned philosopher and mathematician, says that he composed in defence of Roger Bacon in which he shows that all that is said about his marvellous works should be ascribed to his knowledge of nature and mathematics, rather than to a commerce with demons, which he never had, I protest that I would speak no more about him (Roger Bacon) . . . But since this book (by Dee on Bacon) has not yet come to light, so far as I know . . . I must fill this gap, so that the good name of this English Franciscan, who was a Doctor of Theology, and the greatest chemist, astrologer, and mathematician of his time, may not remain perpetually buried and condemned among the crowd of sorcerers and magicians to which he most certainly did not belong . . .

Dee's book on Roger Bacon has still not come to light, but it is profoundly interesting that Naudé brings it into his defence of mathematicians accused of magic.

The other reason why, according to Naudé, people can be falsely accused of magic is if they are 'politiques',[3] that is tolerant in religious matters, not given to persecuting those who disagree with them in religion.

Since Naudé nowhere mentions the Brothers R.C. in his 'Apology' one cannot state definitely that these two reasons for being falsely accused of magic—mathematical interests and a tolerant religious outlook—would be applied by him to explain the current Rosicrucian scare. Yet since he had included a book by Dee in the list of authors

---

[1] John Dee, *Propaideumata aphoristica*, London, 1558, 1568; the title of Dee's book on Roger Bacon is announced in the preface as *Speculum unitatis; sive Apologia pro Fratre Rogerio Bacchone Anglo*. Dee also mentions this book in the dedication of the *Monas hieroglyphica* to Maximilian II, where he says that it was written in 1557.

[2] *Apologie*, p. 350. Naudé says that the speaking head, supposed to have been made by Roger Bacon, was an invention of the English populace; he has heard vaguely of the use of the story by English dramatists.

Salomon de Caus's book, *Les raisons des forces mouvantes*, had been republished at Paris in 1624, with an addition illustrating marvels designed by De Caus for the Heidelberg gardens.

[3] *Apologie*, p. 22.

whom he thought were congenial to the R.C. Brothers, when earlier joining half-heartedly in disapproval of them, one can say that Naudé definitely connects the R.C. Brothers with Dee in the first book, and in the second book uses Dee in his defence of mathematicians from charges of evil magic.

Naudé evidently knew a good deal, but he is still being pretty careful, even in the 'Apology'. The hurricane of the excitement about the R.C. Brothers was still blowing in France.

We are now moving into the time when the new movements of the seventeenth century are gathering strength and the Renaissance animist philosophies with their magical implications are on the wane. The great figure in the attack on Renaissance animism, Hermetism, Cabalism, and all their attendant manifestations, was the French monk, Marin Mersenne, the friend of René Descartes. Through his massive attack on the whole Renaissance tradition, Mersenne cleared the way for the rise of Cartesian philosophy.

It is significant that Mersenne's first onslaught on the Renaissance tradition, his *Quaestiones in Genesim*, was published in 1623, the year of the outbreak of the Rosicrucian scare. In this work he attacks Renaissance Magia and Cabala and all the great names associated with that tradition, Ficino, Pico, Agrippa, and so on, but his fiercest criticism is reserved for the contemporary exponent of that tradition, Robert Fludd. He continued the attacks in later years, Fludd replied, and the Mersenne-Fludd controversy held the attention of all Europe.

I cannot attempt, in the few paragraphs which can be allowed to it in this chapter, to mention all the publications in this controversy. I have attempted to deal with one aspect of it elsewhere, pointing out that it was basically an attack on the Hermetic tradition by Mersenne and a defence of it by Fludd, and that Casaubon's dating of the *Hermetica* was used by Mersenne as a weapon for undermining the Hermetic tradition.[1] All that can be done here is to indicate, very summarily, how the new line of historical approach pursued in this book may affect our understanding of Mersenne's position.

We have seen that the Rosicrucian movement, or its manifestos, was connected with the movement for the installation of Frederick, Elector Palatine, in Bohemia, that the publication of Fludd's works in the Palatinate was a part of the movement of thought behind the politico-religious movement. We have seen how the total collapse of the movement with the defeat at Prague in 1620 ushered in a great

[1] *Giordano Bruno and the Hermetic Tradition*, pp. 432–40.

satirical campaign against all that it had stood for. We have seen that the sudden cessation of Rosicrucian publications in Germany coincided with the collapse of 1620 and that the accusation of magic becomes a strong card in the campaign of the conquerors against Rosicrucianism which becomes merged with the witchcraft scares. We have seen that the Rosicrucian scare started in France in 1623 presented the R.C. Brothers of the manifestos as a diabolical, magical, secret society.

Now it is clear that Mersenne was affected by all this, as indeed was everyone who lived in the early seventeenth century. The Frederickian attempt to break the Hapsburg control of the Empire, the crash of that attempt, and the odour of bad magic disseminated around it by the conquerors, were inescapable facts of the contemporary European scene. The Rosicrucian scare affected Mersenne. It is clear, not only from his books but also from his correspondence, that Mersenne believed in the R.C. Brothers as bogeymen, wicked magicians and subversive agents, whom he imagined moving invisibly in all countries to spread their evil doctrines.[1] Moreover, their real existence seemed proved to him by the works of Robert Fludd, whom he took to be a typical Rosicrucian, and whose addiction to the Hermetic tradition in extreme forms was clear to every reader.

Mersenne's reaction to the Rosicrucian scare was different from that of Naudé. Naudé seems to have believed that important mathematical scientific activities lay behind the good magic of the Rosicrucian movement. Mersenne certainly believed that the magic was evil, and that the growth to these proportions of Magia and Cabala indicated that the Renaissance ways of thinking must be eliminated, root and branch, Renaissance animist philosophy must be destroyed, and Renaissance magic, in its modern or Fluddian manifestations, severely repressed. Mersenne was a gentle and loveable character, very different from Père Garasse, yet his reaction to the Rosicrucian scare was closer to that of Garasse than to that of Naudé, a reaction influenced by fear. We have to remember, too, that Mersenne, like Descartes, was educated at the Jesuit college of La Flèche and would have been influenced in his early years by the Jesuit outlook.

Thus Mersenne in all his writings moves towards eliminating Renaissance influences. This was sometimes difficult to achieve,

---

[1] Marin Mersenne, *Correspondence*, ed. Waard and Pintard, Paris, 1932, I, pp. 37–9, 154–4, 455 etc.; II, pp. 137, 149 (Gassendi and the Rosicrucians); 181 ff., 496 (J. B. Van Helmont and the Rosicrucians); *La vérité des sciences*, Paris, 1625, pp. 566–7. cf. *Giordano Bruno and the Hermetic Tradition*, p. 408 etc.

particularly on the musical side, for Mersenne was a believer in universal harmony and an admirer of Baïf's Academy of Poetry and Music, for the activities of which he is one of the chief sources.[1] In his *Harmonie universelle* (1636) he has to expound universal harmony in a manner which avoids the macro-microcosmical magical philosophy (though he actually uses one of Fludd's diagrams) and eliminates the Renaissance outlook which underlay the work of Baïf's Academy and to which Tyard had given philosophical expression (as Naudé knew).

The seventeenth-century philosophy which was to replace the Renaissance philosophies was Cartesian mechanism, and Mersenne, devoted friend and admirer of Descartes, was instrumental, through his wide connections and correspondence, in encouraging the shift from magic to mechanism.[2] It is one of the more profound ironies of the history of thought that the growth of mechanical science, through which arose the idea of mechanism as a possible philosophy of nature, was itself an outcome of the Renaissance magical tradition. Mechanism divested of magic became the philosophy which was to oust Renaissance animism and to replace the 'conjuror' by the mechanical philosopher.

This fact is not yet generally understood, and whilst awaiting its recognition it is important that we should try to discover and understand all the circumstances leading up to this momentous change in man's attitude to nature. Amongst the historical factors in the situation were those which we have been examining in this book. The failure of the Rosicrucian movement in Germany, its suppression by force and by savagely adverse propaganda, affected the tone of thought in the early seventeenth century, injecting into it an atmosphere of fear. Mersenne, too, was afraid. He had to protect his own interest in mathematics and mechanics from any taint of conjuring. This gave an asperity to his anti-Renaissance movement which, in less excited times, might have been conducted more gently and with less loss of the more valuable aspects of the Renaissance tradition.

And what of Descartes and the R.C. Brothers? Some of the most important mentions of them are to be found in Baillet's fascinating life of Descartes (first published in 1691).[3] Our new knowledge of the historical situation can enable us to read that biography with a new understanding, or, at any rate, with new questions in our minds as we read it.

---

[1] *The French Academies of the Sixteenth Century*, pp. 23 ff.
[2] See R. Lenoble, *Mersenne ou la naissance du mécanisme*, Paris, 1948.
[3] Adrien Baillet, *La Vie de Monsieur Descartes*, Paris, 1691.

In 1618 the young Descartes left France for Holland and enrolled himself in the army of Prince Maurice of Nassau. It was rather a strange step for the Catholic, Jesuit-educated Descartes to take, but the explanation given is that he wanted to see the world and enlarge his knowledge of men and of life. In this reflective mood, Descartes moved in 1619 into Germany, having heard news of strange movements there, of a revolt in Bohemia, and a war between Catholics and Protestants about this. Hearing that the Duke of Bavaria was levying troops, he thought he would join, though without a clear idea as to who the enemy was. Eventually it transpired that the troops were to march against the Elector Palatine whom the Bohemians had elected as their king.[1] Apparently not much exciting himself about this, Descartes went into winter quarters at a place on the Danube, where, warmed by a German stove, he fell into a series of profound meditations. On the night of 10 November 1619, he had dreams,[2] which seem to have been a most important experience, leading him towards the conviction that mathematics were the sole key to the understanding of nature. He lived a solitary and meditative life during the rest of this winter, but not without some contacts with persons from whom he heard about a society established in Germany under the name of the Brothers of the Rose Cross, who promised a new wisdom and a 'veritable science'.[3] These rumours chimed in so well with his own thoughts and efforts that he tried to find these Brothers, but without success. One of their rules was to wear no distinguishing dress, so it was naturally very difficult to find them. But a great stir was being made by the numbers of publications which these Brothers were producing. Descartes, however, did not read them (he had given up reading) and afterwards said that he knew nothing about the Rosicrucians, though when he returned to Paris in 1623 he learned that his sojourn in Germany had earned him the reputation of being a Rosicrucian.

In June 1620 Descartes was at Ulm, where he spent the rest of the summer and where he met a certain Johann Faulhaber who was much struck by his extraordinary intelligence.[4] (This Faulhaber was one of the

---

[1] *Ibid.*, pp. 58–9.

[2] *Ibid.*, pp. 81–6.

[3] *Ibid.*, pp. 87–92.

[4] *Ibid.*, p. 68. See Johann Faulhaber, *Mysterium Arithmeticum sive Cabalistica et Philosophica Inventio . . . illuminatissimis laudatissimisque Fratribus R.C. . . . dicata*, Ulm, 1615. In an earlier work (*Himlische . . . Magia oder Newe Cabalistische Kunst*, Ulm, 1613) Faulhaber includes mechanical arts, mathematical instruments, perspective, and so on, in his treatment of Divine Magic and New Cabalist Art.

first persons to publish a work addressed to the R.C. Brothers.) When Descartes heard that his general, the Duke of Bavaria, was marching on Bohemia, he joined the Catholic and Imperial army, was at the famous battle of Prague (The White Mountain) and entered Prague on 9 November with the victors. It is thought that he may have seen the famous astronomical apparatus of Tycho Brahe in Prague, but Baillet thinks this unlikely since it had been broken or taken away.[1]

After this Descartes spent some time, meditatively, in southern Bohemia,[2] and in 1621 continued his travels through Moravia, Silesia, northern Germany, the Catholic Netherlands, returning to Paris in 1623.

Here he met the full force of the Rosicrucian scare. Baillet's description of this must be given:[3]

When he [Descartes] arrived [in Paris] the affairs of the unfortunate Count Palatine, elected King of Bohemia, the expeditions of Mansfeldt, and the translation of the Electorate from the Count Palatine to the Duke of Bavaria, made at Ratisbon on the 15th of the previous February, were furnishing the matter of public discussion. He [Descartes] could satisfy the curiosity of his friends on this point, but in return they gave him news which was causing them some anxiety, incredible though it seemed. This was that for the last few days there had been talk in Paris of the Brothers of the Rose Cross, whom he had sought for in vain in Germany during the winter of 1619, and it was beginning to be rumoured that he [Descartes] was enrolled in their company.

He was surprised at this news since such a thing was not in keeping with his character nor with the inclination which he had always had to think of the Rosicrucians as impostors and visionaries. In Paris they were called the Invisibles and it was proclaimed that of the thirty-six deputies which their head had sent throughout Europe, six had come to France in February and were lodged at the Marais in Paris; but that they could not communicate with people, or be communicated with, except by thought joined to the will, that is to say in a manner imperceptible to the senses.

[1] *Ibid.*, p. 75.
[2] *Ibid.*, pp. 91–2.
[3] Translated from the abridged version of the *Vie de Monsieur Descartes*, Paris, 1693, pp. 51–3. For the complete version, see the 1691 edition, pp. 106–8.

The chance of their arrival in Paris at the same time as M. Descartes might have had an unfortunate effect on his reputation, if he had hidden himself, or lived in solitude in the town, as he had been accustomed to do on his travels. But he confounded those who wished to make use of this conjunction of events to establish their calumny. He made himself visible to all the world, and particularly to his friends who needed no other argument to convince them that he was not one of the Brotherhood of the Rosicrucians or Invisibles: and he used the same argument of their invisibility to explain to the curious why he had not been able to find any of them in Germany.

His presence served to calm the agitation of his friend Father Mersenne . . . who had been all the more upset by this false rumour because he was less disposed to believe that the Rosicrucians were Invisibles, or merely chimerical, after what several Germans, and Robert Fludd, the Englishman, had written in their favour.

It is surely one of the highlights or greatest moments in the extraordinary history of this extraordinary subject when Descartes shows himself to his friends in Paris to demonstrate that he is visible, and therefore not a Rosicrucian!

So Descartes was in the area of Germany where the Rosicrucian rumour was spreading when he had his dreams and thought his significant thoughts, he actually went into Prague with the Catholic armies, could have seen Frederick and Elizabeth there in that terrible hour, prowled about in Prague, knew exactly what had happened, spent time thinking in southern Bohemia, came to Paris at a time when all the news was of the Elector Palatine being deprived of the Electorate, about which, as Baillet remarks, he could give his friends inside information since he had been an eyewitness of those great events, on the spot in Prague when it all happened, and picking up news of movements in Germany before it happened.

And all this news is mixed up with the Rosicrucians. The Rosicrucian scare started in Paris, says Baillet, when all the news was of the Elector Palatine and his misfortunes. Our other sources for the scare have not told us this, which confirms the view of the connection of the scare in Paris with events in Germany. And as for Descartes's adventures with the Rosicrucians, they follow the normal pattern. He hears of them, tries to find them, and fails. That Descartes makes his own visibility a proof that he is not one of them is a refinement on the normal experiences of Rosicrucian-seekers which is worthy of a great philosopher!

The desire of Descartes was always to live a very quiet, retired, and solitary life, thinking about mathematics, and, some years after the experience described above of what might happen in Paris to a mathematician who kept himself too invisible, he took up his residence in Holland. Many years later, in 1644, he established himself in a quiet little château near Leiden, largely in order to be near the Princess Elizabeth of the Palatinate, eldest daughter of the unfortunate Elector Frederick, who had died in 1632, and whose widow, Elizabeth Stuart, the 'Winter Queen' of Bohemia, had continued to live at The Hague with her family. The Princess Elizabeth had conceived a great passion for the writings of Descartes, who found in her a most discerning disciple and greatly admired both her character and her brilliant intellect. To her he dedicated the *Principia*, in 1644, describing her in the dedication as daughter of the King of Bohemia, giving her father the title which his enemies denied him. In 1649, when the Treaty of Westphalia ended the Thirty Years War and under which provision was made for the restoration of the Lower Palatinate to Charles Louis, eldest surviving son of the 'Winter King' of Bohemia, the Princess Elizabeth was thinking of retiring to the Palatinate when her brother should take up his residence there. She suggested that Descartes, too, should make his home there. Unfortunately, the plan that Descartes might live in the Palatinate came to nothing. The mild climate of the wine-growing Rhineland would have suited his health better than cold Sweden where he was soon to die, having had to accept the invitation of Queen Christina to go there to talk philosophy with her. According to Baillet, one of his reasons for accepting that invitation was that he might plead the cause of the Princess Elizabeth and the Palatinate at the Swedish court.[1] This strong interest in Palatinate affairs in his later life makes one wonder what exactly Descartes had been doing in his early travels in Germany and Bohemia. Is it possible that he had been looking during those early travels for an enlightenment hidden behind Rosicrucian invisibility, for new developments growing out of secret traditions—and looking for such things in the circle of the Princess Elizabeth's unfortunate father?

Wars and witch-crazes have perhaps confused for the historian the vital steps by which the European mind moved out of the Renaissance into the seventeenth century.

---

[1] *Vie de Monsieur Descartes*, 1691, pp. 388–9.

CHAPTER IX

FRANCIS BACON 'UNDER THE SHADOW OF JEHOVA'S WINGS'

The great Rosicrucian furore seemed to arouse little or no public attention in Britain. No floods of pamphlets addressed to the R.C. Brothers poured from the printing presses, as in Germany from 1614 to 1620. No Invisibles put up placards,[1] arousing frantic interest and storms of abuse, as in Paris in the 1620s. The trumpet sounds of the *Fama*, announcing a new era and vast new advances in knowledge impending for mankind, seem to have been muffled in these islands.

There were, however, other trumpet sounds, making a striking announcement, not with the Rosicrucian wild excitement but in measured and reasonable terms. These were the manifestos concerning the advancement of learning issued by Francis Bacon. These manifestos were dedicated to James I, the same monarch as he to whom the Rosicrucian movement in Germany so vainly pinned its hopes.

The Advancement of Learning, published in 1605, is a sober survey of the present state of knowledge, drawing attention to those areas of learning which are deficient, where more might be known if men would give their minds to research and experiment, particularly in natural philosophy which Bacon finds deplorably deficient. Such improved knowledge of nature could and should be used for the relief of man's estate, the betterment of his position in this world. Bacon demands that there should be a fraternity or brotherhood in learning, through which learned men might exchange knowledge and help one another. The universities do not at present promote such exchange, for there is not sufficient mutual intelligence between the universities of Europe. The brotherhood of learning should transcend national boundaries.[2]

---

[1] A placard put up in London in 1626 is mentioned in R. F. Gould, *Concise History of Freemasonry*, London, 1920, p. 76, but I have been unable to trace anything further on this.

[2] Bacon, *Advancement of Learning*, II, dedication to James I, p. 13.

Surely as nature createth brotherhood in families, and arts
mechanical contract brotherhoods in communities, and the
anointment of God superinduceth a brotherhood in kings and
bishops, so in learning there cannot but be a fraternity in learning
and illumination, relating to that paternity which is attributed to
God, who is called the father of illumination or lights.

In reading this passage, after our explorations in this book, one is
struck by the fact that Bacon here thinks of learning as 'illumination',
light descending from the Father of Lights, and that the brotherhood in
learning which he desires would be a 'fraternity in learning and
illumination'. These expressions should not be passed over as pious
rhetoric; they are significant in the context of the times.

Nine years later, in Germany, the Rosicrucian *Fama* was to present
the Brothers R.C. as a fraternity of illuminati, as a band of learned men
joined together in brotherly love; it was to urge that learned magicians
and Cabalists should communicate their knowledge to one another;
and it was to proclaim that the time was at hand of a great advance in
knowledge of nature. This parallel may suggest that comparison of the
Baconian movement with the Rosicrucian movement might be
revealing for both, and particularly, perhaps, for Bacon.

Recent scholarship has made it abundantly clear that the old view of
Bacon as a modern scientific observer and experimentalist emerging
out of a superstitious past is no longer valid. In his book on Bacon,
Paolo Rossi[1] has shown that it was out of the Hermetic tradition that
Bacon emerged, out of the Magia and Cabala of the Renaissance as it
had reached him via the natural magicians. Bacon's view of the future
of science was not that of progress in a straight line. His 'great instauration' of science was directed towards a return to the state of Adam
before the Fall,[2] a state of pure and sinless contact with nature and
knowledge of her powers. This was the view of scientific progress, a
progress back towards Adam, held by Cornelius Agrippa,[3] the author
of the influential Renaissance textbook on occult philosophy. And
Bacon's science is still, in part, occult science. Amongst the subjects

[1] Paolo Rossi, *Francis Bacon: From Magic to Science*, London, 1968.

[2] For one characteristic statement, among many others, of this aim, see the preface to
the *Instauratio Magna* (Bacon, *Works*, ed. Spedding *et al.*, 1857 edition, I, p. 132). Cf.
Rossi, *Bacon*, pp. 127 ff.; and my essay 'The Hermetic Tradition in Renaissance Science'
in *Art, Science and History in the Renaissance*, ed. Charles S. Singleton, Johns Hopkins
Press, Baltimore, 1968, pp. 266–7.

[3] *De occulta philosophia*, III, 40; see C. G. Nauert, *Agrippa and the Crisis of Renaissance
Thought*, Urbana, 1965, pp. 48, 284.

which he reviews in his survey of learning are natural magic, astrology, of which he seeks a reformed version, alchemy, by which he was profoundly influenced, fascination, the tool of the magician, and other themes which those interested in drawing out the modern side of Bacon have set aside as unimportant.

The German Rosicrucian writers hold similar views about the return to the wisdom of Adam and the millennial character of the advance in knowledge which they prophesy. After study of their writings in comparison with those of Bacon, one has the strong impression—when the fantastic Rosencreutz myth is set aside as a *ludibrium*—that both these movements are concerned with magico-scientific advance, with illumination in the sense of enlightenment.

Nevertheless, though one can see both these movements as belonging naturally to the same times, both ultimately products of the Renaissance Hermetic-Cabalist tradition, both leading out of Renaissance into seventeenth-century advance, there are profound differences between them. Bacon is anxious to emphasize his disapproval of the pride and presumption of the Renaissance magus. He warns particularly against Paracelsus, who, as we have seen, was a prophet for the German Rosicrucian movement. Bacon had studied the system of Paracelsus 'reduced into a harmony by Severinus the Dane',[1] and had decided that 'the ancient opinion that man was *microcosmus*, and abstract or model of the world hath been fantastically strained by Paracelsus and the alchemists'.[2] This attacks the macrocosm-microcosm philosophy, so basic for Fludd and the Rosicrucian theories of world harmony.

Another great difference in outlook between Baconian and Rosicrucian schools of thought is Bacon's deprecation of secrecy in scientific matters, his attack on the long tradition of the alchemists of concealing their processes in incomprehensible symbols.[3] Though the Rosicrucian manifestos advise, as does Bacon, an exchange of knowledge between learned men, they are themselves couched in mystifications, such as the story of the cave in which Rosencreutz's body was found, and which was full of geometrical symbols. That symbolism *may* conceal abstruse mathematical studies by members of a group, leading in advanced directions, but, if so, such studies are not announced but concealed in language which whets the appetite to know more of the mathematical

---

[1] *Advancement*, II, 8, v.
[2] *Advancement*, II, 10, ii.
[3] Rossi, *Bacon*, pp. 34 ff.

or scientific secrets hidden in the Rosicrucian cave. This atmosphere is the opposite of that in which the Baconian manifestos move, and it is precisely his abandonment of magico-mystical mystification technique which makes Bacon's writings sound modern.

The *Advancement of Learning* was published in 1605. The *Novum Organum*, which Bacon wrote in Latin to facilitate its diffusion in Europe and which he regarded as the most important statement of his philosophy and programme, was published in 1620. The *De augmentis*, the Latin translation and revision of the *Advancement*, was published in 1623. Thus the Baconian philosophy had begun to appear several years before the first Rosicrucian manifesto; its major statement was published in the year of destiny, the year of the brief reign in Bohemia of the Winter King and Queen; the Latin translation of the *Advancement* appeared at the time of the Rosicrucian scare in Paris. It is important to realize that the Rosicrucian movement is contemporary with the Baconian philosophy, that the strange Rosicrucian excitements were going on in Europe during the years in which the works of Bacon were appearing in England.

There are, I believe, undoubtedly connections between the two movements, though these are difficult to trace and to analyse. On the one hand, the close connections between England and the Palatinate would have facilitated a Baconian influence on the German Rosicrucian movement. On the other hand the differences between Rosicrucianism and Baconianism have to be carefully considered.

The reign of a daughter of the King of Great Britain in the Palatinate made communications easy between England and that part of Germany and led to an influx of English influences, amongst which should be included an influence from Bacon's *Advancement*. We may speculate on how the influence may have been imported. Both Frederick and Elizabeth were readers and interested in intellectual movements. That they had books from England with them is proved by the fact that they took a copy of Raleigh's *History of the World* with them to Prague, where it fell into the hands of the conquerors, but eventually found its way back to London and the British Museum, where it now reposes.[1] They are therefore likely to have had works by Bacon with them at Heidelberg. We know that in later life Elizabeth was interested in the works of Bacon;[2] in her early life before her marriage she would have known Bacon in England; he composed one of the entertainments for

[1] See Carola Oman, *Elizabeth of Bohemia*, London, 1964, p. 178.
[2] See above, p. 14.

her wedding.[1] Perhaps another transmitter of Baconian influence might have been Michael Maier who was in close contact with England during the reign of Frederick and Elizabeth in the Palatinate. Maier transmitted works by early English alchemical writers to the German alchemical movement,[2] and he may well have also carried books by Bacon to Germany. Maier was deeply interested in philosophical interpretation of mythology and that side of Bacon's thought, expressed in his philosophical interpretation of myth in *The Wisdom of the Ancients* (1609), may well have had a fascination for Maier and his school. That his alchemical philosophy was hidden in the ancient myths was a basic tenet for Maier,[3] and Bacon, too, had sought for his own natural philosophy in mythology.[4] However we need not particularize too much as to what the points of contact may have been. It will suffice to say that the Anglophil movement in the Palatinate and surrounding Protestant states at the time when so much was hoped for from James I would have included an interest in the great philosopher of the Jacobean age, Francis Bacon.

There are, however, as already mentioned, obviously basic differences between Baconianism and German Rosicrucianism. The latter is more profoundly Hermetic, more deeply magical than Bacon's more sober-seeming outlook. We have detected in the German movement a strong undercurrent of influences from Giordano Bruno and, above all, from John Dee. We have seen that Dee's *Monas hieroglyphica*, the symbol in which he summed up his philosophy, recurs in the Rosicrucian literature. Bacon nowhere mentions Dee, and nowhere cites his famous *Monas hieroglyphica*.

It has been a well-known objection to Bacon's claim to be an important figure in the history of science that he did not place sufficient emphasis on the all-important mathematical sciences in his programme for the advancement of learning, and that he showed his ignorance of these sciences by his rejection of the Copernican theory and of William Gilbert's theory of the magnet. In an article published in 1968 I argued that Bacon's avoidance of such topics might have been due to a desire to keep his programme as free as possible from implications of magic.[5]

---

[1] See above, p. 6.

[2] Ashmole states that Maier came to England to learn English so that he might translate the work of a noted English alchemist into Latin verse. (Ashmole, *Theatrum Chemicum Britannicum*, ed. Debus, Prolegomena.) See further, below, p. 196.

[3] See above, p. 82.

[4] Rossi, *Bacon*, pp. 73 ff.

[5] 'The Hermetic Tradition in Renaissance Science', pp. 268 ff.

Dee had been heavily suspected as a magician and 'conjuror'; Giordano Bruno, the Hermetic Magus, had associated the Copernican theory, in a work published in England, with a forthcoming return of 'Egyptian' or magical religion;[1] William Gilbert was obviously influenced by Bruno in his work on the magnet. I suggested that Bacon's avoidance of mathematics and the Copernican theory might have been because he regarded mathematics as too closely associated with Dee and his 'conjuring', and Copernicus as too closely associated with Bruno and his extreme 'Egyptian' and magical religion. This hypothesis is now worth recalling because it suggests a possible reason for a major difference between German Rosicrucianism and Baconianism. In the former Dee and his mathematics are not feared, but Bacon avoids them; in the former Bruno is an influence but is rejected by Bacon. In both cases Bacon may have been evading what seemed to him dangerous subjects in order to protect his programme from witch-hunters, from the cry of 'sorcery' which, as Naudé said, could pursue a mathematician in the early seventeenth century.

In thinking about Bacon's attitude to science, and his way of advocating scientific advancement, we ought always to remember the character and outlook of the monarch whom Bacon had to try to propitiate and to interest in his programme for the advancement of learning. In this he was not successful; as D. H. Wilson has pointed out James 'did not understand or appreciate Bacon's great plan', nor did he respond with any offer to help Bacon's projects for scientific institutions. When he was sent the *Novum Organum* in 1620 he was heard to remark that this work was like the peace of God which passeth all understanding.[2]

It has never, I think, been suggested that James's doubtful attitude towards Baconian science might be connected with his very deep interest in, and dread of, magic and witchcraft.[3] These subjects had a fascination for him which was tied up with neuroses about some experiences in his early life. In his *Demonology* (1597) James advocated the death penalty for all witches, though he urges care in the examination of cases. The subject was for him a most serious one, a branch of theology. Obviously James was not the right person to examine the—always rather difficult—problem of when Renaissance Magia and Cabala were valuable movements, leading to science, and when they

---

[1] *Giordano Bruno and the Hermetic Tradition*, pp. 236 ff., etc.
[2] D. H. Wilson, *King James VI and I*, Cape paperback, 1966, pp. 298–9.
[3] *Ibid.*, pp. 103–6, 308–12.

verged on sorcery, the problem of defining the difference between good magic and bad magic. James was not interested in science and would react with fear from any sort of magic.

It is not surprising that when old John Dee appealed to James for help in clearing his reputation from charges of conjuring devils, James would have nothing to do with him. Dee's fruitless appeal to James was made in June 1604.[1] The old man to whose learning the Elizabethan age was so infinitely indebted was disgraced in the reign of James and died in great poverty in 1608. Bacon must have taken good note of James's attitude to Dee, and he must also have noted that survivors from the Elizabethan age of mathematics and magic, of navigational boldness and anti-Spanish exploits, were not sure of encouragement under James, as they had been under Elizabeth. Northumberland and Raleigh pursued their studies in prison in the Tower under James, working at mathematics and alchemy with their learned associate, Thomas Hariot.[2]

Obviously, Bacon would have been careful to avoid, in works intended to interest James, anything savouring of Dee and his suspicious mathematics. Even so, Bacon did not succeed in allaying James's suspicions of scientific advancement, however carefully presented.

And even more obviously, it was not the way to influence James in favour of his son-in-law's plans and projects in the Palatinate and Bohemia to associate him with a movement which wrapped its designs in enchanted vaults and invisible R.C. Brothers, who could easily be turned into sorcerers by witch-hunters. Among the many mistakes made by the friends of the unfortunate Elector Palatine, the Rosicrucian manifestos may have been one of the worst. If any rumour of them came to James's ears, and any rumour of their being associated with Frederick, this would certainly have done more than anything else to turn him against Frederick, and to destroy any hope that he would countenance his projects.

Thus Francis Bacon as he propagated advancement of learning, and particularly of scientific learning, during the reign of James I was moving amongst pitfalls. The old Elizabethan scientific tradition was not in favour, and some of its major surviving representatives were shunned or in prison. The late Queen Elizabeth had asked John Dee

---

[1] French, *John Dee*, p. 10.

[2] Hariot and Dee are sometimes mentioned together by contemporaries as both profound mathematicians; see D. B. Quinn and J. W. Shirley, 'A Contemporary List of Hariot References', *Renaissance Quarterly*, pp. 15, 20.

to explain his *Monas hieroglyphica* to her;[1] King James would have nothing to do with its author. Bacon, when he published *The Advancement of Learning* in 1605, would have been aware that James had repulsed Dee in the preceding year. And moreover the exported Elizabethan traditions, which had gone over to the Palatinate with James's daughter and her husband, were not in favour either. Francis Bacon was one of those who regretted James's foreign policy and urged support of the Elector Palatine. Here, too, the writer of English manifestos for the advancement of learning would have to walk warily, lest he might seem too much implicated in movements in the Palatinate.

Bacon had to steer a cautious course through many difficulties and dangers as he pleaded for advancement of scientific learning in those years of the early seventeenth century when the witchcraft hysteria was mounting throughout Europe.

We too have been moving cautiously through this chapter, struck by the idea that there might be a certain parallelism between the Rosicrucian and the Baconian movements, that these might be, so to speak, differently developing halves of the same problem, that it might be illuminating for both to study them together. Up to now we have had no evidence to give the reader as to what Bacon himself may have thought about the Rosicrucian manifestos. But now comes evidence of a most striking kind, from the *New Atlantis*.

Bacon died in 1626. In 1627 there was published from his papers an unfinished and undated work in which he set forth his Utopia, his dream of an ideal religious and scientific society. It takes the form of an allegory, about the discovery by storm-tossed mariners of a new land, the New Atlantis. The inhabitants of the New Atlantis had built there the perfect society, though remaining entirely unknown to the rest of the world. They were Christians; Christianity had been brought to them in early times, an evangelical Christianity which emphasized brotherly love. They were also in an advanced state of scientific knowledge. In their great college, called Salomon's House, an order of priest-scientists pursued researches in all the arts and sciences, the results of which they knew how to apply for the benefit of men. This fiction sums up the work and aims of Bacon's whole life, the advancement of learning to be applied for the use and benefit of mankind.

This fiction, parable, or *ludibrium*, reflects at several points themes from the Rosicrucian manifestos in such a way as to make it certain that Bacon knew the Rosencreutz story.

[1] French, *John Dee*, pp. 38–9.

Before the travellers landed they were handed a scroll of instructions by an official from New Atlantis. 'This scroll was signed with a stamp of cherubin's wings, not spread, but hanging downwards, and by them a cross.'[1] So was the Rosicrucian *Fama* sealed at the end with the motto 'Under the shadow of Jehova's wings', and the wings, as we have seen, often appear as characteristic emblems in other Rosicrucian literature.[2]

On the following day the travellers were conducted with great kindness to the Strangers' House and here their sick were cared for. The travellers offered payment for these services but this was refused.[3] The *Fama*, it will be remembered, lays it down as a rule for the R.C. Brothers that they are to heal the sick *gratis*.

A few days later, another official of New Atlantis came to visit the strangers in the Strangers' House. He wore a white turban 'with a small red cross on the top',[4] further proof that Bacon's shipwrecked travellers had come to the land of the R.C. Brothers.

On a following day a governor of the country called on them and kindly explained to them all that they asked to know about the history and customs of the country, how Christianity was brought to it, and about the 'house or college' of Salomon's House with its staff of wise men. The travellers were permitted to ask questions about any matter which might still puzzle them. Whereupon they said that what surprised them most was that the inhabitants of New Atlantis knew all the languages of Europe, and seemed also to know all about the affairs of the outside world and the state of knowledge in it, yet they themselves were quite unknown and unheard of outside their own country:[5]

that they should have knowledge of the languages, books, affairs, of those that lie at such a distance from them, it was a thing we could not tell what to make of; for that it seemed to us a condition and propriety of divine powers and beings, to be hidden and unseen to others, and yet to have others open, and as in a light to them.

At this speech the Governor gave a gracious smile and said that we did well to ask pardon for this question we now asked, for that it imported, as if we thought this land a land of magicians, that

---

[1] Francis Bacon, *New Atlantis*, in *Works*, ed. Spedding, Ellis and Heath, London, 1857, III, p. 130.

[2] See above, p. 55, and Frontispiece.

[3] *New Atlantis, ed. cit.*, p. 132.

[4] *Ibid.*, p. 135.

[5] *Ibid.*, p. 140.

sent forth spirits of the air into all parts, to bring them news and intelligence of other countries. It was answered by us all, in all possible humbleness, but yet with a countenance taking knowledge, that we knew he spoke it but merrily; that we were apt enough to think that there was somewhat supernatural in this island, but yet rather as angelical than magical.

Further on, it is explained how it was that the wise men of New Atlantis knew all that went on in the outside world though themselves remaining invisible to it. It was because travellers were sent out from New Atlantis to collect information; they dressed in the dress of the countries they visited and adopted their habits, and so passed unperceived. In terms of a Rosicrucian manifesto, this means that they followed one of the rules of the R.C. Brothers, to wear no special habit or distinguishing mark but to conform in dress and appearance with the inhabitants of whatever country they were visiting. The ordinance laid down in New Atlantis was that every twelve years 'three of the fellows or brethren of Salomon's House' should go forth on a mission to collect knowledge of the state of arts and sciences, to bring back books, instruments and news. This trade, it was explained, was not a commerce in ordinary material commodities, but only a seeking 'for God's first creature, which was light; to have light, I say, of the growth of all the parts of the world'.[1]

Thus, though the name Rose Cross is nowhere mentioned by Bacon in the *New Atlantis*, it is abundantly clear that he knew the Rose Cross fiction and was adapting it to his own parable. New Atlantis was governed by R.C. Brothers, invisibly travelling as 'merchants of light' in the outside world from their invisible college or centre, now called Salomon's House, and following the rules of the R.C. Fraternity, to heal the sick free of charge, to wear no special dress. Moreover the 'cherubin's wings' seal the scroll brought from New Atlantis, as they seal the *Fama*. The island had something angelical about it, rather than magical, and its official wore a red cross in his turban.

Modern students of Bacon are not familiar with Rosicrucian literature, which has not been included in their studies nor recognized as a legitimate branch of history of thought or science. But those who read the *New Atlantis* before the *Fama* and the *Confessio* were forgotten would have immediately recognized the R.C. Brothers and their Invisible College in the denizens of New Atlantis. One such reader

[1] *Ibid,* p. 147.

recorded his recognition. This was John Heydon whose *Holy Guide*, published in 1662, is largely based on adaptation of the *New Atlantis*. When the man in the white turban with the red cross on it comes to visit the sick, Heydon quotes this as follows: 'I am by Office Governour of this House of Strangers, and by vocation I am a Christian priest, and of the Order of the Rosie Cross.'[1] When Bacon speaks of one of the wise men of the House of Salomon, Heydon quotes this as, 'one of the wise Men of the Society of the Rosicrucians'.[2] Heydon speaks explicitly of the House of Salomon in New Atlantis as the same as the 'Temple of the Rosie Cross'.[3] There are very many other points at which Heydon associates *New Atlantis* with the *Fama*; in fact he is reading Bacon's work as practically the same as the Rosicrucian manifesto.

Heydon's significant Rosicrucian interpolations into *New Atlantis* should be studied in more detail than is possible here, but one other of his points must be mentioned. When Bacon says that they have some of the lost works of Solomon in New Atlantis, Heydon expands this into a statement that they have 'the book M', which was written by Solomon, in New Atlantis.[4] The book M was one of the sacred objects found in the tomb of Christian Rosencreütz, according to the *Fama*.

The fact that Bacon's *New Atlantis* shows knowledge of the *Fama*, and that Heydon confirms the parallel, is most certainly not a proof that Bacon belonged to some Rosicrucian or masonic secret society. The historical evidence is spoiled and distorted if it is used to support

[1] John Heydon, *The Holy Guide*, London, 1662, sig. b 6 *recto*. Compare *New Atlantis, ed. cit.*, p. 135: 'I am by office Governor of this House of Strangers, and by vocation I am a Christian priest; and therefore am come to offer you this service.'

[2] 'It so fell out, that there was in one of the Boats, one of the wise men of the Societie of the Rosie Crucians, whose House or Colledge is the very Eye of this Kingdome', Heydon, *Holy Guide*, sig. b 8 *verso*. Compare *New Atlantis, ed. cit.*, p. 137: 'It so fell out, that there was in one of the boats one of our wise men, of the Society of Salomon's House, which house or college, my good brethren, is the very eye of this kingdom . . .'

[3] 'Their king had erected an Order, or Society, which we call the Temple of the Rosie Crosse; the noblest Foundation (as we think) that ever was upon earth; and the Lanthorne of this Kingdome. It is dedicated to the study of the works, and Creatures of God . . .' (*Holy Guide*, sig. c 7 *recto*). Compare *New Atlantis, ed. cit.*, p. 148: 'Ye shall understand, my dear friends, that amongst the excellent acts of that king, one above all hath the preeminence. It was the erection and institution of an order, or society, which we call Salomon's House; the noblest foundation, as we think, that ever was upon earth, and the lantern of this kingdom. It is dedicated to the study of the works and creatures of God . . .'

[4] 'For we have some part of his [Solomon's] works which with you are lost, namely the Rosie Crucian M which he wrote of all things past, present, and to come' (*Holy Guide*, sig. c 7 *recto*). Compare *New Atlantis, ed. cit.*, p. 148: '. . . . for we have some part of his (Solomon's) works which with you are lost, namely that Natural History which he wrote of all plants . . .'

unverifiable claims of this kind. It is perhaps justifiable reaction against such fanciful theories[1] which has prevented serious historians from taking proper note of the fact that there are undeniably influences from the *Fama* in the *New Atlantis*.

This fact will have to be studied very seriously in the future by historians of thought, and studied in connection with the German Rosicrucian movement. The religion of *New Atlantis* has much in common with that of the Rosicrucian manifestos. It is intensely Christian in spirit, though not doctrinal, interpreting the Christian spirit in terms of practical benevolence, like the R.C. Brothers. It is profoundly influenced by Hebraic-Christian mysticism, as in Christian Cabala. The inhabitants of New Atlantis respect the Jews; they call their college after Solomon and seek for God in nature. The Hermetic-Cabalist tradition has borne fruit in their great college devoted to scientific enquiry. There is an unearthly quality in the world of New Atlantis. Though it may be prophetic of the advent of the scientific revolution, this prophecy is made, not in a modern spirit, but within other terms of reference. The inhabitants of New Atlantis would appear to have achieved the great instauration of learning and have therefore returned to the state of Adam in Paradise before the Fall—the objective of advancement both for Bacon and for the authors of the Rosicrucian manifestos. One of the most revealing moments in *New Atlantis* is when the travellers wonder whether they are not in the presence of divine powers and beings, whether the invisibility of the Brothers (whom we now know to have been R.C. Brothers) may not have in it something supernatural, 'yet rather angelical than magical'. Though the Governor treats this doubt 'merrily' (or as a *ludibrium*), and gives rational reason for their invisibility, yet the *New Atlantis* is poised on a knife edge, depending for its favourable reception by the reader on whether that reader accepts the scientific influences in it as 'almost angelical', or as diabolically inspired. For the latter kind of interpretation we need only remember the 'Horrible Pacts' published a few years before in Paris.

---

[1] The fact of the influence of the *Fama* in *New Atlantis* was observed by a crank whose book is otherwise utter nonsense (F. W. C. Wigston, *Bacon, Shakespeare, and the Rosicrucians*, London, 1888). A. E. Waite (*Real History of the Rosicrucians*, p. 333) regards the *Holy Guide* as a kind of perverted version of the *Fama* but does not mention *New Atlantis* in connection with it.

CHAPTER X

ITALIAN LIBERALS AND ROSICRUCIAN MANIFESTOS

This book, in tracing the complexities of a theme which is European rather than national, has to wander from country to country. We left Germany at the end of the furore, followed the scare in France, and came back to England to watch Francis Bacon. Now we have to return to Germany as it was before the outbreak of the Thirty Years War in order to consider how the movements around the Elector Palatine affected, or were affected by, the contemporary situation in Italy. This involves returning to the Rosicrucian manifestos in order to pick out a thread in them which we have not yet examined.

When introducing the *Fama* in an earlier chapter it was mentioned that the first edition of this manifesto is preceded by a German translation from an Italian writer about a 'general reformation of the whole world'. Discussion of this contribution of Italian origin to the German manifesto was deferred until a later stage. That stage has now arrived, and the time has come to consider the slant towards the contemporary situation in Italy given by the inclusion in the volume containing the *Fama* of an appeal by an Italian writer for general reformation.

There was a situation in Italy—or more particularly in Venice—which was significant for those who, in Germany, hoped for a new lead from Frederick V, Elector Palatine, with the supposed support of his father-in-law, King James. This was the current of anti-papal feeling still flowing in Venice since the movement of resistance to the demands of Rome led by Paolo Sarpi earlier in the century, and in which James and the English ambassador in Venice, Sir Henry Wotton, had been intensely interested.[1]

In the controversy of Venice with the papal curia which culminated in the Interdict of 1606, the case of the Venetian government was conducted on strictly legal lines by the Servite friar, Paolo Sarpi, who

[1] See my article, 'Paolo Sarpi's *History of the Council of Trent*', *Journal of the Warburg and Courtauld Institutes*, VII (1944), pp. 113–43.

thus became famous among all those interested in maintaining a spirit of liberty in Europe. James's interest in the Venetian case was stimulated by the supposed similarity of the Venetian stand against Rome to the Anglican position of independence. Sir Henry Wotton, the enthusiastic ambassador, really hoped at one time to induce Venice to adopt a reform similar to the Anglican reform. The English prayer book was translated into Italian and services were held in the embassy.

It was in these circumstances of Anglo-Venetian *rapprochement* that it came about that the great work of the great Italian liberal, Sarpi, was first published, not in Italy, but in England. This was Sarpi's famous *History of the Council of Trent*, designed to bring out that the Protestants had not been invited to the Council, that the advice of the more liberal French Catholic elements in the Council had not been listened to, and that the Council had aimed at introducing more strict controls dominated by the papacy rather than at seeking broad measures of liberal reform. The whole Interdict controversy, and the sympathy with Anglicanism which it aroused, had repercussions on the watching states of Europe. The sensational conversion to Anglicanism of a Catholic archbishop—Antonio de Dominis, Archbishop of Spalato—in 1616 was an event which seemed to presage new movements encouraging to those in Germany who were building hopes on the Elector Palatine and his royal Anglican wife. And it was De Dominis who first published Sarpi's *History of the Council of Trent* in Italian, in England in 1619, with a dedication to James I appealing to him as one in whom those in Italy who are dissatisfied with the state of religion have confidence. In the following year a Latin translation of Sarpi's work came out in London, made by a former tutor to Prince Henry. There was an excited sense in these years that Venice and England were drawing together in religious and political sympathy in the face of the claim of post-Tridentine Catholicism, of the extremes of Counter Reformation supported by the Jesuits and the Hapsburg powers.

No historian seems to have examined the connections of this movement with the movements around the Elector Palatine.[1] Yet

---

[1] These are not mentioned, for example, by W. J. Bouwsma, *Venice and the Defence of Republican Liberty*, University of California Press, 1968. Yet some of the contemporary documents quoted in this book are not understandable without reference to Frederick's Bohemian adventure, the failure of James I to support it, and its collapse. The indignation of Sarpi's friend, Micanzio, at James's failure to act in 1619, discussed by Bouwsma, pp. 526–7, must be wholly referable to that situation, also Micanzio's angry words on the same theme early in 1621: 'To stand looking on for doubtfulness of right and let him that is mighty grow still more mighty and be able to undermine all free states ... If from

Anhalt was in touch with Sarpi, and the chief representative of the Palatinate, Baron Christian Von Dohna, was a frequent visitor to Venice in these years. Like many others in Europe, the Venetian government was eager to obtain information as to whether James intended to support his son-in-law's Bohemian enterprise. A Venetian ambassador, reporting to the Doge in November 1619, pointed out that a rebuff of the imperialists in Bohemia would weaken the designs of the Spanish-Hapsburg powers for the subjugation of Italy, and such a weakening of those powers is 'what your Serenity has every reason to wish'. Therefore 'the common prosperity depends on the success of the Palatine.'[1] Though the affairs of the Palatinate are not mentioned by historians who treat of Venetian relations with England in the early seventeenth century, yet those affairs must have belonged very prominently to the general picture for those who were watching the affairs of Venice. A strong government in the Palatinate, so close to Venice and on the mainland route from Venice to England, might have encouraged Venice to continue longer in a defensive position, to maintain longer a stand for relative freedom as compared with the rest of Italy. Still more, had the Bohemian venture shown any chance of succeeding, this would have strengthened liberal movements in all Europe. As things turned out, James's support of Frederick proved a chimera, and his defeat at Prague in 1620 was a death knell for liberal hopes in Venice, as well as in Bohemia and Germany.[2] The Doge of Venice was heard to remark satirically that if the King of England would do nothing in defence of his own daughter, others could certainly hope nothing from him.[2] Henry Wotton's status with the Doge and senate slumped after 1620. Venice was moving away from the English alliance and sinking, with the rest of Italy, into the torpor of subjugation.

This very brief sketch of the Venetian interest in Anglo-Palatine affairs must suffice as an introduction to the study of the translation

---

England there come not some helpful resolutions and that well accompanied with deeds ... the Spaniards are conquerors of Germany and· have Italy at their discretion' (quoted Bouwsma, p. 527).

[1] Zorzi Giustiniani to the Doge, November 1619, in S. R. Gardiner, *Letters and other Documents illustrating relations between England and Germany*, Camden Society, 1868, II, p. 82.

[2] The anxiety with which the Venetians watched events and their despair at Frederick's failure is vividly conveyed by the despatches in *Calendar of State Papers Venetian*, XVI, 1619–21

from Italian which was published with the *Fama*, and which gave the Rosicrucian manifesto and its plea for general reformation a slant towards Venice, and the Venetian dissatisfaction with the state of religion.

The tract on 'the general reformation of the whole wide world' which is published with the *Fama*[1] is a translation into German of a chapter in Traiano Boccalini's *Ragguagli di Parnaso*,[2] published at Venice in 1612–13. It was thus a recent publication, the latest thing from Italy, when the German translation from it was published with the *Fama* in 1614. Boccalini was an extremely anti-Hapsburg Italian liberal, a friend of Sarpi and of other Italian intellectuals in Sarpi's circle, which included Galileo. The trend of his 'News from Parnassus' is very strongly anti-Hapsburg, deploring the subjugation of Italy by foreign tyrants and lamenting the resultant decay of Italian culture. Boccalini died in 1613. It used to be rumoured that he was murdered by two men who entered his house at night and struck him with sacks filled with sand, but recent research has shown that there is no truth in this legend.[3] Perhaps the legend transferred to Boccalini himself the death by sandbagging which he imagines in his book as having happened to Euclid.[4]

Boccalini's satire, or bitter jesting, takes the form of an allegory. Apollo is supposed to be holding his court on Parnassus and to him come personages, ancient and modern, who complain to him about the present state of things. Boccalini is not a Protestant; in one of the pieces of news from Parnassus, Pico della Mirandola is complaining to Apollo about the noise made by the Reformers which prevents him from thinking.[5] But he is for religious toleration; the defence of Bodin,[6] who has been accused to Apollo of toleration, takes the indirect form of pointing out that Mohammedans are more tolerant than Catholics. One interesting piece of 'news' is the scene in which Thomas More

---

[1] The 'General Reformation' (i.e. the Boccalini extract), appears not only in the first edition of the *Fama*, Cassel, 1614, but also in the editions of Frankfurt, 1615, and of Cassel, 1616l See Appendix, below, pp. 236–7.

[2] Traiano Boccalini, *Ragguagli di Parnaso*, Venice, 1612–13; there is a seventeenth-century English translation, *Advertisements from Parnassus*, by Henry, Earl of Monmouth, London, 1669. I discussed briefly the significance of the publication of the Boccalini extract with the *Fama* in *Giordano Bruno and the Hermetic Tradition*, pp. 357–8, 408–12.

[3] Gaetano Cozzi, 'Traiano Boccalini, Il Cardinal Borghese e la Spagna', *Rivista storica italiana*, LXVIII (1961).

[4] Boccalini, *Ragguagli di Parnaso*, II, 3.

[5] *Ibid.*, II, 16.

[6] *Ibid.*, I, 65.

complains to Apollo of the spread of heresy and asks when it will end; the reply is that it will end when the Hapsburg power is broken; it is this tyranny, according to Apollo, which causes Protestant revolt.[1] The satire is always subtle but the trend of it is always the same; it is a confrontation of representative names of thinkers, poets, scholars, with a reactionary world; a complaint against the 'Spanish Monarchy', its attempted hegemony of Europe, and its enslavement of Italy.

Boccalini's great hero is Henry IV of France. One of the most striking scenes at the court of Apollo is the mourning at the news of his death.[2] Apollo weeps bitter tears and his radiance is obscured, fearing that now that this great man is gone all hope of improvement is lost. But we hear in other chapters of how in the Netherlands they are standing firm. All is not yet lost and men of goodwill must stand together.

The chapter from this work which was thought suitable for printing, in German translation, with the Rosicrucian *Fama*, was the one in which Apollo tries to start a general reformation of the world.[3] Apollo finds the world to be in a very terrible state. He learns that men are so weary of life under such frightful conditions that many, finding life intolerable, commit suicide. Apollo fetches a deep sigh and decides to take counsel with wise men to discover how to remedy the dreadful state of affairs. The wise men produce proposals, but all the remedies suggested are abandoned as impracticable. Finally the reformers busied themselves over unimportant trifles, giving up the attempt at deep and general reformation. Things were dressed up again in their former rags, and the Age remained as wretched as ever.

It seems obvious that the allusion here is to the Council of Trent. To anyone in Sarpi's circle, the Council would represent just such a failed reformation, an attempt at reformation which had produced only rigorous regulations and had not tackled the deep issues. But Boccalini has views as to what chiefly ails the age and in what a true general reformation should consist. These views he put into the mouth of the wisest of men, Solon, who gave it as his opinion that what was mainly wrong with the age was lovelessness:[4]

---

[1] The passage on Thomas More occurs in the *Pietra del Paragone politico*, published in 1615, and added to the *Ragguagli*, as a third part, in later editions.

[2] *Ragguagli*, I, 3.

[3] *Ibid.*, I, 77.

[4] Quoted in Monmouth's English translation.

What hath put the present Age into so great confusion is the cruel hatred, and spiteful envie which in these days is seen to reign generally amongst men. All help then for these present evils, is to be hoped for from infusing Charity, reciprocal affection, and that sanctified love of our Neighbour, which is God's chiefest commandment, into mankind; we ought therefore to employ all our skill in taking away the occasions of those hatreds, which in these days reign in men's hearts.

Thus, in spite of the marked differences in style, the Boccalini extract proclaims a message which is closely parallel to that of the *Fama*, the need for a new reformation since former attempts at reformation have failed, for a movement which should emphasize Christian love and charity as its main inspiration. The Boccalini extract presents in its fiction about the court of Apollo the same message of benevolence as does the fiction of Christian Rosencreutz and his Brotherhood. There is, however, no stress on intellectual enlightenment in the Boccalini extract, as there is in the *Fama*, and Boccalini's tone is sad and hopeless, compared to the springing enthusiasm of the *Fama*.

The inclusion of the Boccalini extract with the *Fama* shows that the author, or authors, of the Rosicrucian manifesto had Italy, or Venice, also in mind in their message, and, of course, Boccalini's politico-religious slant, his anti-Hapsburg views, would be very congenial to the circles whence the Rosicrucian manifestos emanated. And the views of Boccalini would lead on to those of Giordano Bruno, for it is more than probable that there was an influence of Bruno on Boccalini,[1] who held such similar views and whose powers of painting in words a great fresco of mythological figures and inspiring it with politico-religious meaning—as in the presentation of the Court of Apollo—reminds one of Bruno's powerful word-painting in his *Spaccio della bestia trionfante*.

In earlier years, Giordano Bruno had 'hoped great things' of Henry IV,[2] had wandered through Europe looking for supporters against the growing Hispano-Austrian power in Italy, had sought such support from the French Monarchy as represented by Henry III, had sought it also in Elizabethan England with its knights and poets, and in Lutheran Germany. He returned to Italy when the conversion of Henry IV seemed to promise an era of greater liberalism and toleration in Italy,

---

[1] *Giordano Bruno and the Hermetic Tradition*, pp. 411 ff.
[2] *Ibid.*, pp. 340 ff.

and paid at last for this over-hopeful attitude by his death at the stake in 1600.

The Henry IV line of approach to the problems of the age, endorsed by both Bruno and Boccalini, had also been very much the approach of Christian of Anhalt and the Palatinate in earlier years.[1] Anhalt and the Palatinate rulers had been ready to support the entry into Germany of Henry IV, the enterprise which was arrested by the assassination of Henry in 1610. Boccalini expressed the despair of Italian liberals when all these plans failed. By placing the Boccalini extract with the *Fama*, the authors of the Rosicrucian manifesto gave their challenge a slant towards Italy, and 'Rosicrucianism' could thus become associated with secret mystical, philosophical, and anti-Hapsburg currents of Italian origin.

Giordano Bruno as he wandered through Europe had preached an approaching general reformation of the world, based on return to the 'Egyptian' religion taught in the Hermetic treatises, a religion which was to transcend religious differences through love and magic, which was to be based on a new vision of nature achieved through Hermetic contemplative exercises. He had preached this religion, enveloped in mythological forms, in France, England, and Germany. According to himself, he had formed a sect in Germany, called the 'Giordanisti',[2] which had much influence among the Lutherans. I have suggested elsewhere that there might be a connection between Bruno's 'Giordanisti' and the Rosicrucian movement, that a secret Brunian influence might have contributed towards the development of the kind of reform which the Rosicrucian manifestos adumbrate. The use of the Boccalini extract with the *Fama* helps to confirm this suggestion, for Boccalini represented the Brunian type of politico-religious attitude.

In an earlier chapter in the present book, the study of Michael Maier's use of mythology pointed in the same direction.[3] Maier is imbued with the deepest 'Egyptianism' or profoundly mystical Hermetism, suggestive of Bruno. Maier, however, in a direct statement in one of his works about the 'General Reformation of the World' (i.e. the Boccalini extract included with the *Fama*) goes out of his way to minimize its importance. In fact, he actually states that the 'General Reformation' had nothing to do with the *Fama* and was only

---

[1] See above, pp. 15–16, 36.
[2] *Giordano Bruno*, pp. 312–13.
[3] See above, pp. 82–3.

accidentally printed with it.[1] This is very strange since the Boccalini extract is found, not only in the first edition of the *Fama*, but also in two subsequent editions, and it is unbelievable that this can have been accidental. It is probable that Maier's withdrawal was due to nervousness about the effect of the manifestos and the wrong use which was being made in some quarters of their message.

The person who knew most about the Rosicrucian manifestos—Johann Valentin Andreae—gives evidence that Boccalini was an important influence in his circle. In his *Mythologiae Christianae Libri tres* (1619), Andreae has a section on 'Bocalinus', who is here said to have been persecuted by 'wicked fools'.[2] The rush of violent language here reminds one of Giordano Bruno on 'pedants'. I am inclined to see an influence of Boccalini on the whole of Andreae's 'Three Books of Christian Mythology', in which he uses famous names, ancient and modern, to allude obliquely to contemporary events in a satirical vein similar to that of Boccalini in tone. The evidence from the 'Christian Mythology' would seem to confirm that the inclusion of the Boccalini extract with the *Fama* was not an accident.

That Andreae and his circle were deeply concerned with the contemporary Italian situation is also evident from their interest in the works of Tommaso Campanella.[3] Campanella was, like Bruno, a revolutionary ex-Dominican friar. In 1600 he led a revolution in southern Italy against the Spanish occupying powers. This was the year in which Bruno was burned at Rome. Campanella's revolution failed; he was captured, tortured, and imprisoned for most of the rest of his life in the castle at Naples. Whilst in prison he wrote his *City of the Sun*, the description of an ideal city ruled by Hermetic priests who keep the city in happiness and virtue through their benevolent scientific magic. The City of the Sun is in the line of the great Utopias, the fantasies of ideal societies which are characteristic of a Rosicrucian atmosphere. It profoundly influenced Andreae who was himself to be the author of one of the most important of the Utopias.

Campanella had two German disciples who used to visit him in his prison in Naples. They were Tobias Adami and Wilhelm Wense, and

---

[1] Michael Maier, *Themis aurea, hoc est de legibus Fraternitatis R. C.*, Frankfurt, 1618, p. 186.

[2] Johann Valentin Andreae, *Mythologiae Christianae . . . Libri tres*, Strasburg (Zetzner), 1618, p. 237.

[3] On Campanella's influence on Andreae and his friends, see *Giordano Bruno*, pp. 413 ff.; Arnold, *Histoire des Rose-Croix*, pp. 61 ff.

they were both close friends of Andreae. They took manuscripts by Campanella to Andreae in Germany, including a manuscript of the *City of the Sun*, a Latin version of which was published at Frankfurt in 1623. (Like Sarpi's *History of the Council of Trent*, Campanella's *City* is a great and famous Italian work of this period which was first published in a foreign country; such exports as these are evidence of the blight of tyranny which had fallen upon Italy.) Wense and Adami were at Tübingen, in contact with Andreae, at about the time when the Rosicrucian manifestos were being produced. This interest of Andreae and his circle in Campanella, and their direct knowledge of conditions in Italy through Adami and Wense, make it quite natural that the Boccalini extract, expressive of anti-Hapsburg feeling in Italy, should have been printed with the *Fama*.

In his efforts to get out of prison, Campanella was to abandon his earlier revolutionary ideas and to write works advocating that the universal monarchy of the world should belong to the orthodox powers. His *Monarchia di Spagna*, written in prison and published in 1620, offers the world monarchy to Spain.[1] The revolutionary whose vision of a world-wide Hermetic reform had been embodied in the *City of the Sun* had given in to the ruling powers. The date of the publication of Campanella's *Monarchia di Spagna* is interesting, 1620, the fatal date.

The doors which the *Fama* had prophesied might be opening in Europe were slammed shut in 1620. The trial of Galileo in 1633 closed a door in Italy.

Before 1620 ended an epoch, observers in Europe were aware of many tentative, intermingled, strands of development which came to nothing and the very memory of which was blotted out, to such an extent that the modern historian seems unaware that something was going on in the Palatinate which was of interest in Venice. Learned and devout Englishmen of Anglican principles looking out from their country towards the European scene would have been inclined to see in the movement around Sarpi in Venice and the accompanying Anglo-Venetian *rapprochement*, a line of development having obvious connections with the Palatinate movement, and its close English affiliation through the Elector's Anglican wife. We can see how these two lines of thinking, or two hopes for 'religion', merge in the minds of two poets and close friends, John Donne and Henry Wotton. Donne's cult of

---

[1] The reference to Rosicrucians in this work (quoted Arnold, p. 144) is in an appendix which is probably not by Campanella.

Elizabeth Stuart was on a note of religious ecstasy, from the time of her wedding when he adjured her to be a 'new star':

> Be thou a new star, that to us portends
> Ends of great wonder; and be thou those ends.

And Donne was an admirer of Sarpi, whose portrait hung in his study in later years.[1] Similarly, Wotton combined his friendship with Sarpi and profound involvement in the Venetian religious situation with a life-long cult of Elizabeth. Wotton's famous poem 'on his Mistress the Queen of Bohemia', comparing her to the rose, queen of flowers, was written in Greenwich Park in June 1620, just before the disasters.

However, the object of this chapter is not to explore possible literary or poetic interpretations of the situations with which it has been concerned, but only to discuss those situations in so far as they affect the understanding of our Rosicrucian theme. Study of the Rosicrucian *Fama* is incomplete without some attempt at studying the translation from Boccalini which accompanies it.

The Rosicrucian manifesto may now take on a somewhat wider meaning. It calls for a general reformation because other reformations have failed. The Protestant Reformation is losing strength and is divided. The Catholic Counter Reformation has taken a wrong turning. A new general reformation of the whole wide world is called for, and this third reformation is to find its strength in Evangelical Christianity with its emphasis on brotherly love, in the esoteric Hermetic-Cabalist tradition, and in an accompanying turning towards the works of God in nature in a scientific spirit of exploration, using science or magic, magical science or scientific magic, in the service of man.

---

[1] See my 'Paolo Sarpi's *History of the Council of Trent*', pp. 137-8.

THE R.C. FRATERNITY AND THE
CHRISTIAN UNIONS

At some time around 1617, that is, a few years before the outbreak of
the war, Johann Valentin Andreae seemed to change his attitude to
'Christian Rosencreutz' and his 'Brothers'. The myth which he had at
first ardently welcomed as the vehicle for aspirations towards general
reformation and the advancement of learning, now seems to be dis-
paraged by him as a vain 'ludibrium'. In its place, he now urged the
formation of 'Christian Unions', or 'Christian Societies'. These societies or unions were to be inspired by aims very similar to those expressed in the Rosicrucian manifestos. They were to give expression to
a renewal in religion, or a new reformation, to encourage by precept
and example the spread of Christian charity and brotherly love, and to
engage earnestly in intellectual and scientific activities for the good of
mankind. These groupings, though they followed the general lines
laid down in the Rosicrucian manifestos, differed from them in two
important respects. They did not wrap their aims in the Rosicrucian
myth but expressed them in more straightforward terms. And, second,
they came out of the mists of invisibility and possible non-existence
into reality. One of these groups, the 'Societas Christiana', was certainly real. It was a society founded by Andreae between 1618 and
1620, which had a short life in those years just before the war, but
soon foundered in the disastrous years after 1620. It did not, however,
entirely disappear, and it directly influenced the formation of another
society which was to have a very important future.

We have now to look further into the question of what Andreae
may have meant when he called the R.C. Fraternity a *ludibrium*, or a
'play scene', to trace the changes in his attitude to this theatrical mode
of expression, and to discuss the relationship of the *ludibrium* of the
R.C. Fraternity to the real 'Societas Christiana'.

In the minds of men of that age, real stages and real theatres were
dreamily connected with the all-prevalent comparison of the world to a

theatre, and to the life of man as a part played on its stage.[1] 'All the world's a stage' was not a slogan coined by Shakespeare, but a normal part of mental furniture, and in Andreae's writings the theatre simile recurs constantly. In his youth, as we have seen, he had welcomed enthusiastically dramatic influences from travelling companies of English players,[2] and these influences had affected the dramatic form in which he cast his brilliant *Chemical Wedding* of 1616. Andreae's interest in the theatre, his profoundly dramatic cast of mind, must be taken into account, in his numerous references to the R.C. Fraternity as a *ludibrium*. This may not be, with him, always a term of contempt. In fact if one examines the passages in Andreae's writings about the R.C. Brothers one finds that, although a frequent way of denigrating them is to refer to them as mere players, comedians, frivolous and foolish people, yet at other times he highly praises players, plays, and dramatic art generally, as socially and morally valuable. What is one to make of this? But let us turn to look at some examples of how Andreae uses theatrical comparisons.

In the *Menippus*, or 'Hundred Satirical Dialogues', published in 1617 at 'Helicon near Parnassus', Andreae has severe words to say about the Fraternity of the Rosy Cross, which was 'only a ludibrium for the curious, in which those who have tried to follow an artificial and unaccustomed path, instead of the true and simple way of Christ, have been deceived'.[3] This certainly sounds like a condemnation. In the *Peregrini in Patria errores*, said to have been published at 'Utopia' in 1618, there are sad comments on the world as a labyrinth, and on how those seeking knowledge hear only vain fables.[4] And in a passage on the 'Scene', or the stage, the world is compared to an amphitheatre where no one appears in a true light, as himself, but all are disguised.[5] Here the comparison of the world to a theatre implies that it is a place of deception.

Andreae's *Christian Mythology* of 1618, which shows a wide knowledge of contemporary affairs, though presented in a broken and confused way, contains numerous references to drama and the theatre. This work is divided into books, each of which is divided into short

[1] E. R. Curtius, *European Literature in the Latin Middle Ages*, London, 1953, pp. 138 ff.; Yates, *Theatre of the World*, pp. 165 ff.

[2] See above, p. 31.

[3] J. V. Andreae, *Menippus sive Dialogorum Satyricorum Centuria*, 1618, pp. 181–3; cf. Arnold, Rose-Croix, p. 194.

[4] Andreae, *Peregrini in Patria errores*, 1618, p. 65.

[5] *Ibid.*, p. 118.

sections on a bewilderingly varied collection of topics. A section on 'Tragoedia'[1] expresses strong approval of dramatic performances. Another on 'Repraesentatio'[2] states that Comedy can teach decorous modesty and truth. Another section[3] gives the plot of a moral comedy in five acts (which may be compared with the five-act play in the *Chemical Wedding*). A chapter on 'Mimi'[4] discusses actors in a friendly spirit, and in a striking chapter on 'Ludi',[5] Andreae states that it is a Christian act to construct public theatres where plays ('ludos') with rich scenes are shown. These are most useful for training the young, instructing the people, sharpening the mind, delighting old men, portraying women, entertaining the poor. The more severe fathers of the Church, he says, disapproved of the theatre, but more recent ones (*recentiores*) approve of decent comedy. The passage is a remarkable defence of theatres as valuable educative and social institutions of which Christians should approve.

The Jesuits were, of course, 'more recent' theologians who approved of moral and pious use of the drama. But would Andreae have been thinking in this approving fashion of Jesuit drama?

These laudatory references to plays, comedies, 'ludi', in the *Christian Mythology* must be taken into account when studying Andreae's remarks in the same work about the Fraternity of the Rosy Cross as a *ludibrium*, or a comedy. The section on 'Fraternitas' is certaihly an allusion to the R.C. Fraternity. He speaks of it as 'an admirable Fraternity which plays comedies throughout Europe'.[6] Remarks like this are puzzling, and there are many others of a similar character scattered in Andreae's numerous works—he constantly talked of theatre and drama, the subject fascinated him, but always in a vague and inconclusive way.

Without attempting to embark in depth on the entirely new and unfamiliar problems presented by Andreae's interest in the theatre, I would hold it out as an inducement to those who might be thinking of undertaking detailed research into the literature of the Rosicrucian furore in Germany that it is possible that such research might reveal a connection between the activities of English actors and the spread of

---

[1] Andreae, *Mythologiae Christianae . . . Libri tres*, Strasburg (Zetzner), 1618, II, 46 (p. 67).
[2] *Ibid.*, IV, 35 (p. 188).
[3] *Ibid.*, V, 8 (p. 251).
[4] *Ibid.*, VI, 26 (p. 301).
[5] *Ibid.*, VI, 23 (p. 299).
[6] *Ibid.*, VI, 13 (p. 290).

'Rosicrucian' ideas. Ben Jonson, too, in one of his masques (*The Fortunate Isles*, 1625) suggests a connection between 'Rosicrucians' and actors, in a passage in which he shows remarkable knowledge of an out-of-the-way publication of the Rosicrucian furore, and plays cleverly on the Rosicrucian theme of invisibility.[1]

Thus Andreae's discussions of the R.C. Fraternity in terms of theatre may belong to a background which we are only dimly beginning to perceive. Andreae was a highly-gifted and imaginative man whose creative energies were sparked off by new influences in his environment, particularly (as I have argued earlier) the influences from the travelling English players who had inspired his earliest efforts. It is Andreae's strong interest in the drama which helps to explain the *ludibrium* of Christian Rosencreutz and his Fraternity as, not a hoax, but a dramatic presentation of a profoundly interesting religious and intellectual movement. Andreae is a most sad case of a man born in the wrong times, a highly-gifted and original man, perhaps a forerunner of Goethe in the dramatic-philosophical cast of his mind, who was compelled to deny his gifts and to wear himself out in painful anxiety instead of reaping the fruit of reputation which his generous nature and remarkable intellectual and imaginative endowment should have won for him.

For there is no doubt, I think, that Andreae became extremely anxious about the course which the Rosicrucian furore was taking from about 1617 onwards, that he saw that it was becoming damaging to the cause which it had been intended to serve, and that he tried to stem the torrent and to guide it into other channels.

At the end of the *Christian Mythology* there is a dialogue between Philalethes and Alethea (Truth and the Lover of Truth). According to Waite[2] and Arnold,[3] the statements which Andreae makes here are proof that he turned against the Rosicrucian movement, perhaps because he was alarmed at the course events were taking. The Lover of Truth asks Truth what she thinks of the Fraternitas R.C., and whether she belongs to it or has anything to do with it. Truth replies

---

[1] Ben Jonson, *Works*, ed. Herford and Simpson, Oxford, 1923–47, VII, pp. 710–22. Jonson accurately describes the engraving of the winged building on wheels in Theophilus Schweighardt's *Speculum Rhodostaurotichm* (see Frontispiece and pp. 93–4), and makes curious allusions to an 'invisible' Rosicrucian Order, with which he seems to associate actors. The tone is satirical and the allusion should perhaps be related to Jonson's politico-religious position. On other satirical allusions to Rosicrucians by Jonson, see *Theatre of the World*, pp. 89–90.

[2] A. E. Waite, *Brotherhood of the Rosy Cross*, p. 205.

[3] Arnold, *Rose-Croix*, p. 194.

very firmly, 'Planissime nihil', or 'I have nothing whatever to do with it'. She is giving the normal reply to such an enquiry and following the usual evasive pattern. But let us also consider the rest of her speech:[1]

> I have nothing whatever to do with it [the Fraternitas R.C.]. When it came about, not a long time since, that some on the literary stage were arranging a play scene of certain ingenious parties, I stood aside as one who looks on, having regard to the fashion of the age which seizes with avidity on new-fangled notions. As spectator, it was not without a certain quality of zest that I beheld the battle of the books and marked subsequently an entire change of actors. But seeing that at present the theatre is filled with altercations, with a great clash of opinions, that the fight is carried on by vague hints and malicious conjectures, I have withdrawn myself utterly, that I may not be involved in so dubious and slippery a concern.

From this it seems clear that it was not because the R.C. Fraternity could be regarded as 'theatre', as a 'play scene' arranged on the 'literary stage' that Andreae was withdrawing from it. He had approved and enjoyed the 'theatre', the 'comedy', the *ludibrium* of the whole affair, and he admits that he was a 'spectator' of it, knew very well what it was about, and had seen its beginning. And in view of his opinion of theatre as good and morally valuable, the R.C. Fraternity as a *ludibrium* or a play scene could have been the dramatic presentation of good and useful themes. What he objects to is that other people, or other actors, have come into the original movement and are spoiling it.

When the *Christian Mythology* was published, in 1618, the Rosicrucian furore was at full strength, and when more detailed examination of that literature is undertaken it may be possible to identify the damaging contributions, the malicious conjectures—perhaps the start of the witch-scare against the R.C. Brothers—which alarmed Andreae and made him think that it would be advisable to withdraw the myth.

Yet the most piquant and curious part of this whole strange story is that the apparent withdrawal of Christian Rosencreutz was itself a 'ludibrium', a mystical joke which the friends of that fictitious character would have understood. This comes out from careful study of the preface to Andreae's most important work, the description of the ideal or utopian city of Christianopolis.

[1] Andreae, *Mythologiae Christiana . . . Libri tres*, p. 329; cf. Waite, *Brotherhood of the Rosy Cross*, p. 205.

The *Reipublicae Christianopolitanae Descriptio*, published by Andreae's faithful publisher, Lazarus Zetzner, at Strasburg in 1619, is a well-known work which holds a respected position in European literature as a minor classic of the utopian tradition stemming from Thomas More. An English translation[1] has made it accessible to English-speaking readers, and, since it obviously invites comparison with Bacon's almost contemporary *New Atlantis*, *Christianopolis* is a fairly familiar landmark in the field of early seventeenth-century studies. However, we are entering this field by an unfamiliar footpath, overgrown with Rosicrucian brambles, and the landmark itself looks a little different to a reader who arrives at it, not along the smooth and safe highways of textbook history, but fresh from the forgotten terrors of the furore.

The preface to *Christianopolis* begins by deploring the oppression of the church of Christ by Antichrist which has aroused the determination to restore light and dispel darkness.[2] Luther's reformation is now to be succeeded by a new reformation. The drama of Luther's days 'may be played again in our own day', for 'the light of a purer religion has dawned on us.' Men of fervent spirit (he mentions John Gerard, John Arndt, Matthew Moller) have called for a time of meditation and spiritual renewal and for the spread of a new outpouring of the Christian spirit in these times. And 'a certain Fraternity' had promised this but had given rise, instead, to an utter confusion among men. He is of course speaking of the furore which followed the Rosicrucian manifestos.[3]

A certain Fraternity, in my opinion a joke, but according to theologians a serious matter . . . promised . . . the greatest and most unusual things, even those things which men generally want, it added also the exceptional hope of the correction of the present corrupted state of affairs, and . . . the imitation of the acts of Christ. What a confusion among men followed the report of this thing, what a conflict among the learned, what an unrest and commotion of impostors and swindlers, it is entirely needless to say . . . Some . . . in this blind terror wished to have their old, out-of-date and falsified affairs entirely retained and defended by force. Some hastened to surrender their opinions and . . . to reach out after freedom. Some . . . made accusation against the principles of Christian life as heresy and fanaticism . . . While these people

[1] F. E. Held, *Christianopolis, An Ideal State of the Seventeenth Century*, Oxford, 1916.
[2] *Christianopolis*, trans. Held, pp. 133 ff.
[3] *Ibid.*, pp. 137–8.

quarrelled among themselves and crowded the shops, they gave
many others leisure to look into and judge these questions . . .

Thus, according to Andreae, the furore has had at least this good result,
that it has made people think and realize the need for reform. He
suggests that steps should be taken to ensure these reforms. Perhaps it is
here that he first suggests the formation of Christian unions or Christian
societies which should go about their purposes in a straightforward
way.[1]

> For we certainly would not commit such an injury against Christ
> and His Word, as to prefer to learn the way of salvation . . . from
> some society (if there really is such a one), hazy, omniscient only
> in the eyes of its own boastfulness, with a sewn shield for an
> emblem and marred with many foolish ceremonies, than from
> Him who is himself the Way, the Truth, and the Life . . .

This seems to be a condemnation of the (probably) unreal and fictitious
R.C. Fraternity, with its curious emblems and ceremonies, for which
is to be substituted the founding of a real, and not fictitious, Christian
society. Such a society had indeed already been founded by Andreae,
the 'Societas Christiana', to be discussed later.

But what renders all the pretended denigration of the R.C. Fraternity
in this preface of doubtful validity is the concluding paragraph in which
the reader is invited to enter a boat and set sail for Christianopolis.[2]

> The safest way will be . . . for you to embark upon your vessel
> which has the sign of Cancer for its distinctive mark, sail for
> Christianopolis yourself with favorable conditions, and there
> investigate everything very accurately in the fear of God.

In the course of this voyage, after a shipwreck, the island on which was
the ideal city of Christianopolis, described in the book, was discovered.

So did Christian Rosencreutz and his friends embark in ships marked
with the signs of the zodiac on their voyages of further spiritual discovery at the end of the *Chemical Wedding*.[3] By this allusion, at the end
of the preface, to the work of which 'Christian Rosencreutz' was the
hero and which Zetzner had published only three years previously,
Andreae connects the preface to *Christianopolis* with the *Chemical
Wedding*. The island on which Christianopolis stood was really dis-

[1] *Ibid.*, pp. 138–9.
[2] *Ibid.*, p. 141.
[3] See above, p. 64.

covered by Christian Rosencreutz on the voyage on which he was starting at the end of the *Chemical Wedding.*

Thus did the pious mystical joker attempt to elude the furore and continue to preach the Rosicrucian gospel but without the name. After all, as Shakespeare remarks, 'What's in a name? A rose by any other name would smell as sweet.'

The plan of Christianopolis is based on the square and the circle. All its houses are built in squares, the largest external square enclosing a smaller one, which in turn encloses a smaller one, until the central square is reached which is dominated by a round temple. Officials of the city often have angel names, Uriel, Gabriel, and so on, and a Cabalistic and Hermetic harmony of macrocosm and microcosm, of the universe and man, is expressed through its symbolic plan. The description of the city is a fascinating mixture of the mystical and the practical. For example, the city is very well lighted; and this good lighting is of civic importance since it discourages crime and all the evils which walk by night. It has also a mystical meaning, for this is a city in which dwells the light of God's presence.

Whilst extreme piety reigns in the city, and its social life is carefully organized on a pietistic plan, the culture of the city is predominantly scientific. Mechanics and mechanical arts are much cultivated and there is a large, educated, artisan class. 'Their artisans are almost entirely educated men' and this fosters inventive advance for 'workmen are permitted to indulge and give play to their inventive genius'.[1] Natural science, chemistry-alchemy, are taught, and there is great emphasis on medicine. There is a special building devoted to anatomy and dissection. Teaching and study are everywhere helped by pictures. In the natural history laboratory, phenomena of natural history are painted on the walls and there are representations of animals, fishes, gems, and so on. Painting as an art is taught and learned with zeal. The divisions of the art of painting are said to be architecture, perspective, fortification, machinery, mechanics, all subjects linked by mathematics. The concentration on mathematics, in all its branches, is the most distinctive feature of the culture of the city. In the mathematical laboratory the harmony of the heavenly bodies is studied and there are illustrations of tools and machines, and of the figures of geometry. The study of mathematics and number is completed by the study of 'mystic number'.[2]

The combined divinity and philosophy taught in the city is called

---

[1] *Christianopolis*, trans. Held, p. 157.
[2] *Ibid.*, pp. 221 ff.

theosophy. It is a kind of divinized natural science, quite contrary to Aristotle's teachings, though people without insight prefer Aristotle to the works of God. Theosophy deals with the service of angels,[1] highly valued in the city, and with mystical architecture. The inhabitants believe that the Supreme Architect of the Universe did not make his mighty mechanism haphazard but completed it most wisely by measures, numbers, proportions, and added to it the element of time, distinguished by a wonderful harmony. His mysteries he has placed especially in his workshops and 'typical buildings', though in this 'cabala' it is advisable to be somewhat circumspect.[2]

The works of God are meditated upon in the city, particularly through profound study of astronomy and astrology; in the latter study it is recognized that man may rule the stars, and they recognize a new sky where Christ is the moving influence. The study of natural science is a religious duty. 'For we have not been sent into this world, even the most splendid theatre of God, that as beasts we should merely devour the pastures of the earth.'[3]

Of immense importance in the city is music, and to enter the school of music one must pass through those of arithmetic and geometry; musical instruments hang in the theatre of mathematics. Religious choral singing is taught and practised. They do this in imitation of the angelic choir whose services they value so highly.[4] These choral performances are given in the Temple, where they also present sacred dramas.

The inhabitants of Christianopolis are enthusiastically devout Christians. They are also very practical people, interested in improving husbandry, street-lighting, sanitation (sewage is carried away from the houses by an artificial underground river), and education, to which they devote much care and thought. Their culture is highly scientific; indeed, in one of its aspects Christianopolis sounds like an exalted kind of technical college (there is a 'college' at the centre). Their religion is a Christianized form of the Hermetic–Cabalist tradition, with great emphasis on the 'service of angels'. Indeed they seem to live on remarkably close terms with angels, and their streets ring with vocal imitations of the angelic choirs.

It is clear that Christianopolis falls into place in the European

[1] *Ibid.*, p. 218.
[2] *Ibid.*, pp. 221–2.
[3] *Ibid.*, p. 231.
[4] *Ibid.*, p. 226.

tradition as one of the series of Utopias initiated by Thomas More's famous work. Its immediate model was Campanella's City of the Sun —a round city with a round sun temple in its midst—the description of which Tobias Adami and Wilhelm Wense had brought to Andreae's circle direct from Naples. The Hermetic-Cabalist, magico-scientific atmosphere of the City of the Sun[1] is repeated in Christianopolis and many of the details of the two cities—particularly the teaching through pictures on the walls[2]—are recognizably the same.

But in addition to these obvious influences on Andreae's city, there are surely other influences. Andreae's theme of the importance of the mathematical sciences, in association with architecture and the fine arts, though doubtless also implicit in Campanella's city, had been given direct and precise expression by Fludd in the second volume of his *Utriusque cosmi historia*, published at Oppenheim in 1619,[3] the same year as that in which Andreae's *Christianopolis* was published at Strasburg. Fludd was himself following Dee's recommendation of the mathematical sciences in his preface to Euclid.[4] It seems highly probable that the Dee-Fludd influences would have entered into the theme of the mathematical sciences in relation to the fine arts, and particularly to the supremely mathematical art of architecture, which is so noticeable in the description of Christianopolis.

Most striking, too, is Andreae's insistence on the importance of encouraging inventiveness in the artisan class. Though the recognition of the importance of technology had been growing all over Europe, this had been the particular theme of Dee's preface to Euclid with its appeal to the artisan class in London.[5] Andreae's utopian city with its strong, educated, artisan class and its enthusiasm for the mathematical sciences would surely have met with Dee's approval.

And, of course, very much like Dee is Andreae's insistence on the 'service of angels' in the city. Dee, as we know, had tried to secure the service of angels through practical Cabala, or Cabalist magic.[6] That Andreae is not afraid to insist on the 'service of angels' in his mathematically orientated Utopia suggests that he is not afraid to proclaim the major influence on his work.

[1] On this see *Giordano Bruno and the Hermetic Tradition*, pp. 367 ff.
[2] On the relationship to the art of memory of these systems of teaching through pictures, see *The Art of Memory*, pp. 297–8, 377–8.
[3] See above, pp. 78–80.
[4] *Theatre of the World*, pp. 42 ff.
[5] *Ibid.*, 18, 40, 82–3 etc.; French, *John Dee*, pp. 160 ff.
[6] *Theatre of the World*, pp. 5 ff.; French, *John Dee*, pp. 110 ff.

Andreae, as we have seen, used Dee's 'monas' symbol at the beginning of the *Chemical Wedding*,[1] indicating the source of his inspiration. We have seen, too, that Dee's 'monas' and its meanings was the secret philosophy behind the Rosicrucian manifestos,[2] expressed symbolically in the mystico-mathematical marvels in the tomb of Rosencreutz. It is therefore quite natural that Andreae's Christianopolis should be a statement in the form of a symbolic city of the philosophy implicit in the 'monas', Dee's philosophy, with its practical and utilitarian emphasis on technology, its mathematical orientation, its esoteric magical mysticism and mystical magic, and its belief in angelic guidance.

Andreae is, then, repeating in a disguised form in *Christianopolis* the secret themes of the Rosicrucian manifestos and of his own *Chemical Wedding*. He disguises it by his apparent rejection of Rosicrucians, not only in the preface to *Christianopolis* but also in the text of that work.

There was a guard at the eastern gate of Christianopolis who examined strangers wishing to enter the city. Certain low classes of people were not admitted. These included 'stage-players who have too much leisure', and 'impostors who falsely call themselves the brothers of the Rosicrucians.'[3] We have to move carefully here because this is an Andreaen joke. It is the false R.C. Brothers who are excluded from Christianopolis, not the true ones. And those who had read the *Chemical Wedding* would know that he who is trying to enter Christianopolis is a true one, being none other than Christian Rosencreutz himself who had discovered this island on the voyage on which he was starting at the end of the *Chemical Wedding*.

Let us now try to make the inevitable comparison between Andreae's Christianopolis and Bacon's New Atlantis. The salient point which now comes out is that Andreae's Utopia is both much more mathematical and much more explicitly angelical than Bacon's. I would assume this to mean that the Dee influences are stronger, or at any rate more acknowledged, in Andreae's work than in Bacon's. Utilitarianism, the application of scientific knowledge for the improvement of man's estate, is common to both Utopias, though more practical and technical in Andreae's Utopia than in Bacon's. Indeed what has been called 'vulgar Baconianism', the emphasis on the practical utility of the advancement of knowledge, seems already pretty strongly developed

[1] See above, p. 61.
[2] See above, pp. 45–7.
[3] *Christianopolis*, p. 145.

in Christianopolis. Can it be that this is due to the stronger Dee influence in Christianopolis? A problem such as this cannot be quickly solved and must be left to future investigators. My approach here is purely the historical one, which has led to the realization that the Baconian movement in England should be studied with the continental Rosicrucian movement, the two being in some way related.

The formation of a 'real' society or group, devoted to Christian and intellectual renewal, at which Andreae seems to be hinting in the preface to *Christianopolis* had probably already begun when he wrote that preface. The plan or programme of this 'Societas Christiana' was set forth in two little works published in 1619 and 1620 which were believed to have been lost, but copies of them turned up a few years ago in the Hartlib papers.[1] Their Latin titles are translated as 'A Modell of a Christian Society' and 'The Right Hand of Christian Love Offered' in the English translation by John Hall published in 1647. The address to Samuel Hartlib prefixed to this translation is one of the sources from which we know that the society described in these pamphlets was 'real', that it actually existed, that we have come out of the realm of invisible colleges and invisible R.C. Brothers into the presence of a factual foundation. The translator addresses Hartlib thus:[2]

> Your self (who were acquainted with some members of this
> Society in Germany) can witnesse tis more then an Idaea; and tis a
> great deal of pitty both that warre discontinued it when it was
> first instituted: and that it is not again revived . . .

In spite of this positive statement that the 'Societas Christiana' actually existed for a short time just before the war—and this is not to be doubted—I cannot find that anyone is at all distinct as to exactly where it existed. According to the *Modell* its head was a German prince:[3]

[1] G. H. Turnbull, *Hartlib, Dury and Comenius*, Liverpool, 1947, pp. 74 ff. The Latin texts of the two works, together with the English translation of them by Hall, are printed in G. H. Turnbull's article, 'Johann Valentin Andreae's Societas Christiana', *Zeitschrift für Deutsche Philologie*, 73 (1954), pp. 407–32; 74 (1955), pp. 151–85.

Andreae's 'Societas' and its influence on Hartlib and others are discussed in Turnbull's book and article cited above; by H. Trevor-Roper whose chapter on 'Three Foreigners' (Hartlib, Dury, and Comenius) in *Religion, the Reformation and Social Change*, London, 1967, pp. 237 ff. is fundamental for the wide historical importance of this group; by Margery Purver, *The Royal Society: Concept and Creation*, London, 1967, pp. 206 ff.; Charles Webster, 'Macaria: Samuel Hartlib and the Great Reformation', *Acta Comeniana*, 26 (1970), pp. 147–64; and in Webster's introduction to his reprint of some of Hartlib's works, *Samuel Hartlib and the Advancement of Learning*, Cambridge, 1970.

[2] Turnbull, *article cited, Zeitschrift*, 74, p. 151.

[3] *Ibid.*, p. 154.

> The Head of the society is a German Prince, a man most illustrious
> for his piety, learning and integrity, who hath under him twelve
> Colleagues, his privy Counsellors, every one eminent for some
> gift of God.

In a letter written much later, in 1642, to Prince August, Duke of
Brunswick and Lüneburg, Andreae seems to hint that Prince August
was the German prince referred to in the *Modell*, but one would like
to have further confirmation of this. The place, wherever it was, where
the 'Societas' started must soon have become the seat of war because
Andreae says in the same letter that the group was broken up early in
the wars, copies of the book about it were burnt to ashes, and the
members, dispersed and unable to correspond, either died or became
disheartened.[1]

Nothing approaches nearer to God than Unity, states the *Modell* in
its opening address; disunity and dissension among men might be
cured by 'free communication of all things among good men'. For this
reason, wise men have gathered into societies, but Antichrist is against
this. It seems strange, continues Andreae, that at this time when the
world is 'as it were renewed, all its decaies restored under the Sunne of
Religion and noontide of Learning' that so many of the best and
wisest satisfy themselves with the mere desire for a 'Colledge or
society of best things' without taking steps to found such an institution.[2]

The twelve colleagues of the German prince who is the head of the
Society are specialists in different branches of study though the con-
cerns of the first three are all-inclusive, namely Religion, Virtue,
Learning. The rest, in groups of three, are as follows: a Divine, a
Censor (concerned with morals), a Philosopher; a Politician, a Historian,
an Economist; a Physician, a Mathematician, a Philologist.[3] If translated
into the language of the *Fama*, these specialists would sound not unlike
the R.C. Brothers in their groupings under Christian Rosencreutz.[4]

The Philosopher appears to be predominantly a natural philosopher
who 'looks carefully into both worlds'. The description of the Mathematician is worth quoting:[5]

---

[1] Purver, *op. cit.*, pp. 222–3, quoting from a letter published in *Jana Amosa Komenského:
Korrepondence*, ed. Jan Kvačala, Prague, 1902, II, pp. 75–6. See also Peuckert, *Die Rosenkreutzer*, pp. 179–80.

[2] Turnbull, *article cited, Zeitschrift*, 74, pp. 152–3.

[3] *Ibid.*, p. 154.

[4] See Appendix, below, p. 242.

[5] Turnbull, *article cited*, 74, p. 158.

The Mathematician [is] a man of wonderful sagacity, who applyes
the instruments of all Arts and inventions of man: his businesse
lies about number measure and weight: he knows the commerce
that is between heaven and earth; here is there as large a field to be
till'd by human Industry, as in nature: for every part of
Mathematicks requires a severall and that a most laborious Artist,
which neverthelesse must all aim at this mark, namely to
contemplate the Unity of Christ among so many admirable
inventions of numbring measuring and weighing, & to observe
the wise architecture of God in the fabrick of this Universe.
Hitherto will the Mechanicks assist with their slights and
subtilties, which are not so ignoble and sordid as the Sophisters
pretend, but rather set forth the use and practice of Arts, and
therefore very partially disesteem'd in comparison of loquacity.
But it is part of a true Mathematician to adorn and enrich them
with the Rules of Art, whereby mens labours are diminished and
the Prerogative of industry and the strength and dominion of
reason made more manifest . . .

The culture of the 'Societas Christiana' is evidently very like that of the
city of Christianopolis, a scientific culture, based on mathematics, and
orientated towards technology and utility. Since the main twelve are
to be assisted by others, 'physicians, surgeons, chymists, metallists', the
'Societas', when developed, would become, like the city of Christianopolis, a group of mystical Christians contemplating the works of
God in nature, but with a very practical hard core of scientific and
technological expertise. Their main interests are directed, not towards
'loquacity', or the usual rhetorical studies, but towards applied
mathematics 'whereby men's labours are diminished'.

As in the case of *Christianopolis*, I would think that the main influence
on this conception of the role of the mathematician would be that of
John Dee, whose philosophy, as summed up in the 'monas', lay behind
the Rosicrucian manifestos and behind Andreae's own *Chemical
Wedding*. There may well also be some influence from the parallel
Baconian movement, but this presentation of the mathematician in
such a leading role, and in opposition to 'loquacity', is not at all like
Bacon.

The science of the members of the 'Societas' is infused with Christian
charity and this imparts a strongly pietistic atmosphere to the group.
This side of the movement is emphasized in the tract which seems

meant as an accompaniment to the *Modell of a Christian Society*, and which is called *The Right Hand of Christian Love offered*. This is almost entirely pietistic, with hardly any mention of intellectual labours. The author reaches out 'this hand of faith and Christian love to all and everyone of those, who being experienced in the bondage of the World, and wearied with its weight, do desire with all their hearts Christ as their deliverer . . .'[1] It is possible that the *dextera porrecta*, or the Right Hand Offered, became a sign of membership in this society.

Thus, when the *ludibrium* of the invisible, fictitious R.C. Fraternity translates into something real, it becomes the 'Societas Christiana', an attempt to infuse into dawning science a new outpouring of Christian charity.

The membership of the 'Societas' is rather indistinct, like so much else about it. Andreae's old friends, Tobias Adami and Wilhelm Wense, were active in it, and there is a rumour that Johannes Kepler was interested in Andreae's Christian unions.[2] Andreae had studied mathematics at Tübingen under Maestlin, Kepler's teacher, and certainly knew Kepler.

Though the 'Societas Christiana' came to such a sad end with the outbreak of war, it had continuations and ramifications. About 1628 Andreae made an attempt to restart it at Nuremberg. It may have been through the continuous life of this branch that, in later years, Leibniz came into contact with Rosicrucian ideas. There is a persistent rumour that Leibniz joined a Rosicrucian Society at Nuremberg in 1666,[3] and there is the better authenticated report that Leibniz knew that the Rosicrucian Fraternity was a fiction, having been told this by 'Helmont'[4] (probably Francis Mercury Van Helmont). Knowledge of the 'joke' would not have prevented Leibniz from absorbing some of the ideas behind the joke, as he certainly did. As I have pointed out elsewhere, the rules for Leibniz's proposed Order of Charity are practically a quotation from the *Fama*.[5] There is much material in

---

[1] *Ibid.*, p. 165.

[2] The source for the statement that Kepler was associated with Andreae's group is Andreae's funeral oration on Wilhelm Wense, delivered in 1642; see R. Pust, 'Ueber Valentin Andreae's Anteil an der Sozietatsbewegung des 17 Jahrunderts', *Monatshefte der Comenius Gesellschaft*, XIX (1905), pp. 241–3.

[3] See L. Couturat, *La logique de Leibniz*, Hildesheim, 1961, p. 131, n. 3.

[4] See Leibniz, *Otium Hanoveranum*, Leipzig, 1718, p. 222; cf. Gould, *History of Freemasonry* (ed. Poole, 1951), II, p. 72; Arnold, *Histoire des Rose-Croix*, p. 145.

[5] See Yates, *Art of Memory*, pp. 387–8, n. 5. Leibniz believed that scientific advance leading to an extended knowledge of the universe would also lead to a wider knowledge of God, its creator, and thence to an extension of charity.

Leibniz's works for further study of the influence upon him of ideas ultimately stemming from Andreae's movements, but this fragmentary mention of a very important subject is all that can be attempted here.

The mysterious word 'Antilia',[1] the name of an island, seems to have been a kind of password used by various groups who attempted to form 'models' of Christian society, modelled on Andreae's writings, at various places in Germany and elsewhere during the Thirty Years War. Such 'models' were, for the mystical enthusiast, but preparations for the great and universal reformation, which, in spite of all, was still hoped for. And amongst the earnest enthusiasts for the model society, and its vast possibilities for expansion, was Samuel Hartlib. Whether called Antilia, or Macaria, or what you will, it was the Andreaean combination of evangelical piety with science, and the utilitarian application of science, which inspired Hartlib's untiring efforts.

And with Hartlib, and his friends and helpers John Dury and John Amos Comenius, the movement returned to England, for it was in Parliamentarian England, which had returned to the old Elizabethan role of champion of Protestant Europe, that Hartlib saw the best chance of establishing the new reformation. As the R.C. Fraternity had represented hopes raised by the English alliance, through the Elector Palatine's English marriage, so, when those hopes failed, it was towards an England restored to its Elizabethan role that Hartlib and his friends turned for support for their ideas of universal reformation, their continuation of the Rosicrucian dream under other names. I say that the movement 'returned' to England, for, as I have attempted to argue, I believe that it was from England, in the form of influences deriving from Dee's mission to Bohemia, that the strange 'Rosicrucian' myth largely arose. This is, of course, an over-simplification, which leaves out all the complicated enrichments from European influences which fed the movement from all kinds of sources. But I am trying inadequately to express this movement of outgoing and return which has been lost sight of in the confusions of the period, and which it is necessary to try to restore to view if we are to disentangle the complicated web of circumstances leading to the foundation of the Royal Society.

---

[1] Hartlib says that 'Antilia' was as it were a 'tessera' of a society interrupted and destroyed by the Bohemian and German wars (Turnbull, *Hartlib, Dury and Comenius*, p. 73). A 'tessera' might be something like a device used by members of a mystical academy.

CHAPTER XII

COMENIUS AND THE ROSICRUCIAN RUMOUR IN BOHEMIA

Johann Amos Komensky, or Comenius, born in 1592, was six years younger than Johann Valentin Andreae, whose works and outlook influenced him enormously. Comenius was one of the Bohemian Brethren, the mystical branch of the oldest reformation tradition in Europe, that stemming from John Huss. Comenius and Andreae had much in common. Both were devout, reformed clerics; both were interested in new intellectual movements which they grafted on to their native piety, the German Lutheran tradition in the one case, in the other, the Hussite tradition. Both lived through the same terrible period, and had to work on as best they could through wars and persecutions.

Comenius received his first schooling in his native Moravia and afterwards attended the Calvinist university of Herborn, in Nassau. In the spring of 1613, Comenius left Herborn and made for Heidelberg to continue his studies at the university.[1] There were other Bohemians with Comenius at Herborn and Heidelberg. He matriculated at Heidelberg university on 19 June 1613, twelve days after the entry of the Princess Elizabeth as bride of the Elector Palatine. In all probability, Comenius, as a young student, would have been in the streets of Heidelberg to watch that entry, and would have seen the triumphal arches of welcome erected by the faculties of the university.

Comenius was attending the lectures of the Heidelberg professors David Paraeus, Johannes Henricius Altingius, Abraham Scultetus, and Bartholomaeus Scopenius.[2] Paraeus was interested in uniting Lutherans and Calvinists;[3] both he and the other professors who lectured to Comenius were closely associated with the Elector Frederick. Scultetus

---

[1] Wilhelmus Rood, *Comenius and the Low Countries*, Amsterdam, Prague, New York, 1970, p. 22.

[2] *Ibid.*, p. 23.

[3] In his *Irenicum*, 1614; see David Ogg, *Europe in the Seventeenth Century*, p. 107.

was Frederick's chaplain and accompanied him to Prague; Altingius, or Alting, had been his tutor and remained a close friend, even after the misfortunes; Scopenius, an orientalist, is said to have been spiritual counsellor to the Elector.[1] The young Comenius was thus in a position to learn at first hand about spiritual or intellectual movements at Heidelberg. One wonders whether it may have been rumours of future connections between the Palatinate and Bohemia which drew Comenius and his Bohemian friends to Heidelberg at this glorious time when the Elector's marriage to the daughter of James I seemed to portend things of great wonder.

The time at Heidelberg was also important for Comenius because it was there that he met George Hartlib,[2] brother of Samuel Hartlib, who in later years was to collaborate with Comenius in his work in England.

Probably at some time in 1614 Comenius returned to Bohemia. In the following years he was acquiring a vast encyclopaedic culture and developing a system of 'Pansophia' or universal knowledge. Comenius's Pansophia was based on macro-microcosmic philosophy; he himself says that it was Andreae who influenced him towards it. Comenius called his first pansophic encyclopaedia, begun in 1614, a Theatre, or Amphitheatre, of all things in the world.

Comenius could have met Andreae at Heidelberg, or could have picked up there something of the philosophy underlying the Rosicrucian manifestos. Or, looking at yet another alternative, one wonders whether Bohemian influences might have been yet another spiritual colouring behind the Rosicrucian manifestos. Could the philanthropy and benevolence for which the Bohemian Brethren were noted have combined with other strands of influence towards the formation of Brother Christian Rosencreutz?

The years of peaceful life in his native country came to an end for Comenius with the defeat of Frederick at the Battle of the White Mountain in 1620 which meant, for Bohemia, the suppression of the national religion. The Bohemian Brethren were proscribed. In 1621 the little town where Comenius lived was captured by Spanish troops. His house was burned down and he lost his library and manuscripts. He fled for protection to the estate of Charles, Count Zerotin, at Brandeis. During the war, Zerotin, though a patriot and a member of the Bohemian Unity, had not espoused the cause of Frederick of the

---

[1] Rood, p. 23.
[2] Ibid., p. 24.

Palatinate but had remained faithful to the House of Hapsburg. His estates were therefore not immediately confiscated and he was able to shelter Comenius and others like him for a while. During the dangerous journey to Brandeis, Comenius lost his wife and one of his children and arrived in a state of total destitution about the end of 1622.[1]

Whilst at Brandeis Comenius wrote *The Labyrinth of the World*, a great classic of Czech literature and one of the great books of the world. In that book Comenius gives a striking description of the Rosicrucian furore which forms an important addition to the series of Rosicrucian documents.

Before turning to study *The Labyrinth of the World*, the question must be raised of what was Comenius's attitude towards Frederick, Elector Palatine, as King of Bohemia. His stay at Heidelberg must have acquainted him with the character and ideas of Frederick, and he cannot possibly have been ignorant of the historical events leading up to the coronation of Frederick and Elizabeth as King and Queen of Bohemia in Prague cathedral on 4 November 1619. In fact, it is known that Comenius was present in the cathedral during the coronation ceremony[2]—that ceremony which was the last official act of the church to which he belonged before its suppression.

Light can be thrown on Comenius's attitude to Frederick as King of Bohemia through an extremely curious book called 'Light in Darkness', or rather, *Lux in tenebris*.[3] It contains the outpourings of three prophets, three visionaries who claimed to make revelations about coming apocalyptic events, the end of the reign of Antichrist, and the return of light after the darkness of his rule. One of the prophets, Christopher Kotter, promised a future restoration of Frederick to the Kingdom of Bohemia. In 1626 Comenius took the illustrated manuscript containing Kotter's prophecies to The Hague and showed it to Frederick. And, long after Frederick's death, Comenius still thought so highly of Kotter and his prophecies that he published the manuscript in 1657 in *Lux in tenebris*, with engraved illustrations presumably based on the pictures in the manuscript. It is in the preface to this book, introducing

---

[1] Introduction by Count Lützow to his translation of Comenius's *Labyrinth of the World*, London, 1901, pp. 33–6.

[2] Rood, p. 28, n. 4.

[3] *Lux in tenebris* was first published in 1657 (edition used, 1665). It included the prophecies of Christopher Kotter, Nicolas Drabik, and Christina Poniatova, with a preface by Comenius ('Historia revelationum'). On the great importance which Comenius attached to *Lux in tenebris*, see Turnbull, *Hartlib, Dury and Comenius*, pp. 377 ff.

the three prophets, that Comenius states that he showed the manuscript of Kotter's prophecies to Frederick.[1]

Kotter was one of the Bohemian clergy suffering from cruel oppression in Bohemia after 1620. He gives the dates of his visions which run from 1616 to about 1624. In the visions of 1620, before the fatal battle, he is warned to tell Frederick not to use force. In visions after that date, the eventual recovery of Frederick's fortunes is prophesied. The following is an example of one of these prophecies, translated:[2]

> Frederick, Palatine of the Rhine, is by God crowned King.
> Frederick, Palatine of the Rhine, King of Bohemia, crowned by God, the supreme King of all Kings, who in the year 1620 fell into danger, but . . . will again recover all and far greater riches and glory.

Kotter's visions were brought to him by angels, so he believed, who would suddenly become visible to him, show him a vision, and return to invisibility. In the illustrations, the angels are shown as young men, without wings, in long robes. Frederick is usually presented in the form of a lion, of course the lion of the Palatinate whom we have often seen before in pro-Frederick and anti-Frederick propaganda. The famous print of Frederick and Elizabeth with the four lions—of the Palatinate, of Bohemia, of Great Britain, of the Netherlands—appears in a strange form in one of Kotter's visions of a lion with four heads. In other visions, Kotter saw lions bringing down an imperial eagle; or the double-tailed lion of Bohemia embracing Frederick; or Frederick as a lion standing on the moon to show the variability of his fortunes, and embraced by six other lions.[3] The visions thus reverse that savage victory of the Hapsburg Eagle over the Palatinate Lion shown in the prints against Frederick disseminated after his defeat. Assisted by his angels, and by wishful thinking, Kotter sees visions of victorious lions.

One of the most striking of these is the scene in which Kotter, sitting peacefully under trees with two angels, is shown a vision of a glorious lion, nimbed with light, strutting victoriously (Pl. 27a). Behind him, another lion is fiercely attacking a snake, and a snake which has been chopped in pieces is seen in the sky below a star. This may possibly be an allusion to the new star in the constellation Serpentarius,

---

[1] 'Historia revelationum' in *Lux in tenebris*, ed. cit., p. 22. Cf. Rood, pp. 29–30.

[2] *Lux in tenebris*, ed. cit., pp. 42–3.

[3] *Ibid.*, pp. 33, 59.

referred to in the Rosicrucian *Fama* as foretelling new things.[1] The lion of Kotter's vision is perhaps punishing Serpentarius for not having fulfilled the interpretation of the new star as favourable to Frederick's fortunes.

Most striking of all, is the vision in which Kotter saw three young men, or rather angels, sitting at a table and holding hands to protect a diminutive lion which is on the table. Three roses grow out of the table, on the front of which is a cross (Pl. 27b). The rose and cross symbolism invites us to look for 'Rosicrucians', and perhaps there they are, the invisible angels who have become visible for the moment of vision, the guardian angels protecting the Lion of the Palatinate, whose restoration to the Bohemian throne is foretold in Kotter's prophecies.

Kotter's pathetic visions, with their plethora of lions, have a semi-alchemical suggestion about them, reminding one of the emblems from Maier's works, and from other works of Maier's group, with which the Bohemian refugee, Daniel Stolcius, consoled himself in his exile.[2] These visions belong to a world which it is difficult for us to recreate, a world of people who had been fed with wondrous angelic promises, with visions of Lions and Roses bringing in a new dawn, and who, in their abandonment and despair, fed still on the visions.

It is for their insight into Comenius's attitude to Frederick when King of Bohemia that Kotter's visions are important to us here. Thinking again now of the campaign of satirical prints against Frederick circulated after his defeat, we remember that the caricature of Frederick standing on the capital Y (Pl. 16) describes in the letterpress under the picture, how the Bohemians 'married' Frederick to the world, expected a world reformation from his rule, were attempting reforms in society and in education under his auspices, and connecting all this with the 'high society of the Rosicrucians'.[3] Is it possible that among the Bohemians attempting reform during the reign of Frederick was the young Comenius?

There is a big gap in one's knowledge here, an even bigger gap than usual. We know nothing about what may have been the effect in Bohemia of John Dee's reforming movement, whether it was taken up by Bohemian Brethren, whether in Prague—the European centre for alchemical and cabalist studies—the movement took on new lights before its transmission to Germany and expression there in the 'Rosi-

[1] See above, p. 48.
[2] See above, pp. 88–9.
[3] See above, pp. 56–8.

crucian manifestos'. All this remains dark to us, but we have glimpsed that in Comenius's early life he certainly had deeply impressed upon him the figure of Frederick of the Palatinate as having a deep meaning for Bohemia.

It is with this knowledge in our minds that we now turn to what he has to say about the Rosicrucian furore in *The Labyrinth of the World*.[1] He gives in this book a long description of the furore, how the trumpet sounds of the two manifestos aroused intense excitement, how terrible confusion arose through the numbers who reacted in various ways to the excitement. Two things should be noted before we quote Comenius on the Rosicrucian furore. First, that he plays up to the *ludibrium*, pretends not to be able to understand why no one has had a reply from the R.C. Brothers, why they are always invisible. Second, that he is writing in misery in 1622, after the collapse of the Frederickian movement, looking back in deep depression upon the course of the movement which had ended by bringing disaster upon his country.

Comenius's 'Labyrinth of the World' is a city divided into many quarters and streets, in which all the sciences, learning, and occupations of men are represented. It is one of the architectural memory-systems, like Campanella's City of the Sun, wherein the whole encyclopaedia is set out. The Labyrinth is obviously influenced by Campanella's City of the Sun, and also, probably, by Andreae's Christianopolis.

Such a city ought to be at the same time a Utopia, an ideal city, a blueprint for a reformed world of the future. But Comenius is in reaction against the delusive hopes of preceding years; his city as a labyrinth reverses Utopia, because in this labyrinth everything is wrong. All the sciences of man lead to nothing, all his occupations are futile, all his knowledge is unsound. The book represents the state of mind of a thoughtful and idealistic person after the beginning of the Thirty Years War.

It is also a record of the disappointing experiences which have led to this state of despair, a record of the Rosicrucian movement. What Comenius has to say about this must be quoted in full. The heading of chapter 12 is 'The Pilgrim beholds the Rosicrucians' and underneath these words is the note, '*Fama* fraternitatis anno 1612, Latine ac Germanice edita'. This makes it absolutely certain that he is referring

---

[1] Written in 1623, *The Labyrinth of the World and the Paradise of the Heart* was first printed in Czech in 1631. Quotations here are from the English translation by Count Lützow, London, 1901.

to the first Rosicrucian manifesto, which he dates two years earlier than the earliest known printed edition.[1]

And then immediately I hear in the market place the sound of a trumpet, and looking back, I see one who was riding a horse and calling the philosophers together. And when these crowded round him in herds, he began to speak to them in fine language of the insufficiency of all free arts [2] and of all philosophy; and he told them that some famous men had, impelled by God, already examined these insufficiencies, had remedied them, and had raised the wisdom of man to that degree which it had in Paradise before the fall of man. To make gold, he said, was one of the smallest of their hundred feats, for all Nature was bared and revealed to them; they were able to give to, or take from, each creature whatever shape they chose, according to their pleasure; he further said that they knew the languages of all nations, as well as everything that happened on the whole sphere of the earth, even in the new world, and that they were able to discourse with one another even at a distance of a thousand miles. He said that they had the stone, and could by means of it entirely heal all illnesses and confer long life. For Hugo Alvarda,[3] their praepositus, was already 562 years old, and his colleagues were not much younger. And though they had hidden themselves for so many hundred years, only working—seven of them—at the amendment of philosophy, yet they would now no longer hide themselves, as they had already brought everything to perfection; and besides this, because they knew that a reformation would shortly befall the whole world; therefore openly showing themselves, they were ready to share their precious secrets with everyone whom they should consider worthy. If, then, one applied to them in whatever language, and be it that he was of whatever nation, each one would obtain everything, and none would be left without a kind of answer. But if one was unworthy, and merely from avarice or forwardness wished to secure these gifts, then he should obtain nothing.

[1] See appendix, below, p. 236. He might be referring to Haselmayer's 'Reply' which was published in 1612. Or perhaps to some 1612 printed edition of the *Fama* which is lost. Or perhaps to a manuscript copy of the *Fama*, circulating in Bohemia, which he had seen in 1612. So far as I know, the *Fama* was never printed in Latin, but a Latin copy of it might have been circulated in manuscript with the German.

[2] That is, liberal arts.

[3] A Rosicrucian pseudonym: see below, p. 165.

(Varia de Fama Judicia)

Having said this, the messenger vanished. I then, looking at
these learned men, see that almost all of them were frightened by
this news. Meanwhile, they begin slowly to put their heads
together and to pass judgment, some in a whisper, some loudly,
on this event. And walking, now here, now there, among them, I
listen. And behold, some rejoiced exceedingly, not knowing for
joy where to go. They pitied their ancestors, because, during
their lifetime, nothing such had happened. They congratulated
themselves because perfect philosophy had been fully given unto
them. Thus could they, without error, know everything; without
want have sufficient of everything; live for several hundred years
without sickness and gray hair, if they only wished it. And they
ever repeated: 'Happy, verily happy, is our age.' Hearing such
speech I also began to rejoice, and to feel hopes that, please God,
I also should receive somewhat of that for which they were
longing. But I saw others who were absorbed in deep thought, and
were in doubt as to what to think. Were it but true what they had
heard announced, they would have been glad; but these matters
seemed to them obscure, and surpassing the mind of men. Others
openly opposed these things, saying that they were fraud and
deceit. If these reformers of philosophy had existed for hundreds
of years, why, then, had they not appeared before? If they were
certain of what they affirmed, why, then, did they not appear
boldly in the light, but express their opinions in the dark, and in
corners, as if they were whizzing bats? Philosophy, they said, is
already well established, and requires no reform. If you allow this
philosophy to be torn from your hands, you will have none
whatever. Others also reviled and cursed the reformers and
declared them to be divinators, sorcerers, and incarnate devils.

(Fraternitates Ambientes)

Generally there was a noise everywhere in the market-place, and
almost everyone burnt with the desire of obtaining these goods.
Therefore not a few wrote petitions (some secretly, some openly),
and they sent them, rejoicing at the thought that they also would
be received into the association. But I saw that to each one his
petition, after all parts of it had been briefly scanned, was returned
without an answer; and their joyful hope was turned to grief, for
the unbelievers laughed at them. Some wrote again, a second, a

third time, and oftener; and each man, through the aid of the muses, begged, and even implored, that his mind might not be deprived of that learning which was worthy of being desired. Some, unable to bear the delay, ran from one region of the earth to another, lamenting their misfortune that they could not find these happy men. This, one attributed to his own unworthiness; another to the ill-will of these men; and one man despaired, while another, looking round and seeking new roads to find these men, was again disappointed, till I myself was grieved, seeing no end to this.

(Continuatio Famae Roseaeorum)

Meanwhile, behold the blowing of trumpets again begins; then many, and I also run in the direction from which the sound came, and I beheld one who was spreading out his wares and calling on the people to view and buy his wondrous secrets; they were, he said, taken from the treasury of the new philosophy, and would content all who were desirous of secret knowledge. And there was joy that the holy Rosicrucian brotherhood would clearly now share its treasures bounteously with them; many approached and bought. Now everything that was sold was wrapped up in boxes that were painted and had various pretty inscriptions, such as Portae Sapientiae; Fortalitium; Gymnasium Universitatis; Bonum Macro-micro-cosmicon; Harmonia utriusque Cosmi; Christiano-Cabalisticum; Antrum Naturae; Tertrinum catholicum; Pyramis Triumphalis, and so forth.

Now everyone who purchased was forbidden to open his box; for it was said that the force of this secret wisdom was such that it worked by penetrating through the cover; but if the box was opened it would evaporate and vanish. None the less, some of those who were more forward could not refrain from opening them, and finding them quite empty, showed this to others; these then also opened theirs, but no one found anything. They then cried 'Fraud! Fraud!' and spoke furiously to him who sold the wares: but he calmed them, saying that these were the most secret of secret things, and that they were invisible to all but 'Filiae scientiae' (that is, the sons of science); therefore if but one out of a thousand obtained anything, this was no fault of his.

(Eventus Famae)

And they mostly allowed themselves to be appeased by this. Meanwhile, the man took himself off, and the spectators, in very different humours, dispersed in divers directions; whether some of them ascertained something concerning these mysteries or not, I have hitherto been unable to learn. This only I know, that everything, as it were, became quiet. Those whom I had at first most seen running and rushing about, these I afterwards beheld sitting in corners with locked mouths, as it appeared; either they had been admitted to the mysteries (as some believed of them), and were obliged to carry out their oath of silence, or (as it seemed to me, looking without any spectacles), they were ashamed of their hopes and of their uselessly expended labour. Then all this dispersed and became quiet, as after a storm the clouds disperse without rain. And I said to my guide; 'Is nothing, then, to come of all this? Alas my hopes! For I likewise, seeing such expectations, rejoiced that I had found nurture convenient to my mind.' The interpreter answered: 'Who knows? Someone may yet succeed in this. Perhaps these men know the hour they should reveal these things to someone.' 'Am I then to wait for this?' I said. 'I who, among so many thousands who are more learned than I, know not of a single example of one who succeeded? I do not wish to continue gaping here. Let us proceed hence.'[1]

Thus Comenius surveys the Rosicrucian furore. First he hears the trumpet sound of the *Fama*, and his description of the profound impression made by the first manifesto is striking. Then came the blast of the second manifesto, promising secret knowledge taken from the treasures of the new philosophy—perhaps an allusion to the abstract of Dee's *Monas hieroglyphica*, published with the *Confessio*. The blasts of the two manifestos are accompanied by floods of other Rosicrucian literature. The titles on the 'boxes', or best-selling Rosicrucian books, are easily recognizable as real Rosicrucian titles, or close parodies of such titles. A pamphlet called *Fortalitium Scientiae*, supposedly by Hugo de Alverda, an imaginary R.C. character said to be very old, was published in 1617.[2] A *Portus Tranquillitatus* appeared in 1620.[3] The macro-microcosmic titles are probably allusions to Fludd, and the *Harmonia utriusque cosmi* is actually the title of Fludd's publications of 1617–19 at Oppenheim. The young Comenius had evidently steeped himself in all this literature, and had hoped for much from it. Then

---

[1] *Labyrinth of the World*, trans. Lützow, pp. 150–56.

[2] 'Rhodophilus Staurophorus', *Fortalitium Scientiae*, 1617. Cf. Waite, *Brotherhood of the Rosy Cross*, p. 264.

[3] 'Irenaeus Agnostus', *Liber T . . . oder Portus Tranquillitatus*, 1620. Cf. Waite, p. 251.

came the reaction, the fading away of the whole commotion, and the disappointment and disillusion of those who had believed themselves on the threshold of a new age.

Presumably it was in Bohemia that Comenius lived through these experiences, and it is the reactions in his own country to the Rosicrucian furore that he is describing.

The further experiences of the Pilgrim in the Labyrinth of the World are uniformly sad, particularly when he visits the streets of different religions and sects and notes their ferocious quarrels among themselves. And he has one particularly alarming experience.[1]

Now it befell that in my presence a royal throne suddenly shook, broke into bits, and fell to the ground. Then I heard a noise among the people, and looking round, I saw that they were leading in another prince and seating him on the throne, while they joyously declared that things would now be different from what they had been before; and everyone, rejoicing, supports and strengthens the new throne as much as he can. Now I, thinking it well to act for the common welfare (for thus they called it), came nearer and contributed a nail or two to strengthen the new throne; for this some praised me, while others looked askance at me. But meanwhile the other prince recovered himself, and he and his men attacked us with cudgels, thrashing the whole crowd, till they fled and many even lost their necks. Maddened by fear I almost lost consciousness, till my friend Searchall, hearing that they were inquiring as to who had aided and abetted the other throne, nudged me that I also might flee.

As the note to the English translation of the *Labyrinth* remarks, Comenius is here referring to the temporary expulsion of the Austrians from Bohemia and the brief reign of Frederick of the Palatinate. The passage makes it quite clear that Comenius had supported the Frederick regime in some way, had contributed a nail or two to strengthen the new throne.

The Labyrinth of the World reflects the Frederick disaster as a shattering experience for Comenius, a depressive and disillusioning event, like the failure and petering out of the Rosicrucian furore and the hopes it raised. The two were surely connected, as Kotter's visions connecting 'roses' and 'lions' show. In the *Labyrinth* Comenius lives through the years of Rosicrucian hope again followed by disastrous Frederickian

[1] *Labyrinth of the World*, trans Lützow, p. 196.

failure. These experiences left an indelible mark of suffering, resulting in distaste for the whole world and its labyrinthine ways.

The Pilgrim had seen terrible sights. He saw vast armies rolling along and the awful punishments inflicted on the former rebels. He saw death and destruction, plague and famine, contempt for human life and human comfort, instead of the building up of human life and human comfort such as he and his former friends had wished for. He saw, in short, the beginnings of the Thirty Years War.[1]

> Then, unable to bear such sights, or to bear the sorrow of my heart any longer, I fled, wishing to seek refuge in some desert, or rather, were it possible, to escape from the world.

Looking about him, and seeing nothing but the dead and dying, overcome with pity and terror he cried out,

> Oh, most miserable, wretched, unhappy mankind! this then, is your last glory? this the conclusion of your many splendid deeds, this the term of your learning and much wisdom over which you glory so greatly?

And now he heard a voice which cried 'Return!' He looked around but could see no one, and again the voice cried 'Return!' And then again, 'Return whence thou camest to the house of the heart, and then close the doors behind thee!'[2]

Now the Pilgrim, retreating into the heart, is there welcomed with kind and loving words and gives himself over entirely to Jesus.

The intellectual and religious attitudes of Comenius are extremely close to those of Andreae and the actual physical experiences of their lives run parallel. This is because, I suggest, they shared the original hopes expressed in the Rosicrucian manifestos, hopes of a new universal reforming movement and of advance in knowledge for mankind. They both watched with alarm the excitement aroused by the manifestos and the way in which the movement got out of hand and became dangerous. Comenius's account of these developments closely resembles the alarm of Andreae at the entry of so many other actors into the theatre of the Rosicrucian *ludibrium*. The movement took a turn other than that expected by those who started it, and became damaging to the causes it was meant to serve. We learn this from both Andreae

[1] *Ibid.*, p. 274.
[2] *Ibid.*, pp. 276–7.

COMENIUS AND THE ROSICRUCIAN RUMOUR IN BOHEMIA

and Comenius. And both of these two religious idealists were shattered by the disaster of the war and the collapse of Frederick in Bohemia. The tale of damage to libraries and scholarship, of untold suffering for scholars, is the same in Germany and in Bohemia. And both Andreae and Comenius find final refuge in their evangelical piety. Andreae shifts from the Rosicrucian *ludibrium* to the 'Societas Christiana'. Comenius withdraws into his heart to find Jesus there. The strain of piety expressed in the Rosicrucian motto *Jesus mihi omnia* becomes dominant in both of them, and the sadly misunderstood joke about Christian Rosencreutz and his benevolent Order has to be discarded. The movements of the spirit and the historical experiences described in *The Labyrinth of the World* are those through which Andreae and his whole group would also have been passing.

Comenius's philosophy, already developing immediately after his visit to Heidelberg, and more fully developed during his later life of exile, was called by him 'pansophia'. First used in the Renaissance by the Platonic-Hermetic philosopher, Francesco Patrizzi,[1] the word 'pansophia' expressed a doctrine of universal harmonies, and a connection between the inner world of man and the outer world of nature—in short, a macro-microcosmical philosophy. Fludd had called his doctrines 'pansophia' and had said that the Rosicrucian manifestos seemed to him to express a similar outlook.[2] We can now see Comenius and his pansophia as coming directly out of the Rosicrucian movement as now understood.

The last, or almost the last, experience described by Comenius in the *Labyrinth* is a vision of angels:[3]

Now nothing in the world appeared so exposed and subject to divers dangers than the band of the godly, at which the devil and the world looked angrily, menacing to strike and smite them . . . Yet I saw that they were well sheltered; for I saw that their whole community was encompassed by a wall of fire. When I came nearer I saw that this wall moved, for it was nothing else but a procession of thousands and thousands of angels who walked around them; no foe, therefore, could approach them. Each of them also

---

[1] One of the books of Patrizzi's *Nova de universis philosophia* (1592) is called 'Pansophia'. Patrizzi had recommended the teaching of Hermetic-Platonic philosophy as a better way of bringing people back to the Church than 'ecclesiastical censures' or 'force of arms'; see *Giordano Bruno and the Hermetic Tradition*, p. 345.

[2] See above, p. 77.

[3] *Labyrinth of the World*, trans Lützow, pp. 321–2.

had an angel who had been given to him by God and ordained to be his guardian.

I saw also . . . another advantage of this holy, invisible companionship—to wit, that the angels were not only as guards, but also as teachers to the chosen. They often give them secret knowledge of divers things, and teach them the deep secret mysteries of God. For as they ever behold the countenance of the omniscient God, nothing that a godly man can wish to know can be secret to them, and with God's permission they reveal that which they know . . .

To follow Comenius's experiences in *The Labyrinth of the World* right up to the end of the book, with its striking insistence on the 'ministry of angels', is to gain another insight into the Rosicrucian movement through which he had passed and which he describes so vividly in the earlier part of his book.

Angelology was an important branch of Renaissance studies. Cabala professed to teach a mode of approaching angels and set out their hierarchies and functions in great detail. The Christian Cabalist identified the angels of Cabala with the Christian hierarchies of angels set out by Pseudo-Dionysius. The insistence of the Hermetic writings on divine 'powers' was an emanationist philosophy which easily became incorporated with Christian Cabala. The immense importance of this movement in the Renaissance is hardly yet appreciated.

John Dee, when he associated his angelic visions with his work as a scientist and mathematician, was moving within an outlook which emphasized the teaching power of angels, and his angelic science was, for Dee, merely the highest branch of his scientific studies in general. Dee only appears as a peculiar crank when he is isolated from the Renaissance angelogical tradition. The Rosicrucian movement was permeated with Hermetic-Cabalist Christian angelology. Andreae's *Christianopolis* with its tremendous insistence on science, technology, philanthropy, in the ideal city, is founded on a ministry of angels as its basic framework. Comenius in the *Labyrinth* makes explicit the teaching aspect of the ministry of angels.

Though Andreae and his followers, of whom Comenius was one, moved away from the discredited name of 'Rosicrucian' in the war-time years, yet the utopian ideal of an enlightened philanthropic society, in touch with spiritual agencies, was not abandoned. On the contrary, utopianism of the type of Andreae's Christian societies was one of the great subterranean forces of the wartime years, propagated by men like Comenius, Samuel Hartlib, John Dury, all influenced by Andreae, and inheritors of the reforming movement which had met with such catastrophe in its Rosicrucian disguise.

CHAPTER XIII

FROM THE INVISIBLE COLLEGE TO
THE ROYAL SOCIETY

In the years after 1620 the combination of Hapsburg power with Counter Reformation Catholicism came near to absolute victory. The Reformation seemed on the verge of extinction in Europe, and there seemed little place in the world for a failed Lion, for the ex-King of Bohemia who had lost all his lands, been deprived of his electorate, and lived in poverty-stricken dependence as a refugee at The Hague. The Eagle had indeed triumphed. Frederick continued to take part in campaigns for the recovery of the Palatinate and continued to be a failure. Yet this man represented something. In his failure and despair he represented the failure and despair of Protestant Europe. And in the eyes of many Englishmen he represented disgrace and shame, shame for the abandonment by her Stuart successors of Queen Elizabeth's role of protector of Protestant Europe.

It is not easy to seize the character of Frederick. He was certainly a very poor general, a naïve politician, an ineffective leader. As a personality, he is presented as weak, governed by his wife and Anhalt, with no will or judgment of his own. But what was he as, for example, a religious or an intellectual personality? No one, I think, has asked. Those who saw him at Heidelberg before the war were impressed by his sincerity. And, indeed, his sincerity has not been doubted, but some of the hostile propaganda, interested in presenting him as a weak fool, has stuck to him. His case may be rather similar to that of Henry III of France, a religious, intellectual, artistic, and contemplative nature, distorted in history by enemy satire.

The portrait of Frederick by Honthorst (Pl. 28), painted at The Hague after the disasters, may be somewhat idealized, or it may have seized the spiritual tragedy of this man. Here is the representative of an ancient German imperial line, the Wittelsbach line—older than the Hapsburgs—who (perhaps we may imagine) has grasped the religious and mystical meaning of an imperial destiny and has suffered more than personal tragedy, a martyrdom. The face is not one's idea of a Calvinist face, but Calvinism, in the Palatinate, was the carrier of mystical traditions, of the Renaissance Hermetic-Cabalist tradition which had moved over to that side. Frederick's spiritual adviser was an 'orientalist'; perhaps, like Rudolph II, he sought an esoteric way through the religious situation. His is a gentle face. Whatever one may, rightly or wrongly, read into it, anyone who has looked through the portraits of the general run of German princes of the Thirty Years War will see at once that Frederick must have been someone of quite a different order.

When the war had been raging for ten years, with disastrous results for the Protestants, a liberating Lion at last arrived, from the North. The victories of Gustavus Adolphus, King of Sweden, saved the Protestant cause. Though the war had many terrible years still to run, Gustavus Adolphus had checked the Hapsburg power and made it certain that Protestantism would survive in Europe. Frederick went to Germany, saw again his ruined Palatinate, and was very well received by Gustavus who recognized his position as leader of the Protestant princes of Germany.[1] The failed Lion and the victorious Lion saluted one another; strange to say, they both died in the same month of November 1632, Frederick of the plague raging in the devastated country, Gustavus, killed at the Battle of Lutzen. The King of Bohemia and the King of Sweden were mourned together in a funeral sermon preached at The Hague.[2] And it is curious to note that, not only were they both Lions, but that the whole apparatus of new stars, fulfilment of prophecy, and so on, was used of both the Lions, though the one had succeeded where the other failed. The cult of Gustavus Adolphus in England kept alive the memory of his predecessor in the Lion role whose failure many attributed to his desertion by James I.[3]

Even more did Frederick's widow, the Queen of Bohemia, represent for sympathizers in England the policy of support for Protestant Europe which, in their opinion, should have been the policy of James I in regard to his daughter and son-in-law. The Queen of Bohemia in

---

[1] On the meeting between Frederick and Gustavus, see Green, *Elizabeth of Bohemia*, p. 288.

[2] It was published in London in an English translation in 1633; see Ethel Seaton, *Literary Relations of England and Scandinavia in the Seventeenth Century*, London, 1935, p. 79.

[3] See the eulogies of Gustavus Adolphus, published in England, referred to by Seaton, p. 83.

her poverty and exile at The Hague was a living reproach for those who thought in this way. After Frederick's death, Elizabeth reigned alone at The Hague, reigned over nothing, very poor, kept by Dutch charity and by erratically paid pensions from England, no territory, nothing but her royal personality and her large family of royal children to sustain her. We can see her in the time of her early widowhood in the portrait painted by Honthorst (Pl. 29) at The Hague, a worn woman but indomitable. Often accused of frivolity and love of pleasure, Elizabeth was in reality a very strong character. She never broke under all those fearful trials. No doubt pride kept her up, and she had been carefully trained in Low Church Anglican principles by those good people, the Harringtons. So she stands there in Honthurst's portrait, sad but dignified in a garden on a hill with a river beyond (is this reminiscent of Heidelberg?), and drawing attention to roses.

Through the later years of the reign of her father, James I, through the whole of the reign of her brother, Charles I, through the whole of the civil wars and Commonwealth, right up to the Restoration of her nephew, Charles II, Elizabeth kept up her proud, poverty-stricken court at The Hague, and all through that time she was never forgotten in England. In her royal aspect she was indeed unforgettable. Had her brother Charles died in youth—and he was a sickly youth, not expected to live long—she would have come to the throne as Queen of Great Britain. If Charles had had no children, or had his children died before him, she would have succeeded, or if herself no longer alive, her eldest son would have succeeded. In contrast to her father and brother, the Queen of Bohemia was extremely rich in children. Those in England, and they were many, who were dissatisfied with the non-Parliamentarian and anti-Puritan, or even potentially Papist, policies of James I and Charles I, looked with longing towards that Protestant royal family at The Hague which represented a possible succession to the throne. And in years to come, it was through Elizabeth of Bohemia's descendants that a Protestant succession was to be sought and found. Her twelfth child and youngest daughter, born at The Hague in 1630, was to become Sophia of Brunswick, Electress of Hanover, whose son, George I, was the first Hanoverian king of Great Britain.

Englishmen passing through The Hague paid their court to the Queen of Bohemia. As an example, John Evelyn's diary under the date July 1641 may be quoted:[1]

[1] John Evelyn, *Diary*, ed. E. C. de Beer, Oxford, 1955, II, pp. 33-4.

Arrived at The Hague, I went first to the Queen of Bohemia's court, where I had the honour to kiss her Majesty's hand, and several of the Princesses', her daughters . . . It was a fasting day for the Queen for the unfortunate death of her husband, and the presence (chamber) had been hung with black velvet ever since his decease . . .

Elizabeth was not only popular with loyal monarchists of Protestant sympathy; she was also popular with Parliamentarians. The Parliaments under James and Charles had always been sympathetic to her and when Parliament overthrew the monarchy, Parliamentarians still continued to feel respect for Elizabeth of Bohemia. In fact, it may be asked whether if she had succeeded to the throne there might never have been a revolution. Parliamentarians, and Oliver Cromwell himself, did not really object to monarchy as such. Oliver thought that monarchy of the Elizabethan type was the best form of government. The objection was to monarchs who tried to rule without Parliament and whose foreign policy was not directed towards the support of the Protestant cause in Europe. Elizabeth Stuart was free from these objections to her royal relatives. In fact, she and her husband really represented the kind of foreign policy which Parliaments would have wished James and Charles to follow. It is thus not surprising that the revolutionary Parliament recognized the right of the Queen of Bohemia to its support. She had received a pension from Charles I which Parliament continued. From her court at The Hague, Elizabeth was thus in a position of being able to follow vicissitudes in England without entirely losing touch with either side. Though she remained absolutely firm in her sympathy for her brother Charles, and was horrified by his death, there were some aspects of Parliamentarian and Cromwellian thinking which were not so much out of line with her position.

This ambivalence of the Palatine house, its ability to include different points of view within one family, can be studied in the lives of the two most striking of Elizabeth's sons. Prince Charles Louis, her eldest surviving son, heir to the electoral title and to the Palatinate (to which he was partially restored by the Peace of Munster (1648), which ended the Thirty Years War), was an intellectual, alive to new ideas about education and utilitarian application of science, and he inclined to the Parliamentarian side, where new ideas proliferated, and where he had many friends who were interested in restoring him to his domains.

Prince Rupert, on the other hand, was a firm royalist, noted for his courage in cavalry charges on the side of the King. But he, too, had intelligent interests; he is said to have been the inventor of mezzotint engraving.

The court of Elizabeth of Bohemia at The Hague is a subject which awaits serious historical treatment. Though M. A. Green assembled many of the documentary sources, and her book is still valuable, her object was to tell in simple romantic terms the story of a royal widow. The first historian, so far as I know, to suggest a deeper approach, is H. Trevor-Roper, who has briefly noted that the chief lay patron of the 'three foreigners', Hartlib, Dury, and Comenius, was:[1]

> Elizabeth, Queen of Bohemia, the king's sister, the royal figurehead of opposition, the pensioner of Parliament throughout the Civil Wars. With her are her diplomatic supporters, Sir William Boswell, executor of Francis Bacon, now ambassador at The Hague, where the exiled queen kept her Court, and Sir Thomas Roe, former ambassador to Gustavus Adolphus.

These few words are enough to set the lines which a new historical approach to Elizabeth's court at The Hague should follow. It should bring together the names of the important and influential Englishmen with whom she was closely in touch, and for whom she was a symbol of the 'Elizabethan' tradition in monarchy. It should be aware that, as the widow of Frederick, Elizabeth had a significance for Europe as well as for England. Refugees from the Palatinate, from Bohemia, from all the stricken corners of Europe, had come to Frederick at The Hague, and continued to come to his widow, though she could do nothing for them financially. Yet she was, so to speak, the ideological link through whom the thoughts of the three 'foreigners', Hartlib, Dury, and Comenius, could become acclimatized in an England which was throwing off monarchical despotism.

Samuel Hartlib had come to England in 1628, after the Catholic conquest of Elbing in Polish Prussia, where he had been the centre of a mystical and philanthropic society. Though factual information about this group is indistinct, or non-existent, it seems to have been an 'Antilia'. That is to say it was like one of Andreae's Christian Unions, the groups which had thrown off the Rosicrucian ludibrium though

---

[1] H. R. Trevor-Roper, *Religion, the Reformation, and Social Change*, London, 1967, p. 256.

they continued to pursue Rosicrucian ideals.[1] The 'word' of Hartlib's group was 'Antilia', and not 'R.C.', yet Hartlib in his whole life and work was something like what an R.C. Brother, if real and not invisible, might have been.

Arrived in England, Hartlib collected refugees from Poland, Bohemia, and the Palatinate, and set up a school at Chichester, returning from thence to London in 1630.[2] He had already developed his mission in life which was to be the tireless attempt at organizing philanthropic, educational, and scientific undertakings, bound together by an intense, though invisible (in the sense of non-sectarian) religious enthusiasm.

John Dury,[3] a Scotsman but almost a 'foreigner' through his life abroad, met Hartlib at Elbing and became an enthusiast for the same type of idealistic projects. He was closely in touch with Elizabeth of Bohemia, and with Sir Thomas Roe, her adviser, and took an active interest in the restoration of her son, Charles Louis, to the Palatinate, as did also Hartlib.[4]

Comenius, the most famous and the most productive of the three, after the experiences in Bohemia of which we heard something in the last chapter, left his native country in 1628, never to return, and went to Poland where he established a community of exiled Bohemian Brethren and began to publish his educational works. In Poland, too, he began to teach his 'pansophia'.

These three men were all of an age to have lived through the excitements of the Rosicrucian furore and its rumours of universal reformation and advancement of learning, and they may well have understood better than we do the meaning of the mystery of the R.C. Brothers and their Invisible College. They were men whom the disasters of 1620 and the following years had uprooted from their countries and turned into wandering refugees. These were the men who came to England and tried to propagate here, universal reformation, advancement of learning, and other utopist ideals. They represented Bohemia and Germany in exile and dispersion, and if we add to

[1] See above, pp. 146 ff.

[2] Trevor-Roper, pp. 249 ff.; C. Webster, *Samuel Hartlib and the Advancement of Learning*, pp. 1 ff.

[3] Turnbull, *Hartlib, Dury, and Comenius*, pp. 127 ff.; Trevor-Roper, pp. 251 ff.

[4] There are constant references to Charles Louis and the necessity of his restoration to the Palatinate in Dury's letters (see Turnbull, index, under Charles Louis, Elector Palatine). Hartlib was granted a patent from Charles Louis in 1637, enrolling him among the 'ministers of the Elector Palatine in consideration of his services to exiles from the Palatinate and his reputation among great men' (Turnbull, pp. 2, 111–12).

them Theodore Haak, who acted as Comenius's agent in England, we have the Palatinate represented, for Haak was a refugee from the Palatinate.[1]

In 1640 the Long Parliament met, angry at Parliament's long exclusion from the affairs of the nation, angry at the domestic policy pursued by the monarchy, and angry, above all, at its foreign policy, which had been one of 'peace with ignominy while the cause of Protestantism was going down abroad'.[2] When, by the execution of Strafford, this Parliament seemed to have broken the 'tyranny', the way seemed open for a new period in human affairs to begin. A mood of great enthusiasm was generated and thoughts turned to far-reaching vistas of some universal reformation, in education, in religion, in advancement of learning for the good of mankind.

To this Parliament, Samuel Hartlib addressed a Utopia, *A Description of the Famous Kingdome of Macaria*.[3] He describes his conception as a 'fiction', likening it to the fictions of Thomas More (Macaria is the name of the imaginary land in More's *Utopia*) and of Francis Bacon in *New Atlantis*. Hartlib's fiction or *ludibrium* (he does not use this word) presents one of those dreamlands beloved in the Rosicrucian age, where everything is rightly ordered, learning has advanced, peace and happiness reign as in Paradise before the Fall, but Hartlib's recommendations are of a more practical cast than those of previous Utopists. He is thinking, not only of the millennium, but of possible reforming legislation which this Parliament might actually carry through. He is confident that this Parliament 'will lay the corner Stone of the worlds happinesse before the final recesse thereof . . . '[4]

In this thrilling hour when it seemed that England might be the land chosen by Jehovah to be the scene of the restoration of all things, when the possibility dawned that here imaginary commonwealths might become real commonwealths, invisible colleges, real colleges, Hartlib wrote to Comenius and urged him to come to England to assist in the great work. Though Parliament did not actually sponsor the invitation, there was general goodwill behind it, and behind a similar one to Dury. In a sermon delivered to Parliament in 1640, Comenius and Dury were mentioned as the philosophers who should be followed in future reforms. Comenius in far away Poland was

[1] Trevor-Roper, p. 289; Webster, p. 32. Like Hartlib, Haak had a semi-official diplomatic appointment from the Elector Palatine

[2] Trevor-Roper, p. 237.

[3] *Macaria* is reprinted by Webster in *Samuel Hartlib*, pp. 79 ff.

[4] *Macaria*, ed. Webster, p. 79.

overjoyed. He believed that he had a mandate from Parliament to build Bacon's New Atlantis in England.

Comenius was warmly welcomed in England by Haak of the Palatinate, and officially welcomed in a splendid banquet given by John Williams, Bishop of Lincoln,[1] who proffered the right hand of friendship to the religious refugee. This was in 1641, the year in which Hartlib published *Macaria*, and John Dury published a similarly optimistic work, prophesying advancement of learning, Protestant unity, and urging the restoration of the Queen of Bohemia's eldest son to the Palatinate.[2] In this year of jubilation and hope, the enthusiasts believed that the new general reformation would now come in England, bloodlessly, without war, without the sufferings which Germany had endured and was enduring. This was the year of Milton's excitement about a universal reform in education and in all departments of life.

It is as though people are most eager now to take the opportunity which had been lost in earlier years, the opportunity for general reformation and advancement which the Rosicrucian manifestos had proclaimed, the opportunity which had been lost in Germany through the collapse of the Frederickian movement. Those who had suffered from that bitter disappointment come now to England, and those in England who bitterly regretted that that movement had not been supported, welcome them. There is a fresh outpouring of the Rosicrucian type of euphoria, the sense that a new era in the world's history is at hand. And it is remarkable how closely Comenius's language echoes the themes and enthusiasms of that earlier period in his book *The Way of Light* which he wrote in England in 1641 but which was not published until later.

The world, says Comenius, near the beginning of this book, is like a comedy which the wisdom of God plays with men in every land. The play is still on; we have not yet reached the end of the story and greater advances in man's knowledge are at hand. God promises us the very highest stage of light at the very end.[3] Thus does Comenius adapt that theatre analogy which was so deeply embedded in the mind of his earliest teacher, Andreae, to the theme that the world moves towards a time of universal enlightenment before its ending.

---

[1] Trevor-Roper, p. 267.
[2] *Ibid.*, pp. 269–70.
[3] John Amos Comenius, *The Way of Light*, trans. E. T. Campagnac, Liverpool, 1938, pp. 32–3. The *Via Lucis* was first published at Amsterdam in 1668.

When all instances and rules have been collected, continues Comenius, we may hope that 'an Art of Arts, a Science of Sciences, a Wisdom of Wisdom, a Light of Light' shall at length be possessed.[1] The inventions of previous ages, navigation and printing, have opened a way for the spread of light. We may expect that we stand on the threshold of yet greater advances.[2] The 'universal books' (the simplified educational primers planned by Comenius) will make it possible for all to learn and to join in the advance. The book of Pansophia will be completed. The schools of universal wisdom advocated by Bacon will be founded. And the prophets of universal wisdom in all countries must be accessible to one another. 'For though it is true that the world has not entirely lacked intercourse, yet such methods of intercourse as it has enjoyed have lacked universality.' Therefore it is desirable that the 'agents of general happiness and welfare' should be many. They must be guided by some order 'so that each of them may know what he has to do, and for whom and when and with what assistance, and may set about his business in a manner which will make for the public benefit.'[3] There should be a College, or a sacred society, devoted to the common welfare of mankind, and held together by some laws and rules.[4] A great need for the spread of light is that there should be a universal language which all can understand. The learned men of the new order will devote themselves to this problem. So will the light of the Gospel, as well as the light of learning, be spread throughout the world.

The obvious influence here is Bacon and his schemes for colleges and organizations for the spread of light, 'the merchants of light' of the New Atlantis. All the three friends—Comenius, Dury, and Hartlib—were devoted to the works of Francis Bacon and acknowledged him as the great teacher of advancement of learning. Here they made contact with the revived Baconianism in England which was flourishing vigorously in the years after 1640. One may however surely detect another influence in this passage from Comenius. Bacon's 'merchants of light' are here merged with the R.C. Brothers, with the intense awareness of the *Fama* of the world moving towards light at the end, with the intense evangelical piety of the Rosicrucian manifestos. And we have seen that Bacon himself seemed aware of such connection, that parts of the myth of New Atlantis are actually modelled on the

[1] *Ibid.*, p. 38.
[2] *Ibid.*, pp. 108 ff.
[3] *Ibid.*, pp. 170–2.
[4] *Ibid.*, p. 173. Peuckert (*Die Rosenkreutzer*, p. 206) has rightly called the *Via Lucis* 'a Comenian *Fama*'.

myth of the invisible R.C. Brothers and their charitable aims, their great college unknown to the rest of the world.

It is difficult to get this clear, but what I am trying to say is that with the coming to England of the three foreigners and their foreign version of the movement for the advancement of learning, one would have the coming together of what we have thought were strands of a movement which had developed as Baconianism in England, as Rosicrucianism in Germany, the two lines being in some way related or in touch with one another. The Rosicrucian manifestos and some of the literature of the Rosicrucian furore may be aware of Bacon. Bacon was certainly aware of the Rosicrucian myth when he wrote *New Atlantis*.

The year 1641 turned out to be a false dawn. The great advancement of learning, the spread of millennial light, was not immediately at hand. No such vision would come peacefully in England, without suffering such as Germany had endured. Long years of anarchy and bloodshed lay ahead. By 1642 it was clear that the country was drifting towards civil war, that Parliament had other work on its hands than legislating for the golden age, that the universal reformation would have to be indefinitely postponed.

The three enthusiasts realized this. Comenius and Dury left England in 1642 to work elsewhere, Comenius in Sweden, Dury at The Hague. But Hartlib stayed, and continued to write, and to plan and organize in England societies which might form models for the future.

Readers who have followed the argument of this book may have at this point (as I do) a curious sense of *déjà vu*. The excitement of 1641 is like the excitement of the Rosicrucian manifestos; advancement of learning is at hand; man is about to step out into larger spheres. The outbreak of the civil wars puts a stop to such foolish ideas, just as the Thirty Years War effectively damped down Rosicrucian hopes. And the remedy, to continue to work towards the ideal through small 'models' of a better society, is the same. Hartlib was continuing in England through 'Macaria', or whatever he liked to call his groups, the same process as that by which Andreae had retreated from the universal ideal into the organization of model groups, Christian societies, the enthusiasm for which had been transmitted to Hartlib before he came to England, through 'Antilia'.

Hartlib was deeply interested in educational reform, in philanthropic and benevolent schemes, and in the utilitarian application of science for practical purposes.[1] He was well aware of the importance of

---

[1] Trevor-Roper, pp. 249 ff.; Webster, pp. 2 ff.

mathematics for applied science, and indeed his 'model' for the improved society is likely to have been nearer to Christianopolis than to New Atlantis. As we have seen, Christianopolis was the model provided by Andreae, and Christianopolis was based, like John Dee's thinking, on a view of mathematics which was both practical and utilitarian, when applied to technical improvements, but reached up from such activities into higher abstract and angelic spheres.

The Dee tradition was very much alive in England in the form of interest in the teaching of mathematics, and its utilitarian application in technology. Hartlib could have picked up this tradition in England, to add to the Christianopolis tradition as the true model of Christian society, which the influence of Andreae would have impressed upon him, before he came to England. And in fact, various points seem to indicate that this type of influence may have been paramount on Hartlib's efforts for the advancement of learning. He certainly greatly admired Dee's Preface to Euclid, for in 1655 he was strongly urging that it should be translated into Latin.[1] And prominent among the English helpers and colleagues whom Hartlib chose were John Pell and William Petty, who were both mathematicians and mechanicians in the Dee tradition. Pell's *Idea of Mathematics* (1638) is surely strongly influenced by Dee's Preface,[2] and Petty, as surveyor and authority on navigation,[3] must surely have owed more to Dee than to Bacon?

I would therefore suggest, though tentatively, that Hartlib's 'vulgar' or utilitarian Baconianism may not be Baconian at all. It may rather come out of the Dee tradition, though Hartlib, like his friends, tends to regard any kind of effort for advancement of learning as Baconian, and there certainly are also strong influences from New Atlantis at the roots of the Hartlib utopianism.

The intense Christian piety of Dee-inspired Christianopolis would perhaps be nearer to Hartlib's strong evangelical pietism and mysticism than Bacon's cooler temperament.

We are now going to begin to cover the familiar ground of the antecedents of the Royal Society,[4] the goal towards which this chapter

---

[1] Peter French, *John Dee*, p. 175.

[2] I do not know whether anyone has yet pointed out this obvious fact.

[3] On Dee as an expert on navigation, see D. W. Waters, *The Art of Navigation in Elizabethan and Early Stuart Times*, London, 1958.

[4] The literature on this subject is very large: see, for example, Christopher Hill, *Intellectual Origins of the English Revolution*, Oxford, 1965; Henry Lyons, *The Royal Society*, Cambridge, 1944; *The Royal Society, its Origins and Founders*, ed. Harold Hartley, London, 1960. The various theories have been brought together by Margery Purver,

has been moving. It may be that familiar pieces in that puzzle may now come together into a more coherent pattern.

According to a statement made by John Wallis, some meetings organized in London in 1645, during the civil wars, for enquiry into natural philosophy, particularly the new experimental philosophy, and other parts of human learning, were the origin of the Royal Society.[1] Amongst those who took part in these meetings, Wallis mentions 'Dr. John Wilkins (afterwards Bishop of Chester) then chaplain to the Prince Elector Palatine in London', and 'Mr. Theodore Haak (a German of the Palatinate, and then resident in London, who, I think, gave the first occasion and first suggested these meetings) and many others.' The reliability of this account of the origins of the Royal Society has been questioned because these London meetings of 1645 are not mentioned by Thomas Sprat in his official history of the Royal Society.

What, however, now stands out in this account is the predominance of influence from the Palatinate in it. Haak, a German from the Palatinate, is credited with having started the meetings which gave rise to the Royal Society. And it is pointed out that John Wilkins (afterwards so prominent in the Royal Society) was, at the time these meetings were started, chaplain to the Elector Palatine (eldest son of the King and Queen of Bohemia). This account seems to give a curiously 'Palatinate' colouring to the origins of the Royal Society, in meetings begun by a German from the Palatinate, the representative of religion at the meetings being chaplain to the Elector Palatine.

Coming now to the next in date of the pieces belonging to the puzzle about the origins of the Royal Society, we find that these are the mentions by Robert Boyle, in letters of 1646 and 1647, of an 'Invisible College'.

Writing in October 1646 to his former tutor, the young Boyle says that he is applying himself to natural philosophy according to the principles of 'our new philosophical college' and he asks his tutor to send him books which might be useful 'which will make you extremely welcome to our Invisible College'.

A few months later, writing to another friend in February 1647, Boyle says:[2]

The Royal Society: Concept and Creation, London, 1967. An important essay is that by P. M. Rattansi, 'The Intellectual Origins of the Royal Society', *Notes and Records of the Royal Society*, 23 (1968).

[1] Wallis wrote two slightly different accounts of these meetings, one in 1678, another in 1697. For full quotation of the passages, see Purver, pp. 161 ff.

[2] Robert Boyle, *Works*, ed. Thomas Birch, 1744, I, p. 20. Cf. Purver, pp. 193 ff.

The best on't is, that the cornerstones of the *Invisible* or (as they term themselves) the Philosophical College, do now and then honour me with their company . . . men of so capacious and searching spirits, that school-philosophy is but the lowest region of their knowledge; and yet, though ambitious to lead the way to any generous design, of so humble and teachable a genius, as they disdain not to be directed to the meanest, so he can but plead reason for his opinion; persons that endeavour to put narrow-mindedness out of countenance, by the practice of so extensive a charity that it reaches unto everything called man, and nothing less than an universal good-will can content it. And indeed they are so apprehensive of the want of good employment, that they take the whole body of mankind to their care.

And in May 1647, writing probably to Hartlib, Boyle speaks again of the 'Invisible College' and its public-spirited plans.

This 'Invisible College' has given rise to much speculation as a possible ancestor of the Royal Society. What was it, where did it meet, who belonged to it? Did it refer to any particular group engaged on the study of natural philosophy, to the group just begun in London by Haak, for example? Or to Hartlib's group?[1] The description of its charitable outlook fits Hartlib perhaps. But this word 'Invisible College' does not sound strange to us. It is the old *ludibrium*, the old joke about invisibility always associated with the R.C. Brothers and their college. Descartes had had to prove his visibility to escape being associated with it. Bacon knew the joke; the benevolent brothers of New Atlantis and their great college were invisible to the outside world. It would apply to the activities of 'Antilia' or of any group, however called, descended from Andreae.

The use by Boyle of the expression 'Invisible College' of the group which he has come to know suggests that, though the word 'Rosicrucian' is not used, Boyle and his friends knew something about it, since they were able to use the old *ludibrium*. We have thus here a chain of tradition leading from the Rosicrucian movement to the antecedents of the Royal Society.

These are well-known pieces in the puzzle. I now put in another piece for consideration, the fact that John Wilkins, chaplain to the Elector Palatine and pillar of the movements leading to the Royal

[1] As suggested by R. H. Syfret, 'The Origins of the Royal Society', *Notes and Records of the Royal Society*, 5 (1948).

Society, and of the Royal Society itself, quotes from the Rosicrucian *Fama*.

In his *Mathematicall Magick* (1648), when discussing a kind of lamp for use underground, Wilkins says that such a lamp 'is related to be seen in the sepulchre of Francis Rosicrosse, as is more largely expressed in the Confession of that Fraternity.'[1] Though he speaks of Francis, instead of Christian, Rosy Cross (probably mistaking the 'Fra' for 'Frater' of the manifestos as an abbreviation of 'Francis'), and though the sepulchre with the lamp in it (the famous vault) is described, not in the *Confessio*, but in the *Fama*, this quotation shows that Wilkins was certainly aware of the Rosicrucian manifestos.

As I have pointed out elsewhere,[2] Wilkins's *Mathematicall Magick* is largely based on the section on mechanics in Robert Fludd's *Utriusque Cosmi Historia*, published at Oppenheim in the Palatinate in 1619, and Fludd himself was inspired by the outline of mathematical or 'Vitruvian' subjects given by Dee in his preface to Euclid of 1570. Wilkins does not conceal his debt to Dee and Fludd but frequently acknowledges both Dee's preface and Fludd's work. Wilkins displays great interest in this book in automata, speaking statues and the like, worked by mechanical magic. He describes a magico-scientific speaking statue of Memnon. Wilkins's mechanical interests here are very much at the stage fashionable at Heidelberg, before the disasters, and his quotation from the marvels of the tomb of Christian Rosencreutz in the *Fama* shows (I think) that he interpreted these as a *ludibrium* for scientifically produced marvels.

Wilkins also frequently mentions the Lord Verulam (Francis Bacon) in this book, which shows that, at this stage in his career, he did not disconnect Baconian science from the Dee-Fludd tradition. Both were 'advancement of learning'. He states that he has called his book 'Mathematical magic' because the kind of mechanical inventions treated in it have been so styled by Cornelius Agrippa.

The book is important for its indications of Wilkins's outlook and interests in the year 1648, for this was the year in which the meetings at Oxford began which are stated by Thomas Sprat in his official history of the Royal Society to have been the origin of the Royal Society.[3] Sprat makes no mentions of the earlier London group

---

[1] John Wilkins, *Mathematicall Magick, or, The Wonders that may be Performed by Mechanicall Geometry*, London, 1648, pp. 256-7.

[2] *Theatre of the World*, p. 51, n. 19.

[3] Thomas Sprat, *History of the Royal Society*, London, 1667, pp. 53 ff.

described by Wallis. These Oxford meetings were held in Wilkins's rooms at Wadham College and they ran from about 1648 to about 1659, when the group moved to London and formed the nucleus of the Royal Society, founded in 1660. Among the members of this Oxford group were Robert Boyle, William Petty, and Christopher Wren. Describing 'rarities' that he had seen in Wilkins's rooms at Wadham in 1654, Evelyn says that Wilkins had contrived a hollow statue which uttered words by a long, concealed pipe, and that he possessed many other 'artificial, mathematical, and magical curiosities',[1] which suggests the atmosphere and the interests of his *Mathematicall Magick*.

During the years covered by the Oxford meetings, 1648–59, many books were published, a few of which we must glance at as relevant for the way that things were going in these pre-Royal Society years.

One of these is certainly highly relevant for the history of Rosicrucianism. In 1652 Thomas Vaughan published an English translation of the *Fama* and the *Confessio*, under the pseudonym of 'Eugenius Philalethes'.[2] This was indeed an epoch-making event. English translations of the Rosicrucian manifestos had certainly been circulating in manuscript long before this, and, in fact, the translation which Vaughan published was not his own but based on a much earlier manuscript version.[3] That these texts now appeared in cold print, and in English, must have made the Rosicrucian manifestos known to a much wider public. Why it was thought opportune to publish them at this moment, I do not know. Vaughan was the author of other mystical works in which he mentions the Rosicrucian myth. He was the brother of Henry Vaughan, the poet, and he had a controversy with Henry More, the Cambridge Platonist. Thomas Vaughan's patron is said to have been Sir Robert Moray,[4] afterwards very influential in the formation of the Royal Society.

The, as it were, public acknowledgement of the *Fama* and the *Confessio* may have encouraged John Webster, a Puritan divine, to

[1] Evelyn, *Diary*, ed De Beer, III, p. 110.

[2] 'Eugenius Philalethes' (Thomas Vaughan), *The Fame and Confession of the Fraternity of R. C. Commonly of the Rosie Cross*, London, 1652. Reprinted in facsimile with a preface by F. N. Pryce, Margate, 1923 (printed for the 'Societas Rosicruciana in Anglia'). See Appendix, below, p. 235.

[3] F. N. Pryce, preface, pp. 3–8. Pryce concludes that the manuscript translation which Vaughan was using must have been composed well before 1633, and probably before 1630. See Appendix, below, p. 237.

[4] Pryce, preface, p. 2.

come out with a remarkable work in which he urges that 'the philosophy of Hermes revived by the Paracelsian school' should be taught in the universities.[1] Webster goes very deeply into the kind of doctrines that are behind the Rosicrucian manifestos, urging, like them, the replacement of Aristotelian scholasticism by a Hermetic-Paracelsist type of natural philosophy, through which to learn the language of nature rather than the language of the schools. His only mention of the 'highly illuminated fraternity of the Rosie Crosse' is in connection with the 'language of nature', which he speaks of as a secret known to the 'divinely inspired Teutonic Boehme' and 'in some measure acknowledged' by the Rosy Cross Fraternity,[2] an interesting (and undoubtedly correct) insight into the affinity between Boehme and the Rosicrucian manifestos.

Within the 'philosophy of Hermes', Webster includes mathematics, particularly as recommended by John Dee in his Preface to Euclid from which Webster quotes at length, with ecstatic encomiums of Dee.[3] He also profoundly reveres that 'profoundly learned man Dr. Fludd',[4] and he is under the impression that if authors like these—and his book is an amalgam of Paracelsist, Agrippan and similar Renaissance magico-scientific type of thinking, with Dee and Fludd as his favourites—were taught in the universities, 'the arcana and magnalia of nature'[5] arrived at by Francis Bacon might be brought to perfection. That is to say, Webster sees Bacon as a 'Rosicrucian' type of thinker whose teaching needs to be supplemented, above all, by Dee's mathematical Preface.

In the heart of Puritan England, this Parliamentarian chaplain produces a work which is right in the Renaissance magico-scientific tradition, culminating in Dee and Fludd, and he thinks that this is what should be taught in the universities, together with Baconianism, which he sees as incomplete without such authors. Webster ignores the fact that Bacon expressly states that he is against the macro-microcosmic

[1] John Webster, *Academiarum Examen, or the Examination of Academies*, London, 1654. On Webster, see P. M. Rattansi, 'Paracelsus and the Puritan Revolution', *Ambix*, XI (1963).

[2] Webster, *Examen*, p. 26.

[3] *Ibid.*, pp. 19-20, 52. Webster outlines the survey of the mathematical sciences made by 'that expert and learned man, Dr. John Dee in his Preface before Euclide', and exclaims at the 'excellent, admirable, and profitable experiments' which these afford, the least of which is of more use, benefit, and profit to the life of man than the learning of the universities.

[4] *Ibid.*, p. 105.

[5] *Ibid.*, Epistle to the Reader, Sig. B 2.

philosophy of the Paracelsians, and is under the impression that Bacon can be reconciled with it. And he seems to underline Bacon's omission of the Dee mathematics.

Seth Ward, one of the Oxford group of predecessors of the Royal Society meeting in Oxford at this time under the aegis of Wilkins, very severely snubbed Webster in his *Vindiciae Academiarum* (1654).[1] Ward is very angry with Webster for trying to assimilate Bacon to Fludd: 'there are not two waies in the whole world more opposite, than those of L. Verulam and D. Fludd, the one founded upon experiment, the other upon mystical Ideal reasons . . .'[2] Ward is disgusted with Webster's 'canting Discourse about the language of nature, wherein he doth assent unto the highly illuminated fraternity of the Rosicrucians'.[3] Ward even goes so far as to say that he suspects Webster of being a Friar, and likens his enthusiastic speech about Dee's Preface to the utterance of some 'moping Friar': 'praying (like some moping Friar to the Lady of Lauretto, or like) the nephew of the Queen of Faery, and uttering a speech to her, made by John Dee in his preface . . .'[4] This seems very odd language from the Oxford group, particularly since the head of it, Wilkins, only six years previously had been drawing quite openly on the Dee-Fludd tradition for his work on 'mathematical magic'.

What has been going on in the Oxford group? I suggest, as a possibility, that there may have been a movement among some of them to disassociate it as completely as possible from imputation of magic, still a danger for scientific groups. To do this, they intensify their interpretation of Bacon as the teacher of 'experimental philosophy', disinfecting him from all other associations, whilst at the same time carefully drawing away from Dee's mathematical preface, and the Dee mathematical tradition, which they are associating with 'enthusiasm', the enthusiasm of a 'canting Puritan' or a 'moping Friar'.

The way was now prepared for the unleashing of a witch-scare, a phenomenon of which we have had considerable experience in earlier chapters, and which now took the form of a publication which was to blast Dee's reputation for three hundred years and to confuse the

---

[1] Seth Ward, *Vindiciae Academiarum*, Oxford, 1654. The laudatory letter to Ward which is printed as a preface to the book is usually attributed to Wilkins, who is, however, not mentioned by name and the letter is signed 'N.S.'.

[2] *Vindiciae*, p. 46.

[3] *Ibid.*, p. 5.

[4] *Ibid.*, p. 15.

history of thought by knocking out from serious consideration one of its most important figures.

This was the publication in 1659 of Dee's Spiritual Diary, or the records of his supposed conversations with angels, with a damning preface by Meric Casaubon accusing Dee of diabolical magic.[1] It appears that Casaubon had personal reasons for the publication, through which he hoped to establish his own orthodoxy, and it was also aimed at discrediting those pretending to 'so much Inspiration', that is, it was against 'enthusiasts'. The government was against the publication of the book and tried to suppress it, but was unable to do so as it had been quickly bought up as 'a great and curious Novelty'. It will no doubt be a long time before the motives behind the publication of this book are fully unravelled. The year of publication is significant, 1659, when Oliver Cromwell was dead, when the weak government of his son was producing chaos, when no one knew what would happen next. What happened next was, of course, the Restoration of Charles II in 1660. Who were the 'enthusiasts' that Meric Casaubon's publication aimed at discrediting and excluding from influence in the years ahead?

The publication of Dee's diary was certainly part of a general campaign against enthusiasts and illuminati being worked up at the time.[2] In his preface, Casaubon states that Dee, like Trithemius and Paracelsus, was inspired by the devil. The mention of Paracelsus gets rid of the whole Rosicrucian movement. This campaign ruined Dee's reputation and deprived him for centuries of the credit for his important scientific work. Robert Hooke, who, as one of the best mathematicians in the Royal Society, would have known of Dee's work, later tried to rescue his reputation by arguing that the Spiritual Diaries were a 'concealed history of art and nature' relating to contemporary events.[3]

As the natural philosophers moved towards the consummation of the Royal Society, they had to be very careful. Religious passions were still high, and a dreaded witch-scare might start at any moment to

[1] John Dee, *A True & Faithful Relation of what passed for many Years Between Dr. John Dee . . . and Some Spirits*, ed. Meric Casaubon, London, 1659. On this book and its effect on Dee's reputation, see French, *John Dee*, pp. 11–13. John Webster published a defence of Dee in which he exposed Casaubon's motives for the publication (John Webster, *The Displaying of Supposed Witchcraft*, London, 1677).

[2] Rattansi, 'Paracelsus and the Puritan Revolution', p. 31.

[3] R. Hooke, *Posthumous Works*, London, 1705, pp. 204 ff. Hooke may have known something about Dee's mission in Bohemia.

stop their efforts. So they drop Dee, and make their Baconianism as innocuous as possible.

One wonders what they did with the references to the R.C. Brothers, their invisibility and their college, in the *New Atlantis*. They must surely have recognized the fiction of Christian Rosencreutz and his benevolent order behind the fiction of New Atlantis. And they were not allowed to forget the parallel, for, between 1658 and 1664—years just before and just after the Restoration and the founding of the Royal Society—that strange character, John Heydon, who abandoned all precedent by loudly claiming that he *was* a Rosicrucian, published a series of works in which the Rosicrucian tendency to fanciful utopianism reached unprecedented heights. Heydon is an astrologer, geomancer, alchemist, of a most extreme type. And Heydon in *The Voyage to the Land of the Rosicrucians* (1660) and in *The Holy Guide* (1662) points out as clearly as possible the parallels between Bacon's *New Atlantis* and the *Fama Fraternitatis*, through which the wise men of Bacon's House of Salomon become the wise men 'of the Society of the Rosie Crucians'.

These parallels between Bacon's imagery in the *New Atlantis* and the fictions of the Rosicrucian *Fama* do undoubtedly exist, and we have pointed out the significance of this in an earlier chapter.[1] That Heydon should choose to take up these parallels and underline them just at this time is indeed curious, and I think that Heydon should be read in the context of the campaign against 'illuminati' and the discredited Dee.

What Heydon may in effect be saying to the Baconians may be: 'Your Francis Bacon was himself a Rosicrucian.'

The Restoration of Charles II in 1660 passed off with remarkable smoothness; the parliamentarian army quietly disbanded and men were eager to forget the past and to turn to peaceful pursuits. In this atmosphere of reconciliation, the Royal Society was founded, with Charles II as its patron. The Society included a number of men who had been on the parliamentarian side in previous years; science brought them together with the royalists in peaceful co-operation, but the situation was tricky. There were many subjects which had to be avoided: utopian schemes for reform belonged to the revolutionary past which it was now better to forget. The Society had many enemies in its earlier years; its religious position seemed unclear; witch-scares were not altogether a thing of the past.

The rule that religious matters were not to be discussed at the meetings, only scientific problems, must have seemed a wise precaution,

[1] See above, p. 128.

and, in the earlier years, the Baconian insistence on experiment, and on the collecting and testing of scientific data, guided the Society's efforts. A permanent Society for the advancement of natural science had arrived, a real and visible, not an imaginary and invisible, institution, but it was very restricted in its aims compared with earlier movements. It did not envisage the advancement of science within a reformed society, within a universal reformation of the whole world. The Fellows of the Royal Society were not concerned with healing the sick, and that gratis, nor with schemes for the reform of education. These men could have had no idea of what lay before the movement they were encouraging. To them its weakness would be more apparent than its strength, the dangers of extinction which still beset it. They had arrived; they had made an Invisible College visible and real, and in order to preserve its delicate existence great caution was required. It all seemed, and was, very sensible. And although Baconian experiment was not in itself the infallible high road to scientific advance, yet the Royal Society, so respectable, so well organized, was a statement clear to all that science had arrived. Nothing could stop it now.

Comenius's book, *The Way of Light*, which he had written in England in the time of hope and illumination, was published at Amsterdam in 1668, twenty-six years after he wrote it, and when the Royal Society had been in existence for eight years. He dedicated the book to the Royal Society in an enthusiastic preface. The aged Bohemian Brother made the strange mistake of addressing the Fellows as 'illuminati'.[1]

> To the Torch Bearers of this Enlightened Age, Members of the
> Royal Society of London now bringing real philosophy to a happy
> birth, greeting and good fortune.
> Illustrious Sirs,
> It is not unfitting that a book entitled *The Way of Light* should be
> sent to you, illustrious men whose labour in bringing the light of
> Natural Philosophy from the deeper wells of Truth is coming to be
> proclaimed and published throughout Europe. It is the more
> appropriate since the work was conceived in that country where the
> territory offered to us for the search for Light and Truth has passed
> into your keeping, according to that word of Christ (applicable in its
> proper sense to this occasion): Others have laboured and you have
> entered into their labours.

[1] *The Way of Light*, trans. Campagnac, p. 3.

Comenius is evidently under the impression that the Royal Society is the inheritor of the earlier labours of himself and his friends. He feels no envy at this but hears with joy the trumpets sounding once again.[1]

> Throughout the world the news will be trumpeted that you are engaged in labours the purpose of which is to secure that human knowledge and the empire of the human mind over matter shall not for ever continue to be a feeble and uncertain thing.

Comenius also utters words of warning. Foundations are being laid by these new investigations into nature, but is it being considered what is going to be built on these foundations? If ends beyond the cultivation of the natural sciences for themselves alone are not being envisaged, the work might turn out to be 'a Babylon turned upside down, building not towards heaven, but towards earth'.[2]

Comenius has been derided for not having understood how different the aims of the Royal Society were from the old pansophic ideals. But I think that he did understand that. And I also think that he was historically right in the connection which he saw between the Royal Society and the past efforts of himself and his generation.[3] And he may also have been right in his warning.

In 1667 the official account of the origins and growth of this great undertaking was published, Thomas Sprat's *History of the Royal Society*. The Society is said to have grown out of the meetings at Oxford of a group of persons interested in natural and experimental philosophy, the group which met at Wadham College from 1648 onwards and became the nucleus of the Royal Society. Nothing is said by Sprat about an earlier group in London, or of the hint that Theodore Haak of the Palatinate might have been the first to suggest such meetings. That earlier group would take one back too far towards the wild revolutionary ideas of the parliamentarian period, and Sprat wants to give the impression that the Society started with the sedate Oxford meetings.

Nevertheless, great is Truth, and it does in spite of all have a tendency to prevail. To end this chapter let us look at the familiar frontispiece

---

[1] *Ibid.*, p. 11.

[2] *Ibid.*, p. 51.

[3] Of course the Royal Society was also influenced by more recent academic movements, particularly in France (I have discussed the early seventeenth-century French academies in my *French Academies of the Sixteenth Century*, pp. 275 ff.), yet its organic connections with the kind of 'academy' adumbrated in the Rosicrucian manifestos are attested by what we now know of Bacon's allusions to these in *New Atlantis*, for Bacon's work was very influential on the early members of the Royal Society.

to Sprat's book (Pl. 30). In the centre is the bust of Charles II, the royal founder, with Francis Bacon on his left, and William Brouncker, the first president, on his right. In the background is a bookcase filled with books by members of the Society and an array of the instruments which they use in their scientific labours. This frontispiece was designed by John Evelyn and engraved by Wenceslas Hollar, a Bohemian artist who left Bohemia, presumably for religious reasons, in 1627 and was apprenticed at Frankfurt to Matthieu Merian.[1] This history makes one look with renewed interest at the engraving, where one now notices the prominent winged angel, blowing a blast on a trumpet, and crowning Charles II with a wreath of fame as the founder of this famous Society. Bacon is under the angel's wing. One cannot help noticing this now, and wondering whether it could be an allusion to 'under the shadow of Jehova's wings', and whether the trumpeting angel was meant to recall the *Fama*, and those hopes of long ago, so long deferred and now, at last, realized.

---

[1] See Hollar, Wenzel, in *Allgemeines Lexicon der Bildenden Künstler.*

CHAPTER XIV

ELIAS ASHMOLE AND THE DEE TRADITION:
Isaac Newton and Rosicrucian Alchemy

Whilst the early Royal Society appeared to be carefully excluding
dangerous topics, concentrating on safe Baconianism, avoiding all
mention of Rosicrucian manifestos (unless indirectly in a frontispiece),
and certainly avoiding all mention of John Dee, now made notorious
by Casaubon's publication, its membership included at least one
scholar in whom the Dee tradition was very much alive. For Elias
Ashmole, Dee was an immensely revered magus whose writings he
collected and whose alchemical and magical teachings he endeavoured
to put into practice. Ashmole's presence in the Royal Society as a
foundation member[1] is a significant indication that 'Rosicrucianism',
if this should be identified with influences from Dee, still found a
place within the Society, if only as a private interest of one of its
members.

Elias Ashmole (1617–92) was a staunch royalist who lived in retire-
ment during the civil wars and commonwealth pursuing his many
interests. Alchemist, astrologer, antiquary, assiduous collector of
records of the past, Ashmole's roots were in that Hermetic universe
governed by magical correspondencies whence the new science was
emerging. Yet he was not exactly out of date for his interest in alchemy reflects the very strong revival, or renaissance, of alchemy in the
seventeenth century, a movement which influenced many notable
figures. Paracelsist alchemy was a major influence on the new medicine;
Robert Boyle's chemistry was a child of the alchemical movement;
and there was an extraordinary background of alchemy even in the
mind of Isaac Newton.

The alchemical renaissance as a historical phenomenon has hardly

---

[1] Ashmole's name was mentioned at the first meeting of the Royal Society as one of
those suitable for membership; he was formally elected a Fellow in January 1661, thus
becoming one of the 114 foundation members; see C. H. Josten, *Elias Ashmole*, Oxford,
1966, I, p. 135.

yet received adequate historical treatment. Alchemy as the Hermetic art par excellence belongs to the Hermetic tradition, but revival of alchemy was not noticeably a part of the revival of the Hermetic tradition in the Italian Renaissance. With the advent of Paracelsus, a reformed, renaissance type of alchemy came into being, and to this tradition John Dee made his contribution. The triple strand of 'Magia, Cabala, and Alchymia' runs through the Rosicrucian manifestos, typifying their inclusion of alchemy with Hermetic-Cabalist tradition.

A notable missionary of the alchemical movement was Michael Maier, whose life work was the collection and publication of alchemical texts, and the propagation of his alchemical religious philosophy through his own publications. We have seen that Maier was most important in the movement around Frederick, Elector Palatine, and that alchemy was associated with the movement and with its appeal to Bohemia.[1] One wonders how far the alchemical movement in seventeenth-century England may have been stimulated by refugees, coming both from Germany and from Bohemia. We have seen that Daniel Stolcius, the Bohemian exile who solaced his sadness with Maier's emblems, came to England,[2] and there must have been others like him.

As the chief representative of the alchemical movement in seventeenth-century England, Elias Ashmole might form a point of departure for the exploration of these themes. Those vast manuscript collections, the Ashmole papers, are not only the work of an antiquarian, a man living in the past (though that side of Ashmole was very strong); they are also full of evidence of the contemporary, one might almost say the modern, alchemical movement in the England of his time.

Amongst those papers, the seeker after the Rosicrucian manifestos finds a curious phenomenon. For Elias Ashmole took the trouble to copy out in his own hand an English translation of the *Fama* and the *Confessio*, and to add to these copies an elaborate letter in Latin, also written in his own hand, addressed to the 'most illuminated Brothers of the Rose Cross', petitioning to be allowed to join their Fraternity.[3] The address is enthusiastic about the Fraternity, but vague, and consists largely of quotations from the *Fama* and the *Confessio*. The original of the English translation of the manifestos which Ashmole copied exists

---

[1] See above, pp. 81 ff.

[2] See above, pp. 88–9.

[3] Bodleian Library, Ashmole MSS., 1459; ff. 280–2 (Latin address headed 'Fratribus Rosae Crucis illuminatissimis'); ff. 284–31 (English translation of the *Fama* and the *Confessio*). See W. H. Black, *Catalogue of the Ashmolean Manuscripts*, 1845, no. 1459.

elsewhere in his papers,[1] written in an early seventeenth-century hand, certainly not later than the reign of Charles I. It is not the same as the English version published by Vaughan but a different version.

Ashmole's procedure would appear to have been to copy out in his own hand a manuscript of an English translation of the manifestos in his possession, and to preface this copy with an address to the R.C. Brothers by himself, expressing profound admiration for these illuminated men and asking to join their order. I do not believe that Ashmole was addressing any real contemporary group of 'Rosicrucians'. I think that the whole operation was in the nature of a pious exercise. Ashmole knew that it was correct for those who approved the aims expressed in the manifestos to address the R.C. Brothers. He identifies himself with the manifestos by writing a prayerful address to the imaginary Brothers. The writing out of the manifestos and of his prayer was in itself a prayer, probably an entirely private exercise.

This glimpse into Ashmole's inner life is a valuable introduction to the study of his well-known published volume, the *Theatrum Chemicum Britannicum* (1652).[2] This is a collection of alchemical writings which was very important in stimulating the contemporary alchemical movement in England. It is a collection of a similar type to the 'theatres' or collections of alchemical material which had been published in the early seventeenth-century German alchemical movement which derived partly (though certainly not entirely) from the impetus to alchemical studies given by Michael Maier as part of the 'Rosicrucian' movement (Pl. 26b). Ashmole's collection includes only English alchemists, but Maier had been particularly interested in English alchemy, and had published in a Latin translation Thomas Norton's *Ordinall of Alchemy*,[3] a poem in English by a famous medieval English alchemist, the original English version of which was published for the first time by Ashmole in his *Theatrum* of 1652.

Now it would have been clear to the attentive reader of Ashmole's *Theatrum* that this work was 'Rosicrucian' in sympathy, that it was in fact a kind of continuation of Michael Maier's revival of English alchemy in the German Rosicrucian movement. For in the opening

---

[1] Ashmole MSS., 1478, ff. 125–9. Black, *Catalogue*, notes that these translations of *Fama* and *Confessio* seem to have been transcribed by Ashmole into 1459.

[2] Elias Ashmole, *Theatrum Chemicum Britannicum*, London, 1652; reprinted in facsimile with introduction by Allen G. Debus, Johnson Reprint Corporation, New York and London, 1967.

[3] Maier's translation of Norton was published in his *Tripus aureus*, Frankfurt (Luca Jennis), 1618; see Read, *Prelude to Chemistry*, pp. 169 ff.

paragraph of the *Theatrum*, Ashmole quotes from the *Fama* and speaks of Maier's efforts to popularize English alchemy in Germany. Ashmole's words are as follows:[1]

> Our English Philosophers generally, (like Prophets) have received little honour . . . in their owne Countrey: nor have they done any mighty workes amongst us, except in covertly administering their Medicine to a few sick, and healing them . . . Thus did I.O. (one of the first foure Fellowes of the Fratres R.C.) in curing the young Earle of Norfolke of the Leprosie . . . But in parts abroad they have found more noble Reception, and the world greedy of obteyning their workes; nay, (rather than want the sight thereof) contented to view them through a Translation, though never so imperfect. Witnesse what Maierus . . . and many others have done; the first of which came out of Germanie, to live in England; purposely that he might so understand our English Tongue, as to translate Norton's Ordinall into Latin verse, which most judiciously and learnedly he did: Yet (to our shame be it spoken) his Entertainment was too coarse for so deserving a scholar.

The story about the legendary R.C. Brother who healed a young earl of leprosy in England comes out of the *Fama*,[2] and Ashmole immediately follows this with the account of Michael Maier's eagerness to spread knowledge of English alchemy abroad, how he came to England to learn English so that he could translate Norton, but his efforts were not well supported.

'To our shame be it spoken', Maier received but coarse treatment for his scholarly efforts. Reading between the lines of Ashmole's remarks in the light of what we now know about the Rosicrucian movement in Germany, the impression is gained that Ashmole knew of Maier's role as intermediary between England and Germany in fostering the alchemical movement as part of the building up of an Anglo-Palatinate-Bohemian alliance[3]—the movement which James I had not encouraged. Maier had indeed received very hard treatment as the result of his misplaced confidence in the English alliance; he had perished, we know not how, soon after the outbreak of the Thirty Years War. We are beginning to understand how Ashmole's *Theatrum Chemicum Britannicum* is yet another of those efforts to restore, or to continue, a movement

---

[1] Ashmole, *Theatrum*, Prolegomena, sigs A 2 *recto* and *verso*.
[2] See Appendix, below, p. 244.
[3] See above, pp. 81 ff.

which had been disastrously interrupted by the collapse of the cause of the King and Queen of Bohemia.

The *Theatrum Chemicum Britannicum* opens with Norton's *Ordinall* and contains many other writings by English alchemists, including one by George Ripley whose work had also been admired in the Maier circle.[1] And Ashmole continued his collection of English alchemical writers up to more modern times by including an alchemical poem said to be by Edward Kelley[2] and a few verses described as the 'Testament' of John Dee.[3]

In his commentary on the work attributed to Kelley, Ashmole tells the story of Dee,[4] dwelling on his proficiency in mathematical studies and the general brilliance of his scientific work, the prejudice against him and the attack on his library, his departure for the continent with Kelley and residence at Trebona in Bohemia where Kelley's supposed transmutations aroused great excitement, the quarrel with Kelley and Dee's return to England. Ashmole notes that Queen Elizabeth continued her favour towards him after his return, but he does not mention the renewed charges of conjuring against him after his return, nor how James I would have nothing to do with him. Brushing aside all rumours, Ashmole states firmly that Dee deserves 'the commendations of all Learned and Ingenious Schollers, and to be remembered for his remarkable abilities'. He particularly excelled in mathematical studies 'in all parts of which he was an absolute and perfect master'.[5]

The short poem called the 'Testament' of Dr Dee in the *Theatrum Chemicum Britannicum* is a description in veiled terms of the famous 'monas'.

Through his allusions to Dee and to Maier in the *Theatrum* Ashmole is, I believe, indicating the connection with Dee of the German Rosicrucian movement. And he was aware of the dangers which such a movement encountered:[6]

it is not less absurd, then strange, to see how some Men . . . wil
not forebeare to ranke True Magicians with Conjurors,
Necromancers, and Witches . . . who insolently intrude themselves

---

[1] Among the representatives of English alchemy in the collection edited by Maier under the title *Symbola Aurea Duodecim Nationum* (Frankfurt, Luca Jennis, 1617) are Roger Bacon, Ripley, Norton, and Edward Kelley; see Read, *Prelude*, p. 227.

[2] *Theatrum*, pp. 324 ff.

[3] *Ibid.*, p. 334.

[4] *Ibid.*, pp. 480–4.

[5] *Ibid.*, p. 480.

[6] *Ibid.*, p. 443.

into Magick, as if Swine should enter into a faire and delicate Garden, and (being in League with the Devill) make use of his assistance in their workes, to counterfeit and corrupt the admirall wisdome of the Magi betweene whom there is as large a difference as between Angels and Devils.

Ashmole is defending Dee as a good magus, and defending him with pretty full knowledge of his career.

Ashmole was not yet of course a member of the Royal Society which had not yet been formed when he published this book in 1652. But the book was well known and it did not prevent Ashmole from being invited to join the Royal Society in 1660 as one of the foundation members.

The kind of alchemy on which Ashmole was so intent may have been 'Rosicrucian' alchemy. By this I mean alchemy as revised and reformed by John Dee and of which his 'monas hieroglyphica' was the mysterious epitome. This alchemy included an intensive revival of the old alchemical tradition, but in some way added to the basic alchemical concepts notions and practices deriving from Cabala, the whole having also a mathematical formulation. The adept who had mastered these formulae could move up and down the ladder of creation, from terrestrial matter, through the heavens, to the angels and God. This most ancient conception was in some manner brought alive in a new way through integration with Cabalistic and mathematical procedures. But Ashmole did not have the brilliant mathematical equipment which, for a man of genius like Dee, made the 'monas' above all a statement of unity, a vision of the One God behind all creation.

Ashmole, the alchemist, was doubled by Ashmole, the antiquarian, the collector of historical documents and zealous preserver of the vestiges of the past. This double role had also been characteristic of his hero, John Dee, whose antiquarian studies,[1] particularly in British antiquities, had been almost as important to him as his scientific interests.

Ashmole's antiquarian enthusiasm was also directed towards British history, in the form of the history of the British chivalrous order, the Order of the Garter.[2] He began accumulating material for a book on this subject in 1655; it was eventually published in 1672 with a dedication to Charles II, and a copy of it was formally presented to the Royal Society by John Wilkins.[3] The book is a landmark in antiquarian

---

[1] See French, *John Dee*, pp. 188 ff.

[2] Elias Ashmole, *The Institution, Laws & Ceremonies of the most Noble Order of the Garter*, London, 1672.

[3] Josten, *Ashmole*, I, p. 182.

scholarship and still unsurpassed as the main authority on its subject. In the preface Ashmole tells of his distress at seeing the honour of the Garter trampled on in 'the late unhappy times' of the civil wars. His purpose was to restore the image of the Order as a step towards the Restoration. When his great book was published, copies were sent abroad, almost like embassies, to foreign potentates.

When recounting the 'Magnificence of the Embassies, sent with the Habit, to stranger Kings and Princes',[1] Ashmole quotes from Cellier's account of the embassy sent to confer the Garter on Frederick, Duke of Württemberg, in 1603, the occasion which may have had a great influence on the imagination of Johann Valentin Andreae and may have contributed towards the formation of the 'Christian Rosencreutz' legend and the birth of Andreae's *Chemical Wedding*.[2] The Order of the Garter and the fact that it had been conferred on the Elector Palatine had formed an important strand in the building up of the Frederickian movement, and the collapse of Frederick had involved the Garter in his disgrace.[3] It had represented the English alliance and had been covered with ignomony in the enemy satires on Frederick. It is thus possible that the restoration of the honour of the Garter was connected in Ashmole's mind with the restoration of the English alchemical tradition in his other book, the *Theatrum Chemicum Britannicum*.

Memories of the dire past must surely have been revived when the young Prince Charles, Elector Palatine and grandson of the unfortunate King and Queen of Bohemia, was presented to Ashmole 'and had much discourse with him about the Order of the Garter'.[4] This was in 1690. The young Elector had just succeeded his father (Charles Louis, Hartlib's patron) in the Palatinate and was travelling in England. Ashmole presented the young prince with a copy of his book, and the Prince presented Ashmole with his father's Garter medal, a gold medal showing Charles Louis wearing the collar and George of the Order. At Heidelberg, after the Elector's return, Ashmole's book was handed round at the court and the company discoursed for several hours on the 'curiosities' it contained.[5]

---

[1] Ashmole, *Garter*, pp. 411–16.
[2] See above, pp. 31–3, 66.
[3] See above, p. 23.
[4] Josten, *Ashmole*, I, pp. 237–8.
[5] *Ibid.*, pp. 238, 240–1. One 'curiosity' in the book which they might have noted at Heidelberg is the illustration showing a medal issued 'in the year when Frederick, Prince Palatine of the Rhyne, was crowned King of Bohemia' (*Garter*, p. 207). It shows on one side the Garter, and on the other, the Lions of the Palatinate and of Bohemia.

Thus Ashmole, both as alchemist and antiquarian, may be looking back to the movement that failed and seeking to restore its memory in the present. And both as alchemist and in his concern for British antiquities, Ashmole was following in the Dee tradition.

The Royal Society soon left 'Baconian experiment' far behind, and the second generation of Fellows was dominated by the tremendous figure of Isaac Newton, one of the greatest of mathematical geniuses. As is well known, Newton, in addition to his stupendous published discoveries, had other interests concerning which he was rather secretive in his lifetime but evidence about which exists in the large mass of his unpublished papers. One of these unpublicized interests was alchemy, and curiosity has been growing of late years about this side of Newton. Can it be true that this great hero of rational science was secretly an alchemist? Or was his interest in alchemy merely a fad, or something which would admit of some other interpretation?

What I have to say on this subject is put forward with extreme modesty. I have not examined Newton's unpublished papers, yet merely by putting this problem into the context of the series of historical inventigations with which this book has been concerned, it is possible that a historical angle for the approach to Newton's alchemy might be suggested.

Newton certainly knew the Rosicrucian manifestos. He possessed a copy of *The Fame and Confession of the Fraternity R.C.*, the English translation of the manifestos published by Thomas Vaughan in 1652. The copy of this book in Yale University Library contains a manuscript note by Newton, with his signature.[1] Newton in this note quotes from the *Fama* the description of the finding of the body of Christian Rosencreutz, and he has looked up two of Michael Maier's works for more information, the books of the 'Laws of the R.C. Fraternity', that is the *Themis aurea*, where Maier gives such laws, based on what is said in the *Fama*, and the *Symbola aureae mensae duodecim*, where Maier has other references to the manifestos and the date at which they were published. Newton ends his historical note, based on study of both the manifestos and Maier, with the remark, 'This was the history of that imposture.' This, however, need not necessarily imply contempt; it could merely mean that Newton knew that the Rosencreutz story was a myth, a *ludibrium*.

---

[1] For the full text of Newton's note in his copy of the *Fame and Confession*, see Ian Macphail, *Alchemy and the Occult, Catalogue of Books from the Collection of Paul and Mary Mellon given to Yale University Library*, Yale, 1968, II, 102.

25a Grotto at Heidelberg Castle: Fountain with Coral. From
Salomon de Caus, *Les raisons des forces mouvantes*

25b Fishing for Coral (the Philosopher's Stone). From *Atlanta
fugiens*

26a   The Marriage of the Alchemical King and Queen

26b   The Alchemists (Thomas Norton, Abbot Cremer, Basil
Valentine) Both from Daniel Stolcius, *Viridarium Chymicum;* reprinted
from Michael Maier, *Tripus Aureus*

27a   Vision of a Triumphant Lion

27b   Vision of a Lion with Angels and Roses. From Christopher
Kotter, *Revelationes . . . ab anno 1616 ad annum 1624*, in *Lux in tenebris*

28 Frederick V, King of Bohemia, by Gerard Honthorst

In his book on Newton, Frank E. Manuel has a chapter on Newton and alchemy, based on study of the Newton manuscripts.[1] From this it appears that Newton made many copies from alchemical works, even copying out obscure alchemical poems. Prominent among the printed alchemical collections which he used was Ashmole's *Theatrum Chemicum Britannicum* which he 'combed over and over again'.[2] In the process of this careful combing of the volume, Newton would have observed that Ashmole begins the book with quotation from the *Fama*, that he speaks of Michael Maier's work in collecting English alchemical authors, and how 'to our shame' he was but ill rewarded. He would have realized that Ashmole's collection really represents the English alchemists whom Maier admired, including the notable Dee and Kelley. In Ashmole's commentary on Kelley's work he would have read the whole story of John Dee, and of how he should be respected for his brilliant mathematical and scientific work. And in the 'Testament' of Dee in the book, he could ponder over a brief rendering in verse of the nysteries of the 'monas'.

In Michael Maier, Newton seems to have been particularly interested, copying out extracts from his works,[3] and even sometimes describing in his own words Maier's alchemical emblems, such as 'Two women cloathed riding on two lyons: each with a heart in her hand . . .'[4] Newton had entered that world of the Maier alchemical revival, had studied the alchemical sources which it brought together, and had pored over the strange expression of its outlook in the alchemical emblems.

We have seen that there is pretty certainly an influence of Dee on Maier's emblems,[5] and the Dee influence was present in Maier's whole effort of alchemical revival, and particularly of the revival of English alchemy. The historical approach thus suggests that it might be of use to approach Newton's alchemy along the lines of the German Rosicrucian movement and the influences on it of the Dee, or 'Rosicrucian', type of alchemy.

As a deeply religious man, like Dee, Newton was profoundly pre-occupied by the search for One, for the One God, and for the divine Unity revealed in nature. Newton's marvellous physical and

---

[1] Frank E. Manuel, *A Portrait of Isaac Newton*, Cambridge, Mass., 1968, pp. 160–90.

[2] Manuel, *Newton*, p. 163.

[3] He made excerpts from the *Symbola Aureae Mensae Duodecim* (Manuel, *Newton*). This was one of the works by Maier which he consulted for evidence about the Rosicrucian manifestos (see n. 25, above).

[4] Manuel, *Newton*, p. 171.

[5] See above, p. 83.

mathematical explorations of nature had not entirely satisfied him. Perhaps he entertained, or half-entertained, a hope that the 'Rosicrucian' alchemical way through nature might lead him even higher.

At any rate, it can be said that the alchemical revival which affected Newton owed much to Ashmole's *Theatrum Chemicum Britannicum*, and that was inspired by John Dee and the Maier alchemical movement. It would thus not be historically fantastic to entertain as a hypothesis basis for future study, the possibility that a 'Rosicrucian' element, in some revised or changed form no doubt, might enter into Newton's interest in alchemy.

As a footnote to this chapter, mention may be made of the collection of 'Rosicrucian' texts preserved among the Harley manuscripts in the British Museum. Though of infinitely less importance than the great personages whom we have been discussing, the man who wrote out these Harleian manuscripts resembles them in that he was copying documents belonging to the German Rosicrucian movement.

The Harley codices 6485 and 6486 are both written in the same hand and probably at the same time: one is dated 1714. Since a 'Dr Rudd' is rather frequently mentioned in these manuscripts, the scribe may be connected in some way with the Thomas Rudd who published an edition of Dee's mathematical preface to Euclid in 1651.[1] The scribe is certainly an ardent admirer of Dee.

The first item in Harley 6485 is a treatise entitled 'The Rosicrucian Secrets' which used to be attributed to Dee on the strength of this manuscript. As a matter of fact, the scribe does not actually say that Dee is the author of this work; what he says is that he is copying it from 'sheets' which he believes were written by Dee.[2] From internal evidence it is clear that 'The Rosicrucian Secrets' is not by Dee. The same codex also contains two other items, 'also said to be copied from 'sheets of Dr Dee'. One is called 'Of the Laws and Mysteries of the Rosicrucians'. Most of this is copied from the English translation of Michael Maier's *Themis aurea*, published in 1656 with a dedication to Ashmole.[3]

---

[1] Euclid, *Elements of Geometry*, ed. Thomas Rudd includes a reprint of Dee's Preface; see French, *John Dee*, pp. 174, 217.

[2] The codex contains three items: (1) 'The Rosicrucian Secrets', a Paracelsist alchemical treatise which uses Lullist-type diagrams. (2) *Clavis Chymicus*, a glossary of alchemical vocabulary, particularly Paracelsist vocabulary. (3) 'The Laws and Mysteries of the Rosicrucians', based on the English translation of Michael Maier's *Themis aurea*. All these items are said to be copied from 'sheets of Dr. Dee'. None of them are by Dee.

[3] *Themis Aurea, The Laws of the Fraternity of the Rosie Crosse, Written in Latin by Count Michael Maierus*, London, 1656. The dedication to Ashmole is signed N.L., T.S., H.S.

The compiler of the Harley codex belongs to the alchemical tradition in which assignment of authorship and of sources was always extremely lax and it was customary to attribute to a well-known name works certainly not written by the possessor of that name (for example, the vast alchemical literature which goes under the name of Raymond Lully was written after the death of the real Ramon Lull). What is interesting here, and what makes it worth our while to pause over Harley 6485, is the evidence which it gives that in an alchemical tradition still surviving in the early eighteenth century the literature of the German Rosicrucian movement is fathered on Dee. If you want to meditate on the rules of the Rosicrucian Order as given in the *Fama* and as expanded in Maier's *Themis aurea* you copy these from supposed 'sheets of Dr Dee', though you are really copying from a translation of Maier's book. In its obscure way, the Harley collection confirms the fact that the influence of Dee lay behind the German Rosicrucian movement.

Harley 6485 is immediately followed by Harley 6486 which consists of a work of which the (abbreviated) title is 'The Famous Nuptials of the Thrice Great Hermes ... Composed by C.R. a German of the Order of the Rosie Cross ... and from the Latin manuscript now faithfully translated into English by Peter Smart, 1714'. On the following page is the further statement: 'In the margin are brief notes by the late Dr Rudd.'

This manuscript is an almost word for word copy of Ezechiel Foxcroft's English translation of Andreae's *Chemical Wedding*, published in 1690.[1] 'Peter Smart' would thus appear to be lying in stating that this is an original translation by himself; so far as I know, there was no 'Latin original' of the work which was only published in German; moreover the marginal notes in the manuscript are also all copied from Foxcroft's translation, and so cannot have been by 'the late Dr Rudd'.

However, 'Peter Smart' may perhaps be partially exonerated on the grounds that his was an alchemical-tradition type of evasiveness and

[1] *The Hermetick Romance: or the Chymical Wedding, Written in high Dutch by Christian Rosencreutz*, translated by E. Foxcroft, late Fellow of King's College in Cambridge, London, 1690. Foxcroft's translation is reprinted in A. E. Waite, *Real History of the Rosicrucians*, pp. 65 ff.; and in *A Christian Rosencreutz Anthology*, ed. Paul M. Allen, New York, 1968, pp. 67 ff. See above, p. 60 n.

Ezechiel Foxcroft is often mentioned in the letters of Henry More to Lady Conway; see Marjorie Nicolson, *Conway Letters*, London, 1930, index. More introduced him to Francis Mercurius Van Helmont 'they both haveing a genius to Chymistry' (*Conway Letters*, p. 323).

confusion, which should not be judged from the strictly veracious standpoint. For the most noticeable thing in Harley 6486 is the large drawing of Dee's 'monas hieroglyphica', copied from Foxcroft's translation (where it is actually more like the 'monas' than the version of it shown in the German text). Though not actually stated to be copied 'from the sheets of Dr Dee', it is clear that the important thing about the *Chemical Wedding* for the compiler of the Harley codices is that he believes it to be infused with the influence of Dee.

Thus the compiler of the Harley codices is looking at 'Rosicrucianism' from an angle which can be recognized as similar to that of Ashmole, seeing German Rosicrucianism as fundamentally the result of Dee influences. Though the scholarly Ashmole would not have confused sources and authorship in the more primitively alchemical manner of the Harley codices, yet Ashmole, too, saw Rosicrucian manifestos, Maier and his alchemical school, and Dee in a historical sequence. And he probably recognized the history behind that sequence, the 'Rosicrucian' movement in its relation to Frederick, Elector Palatine and those dreams of universal reformation through the union with Bohemia which came to naught, and involved the Order of the Garter in Frederick's downfall.

This chapter is somewhat in the nature of a fragmentary hypothesis rather than the full working out of a theme. The hypothesis is that, behind the great exoteric movement typified by Newton's achievements in the fields of mathematics and physics, there was also an esoteric movement, connected with the exoteric movement through the importance which it attached to number, but developing this through another approach to nature, the approach through alchemy. Newton's great work would typify the exoteric approach, whilst Ashmole would have been keeping alive the alchemical approach. And both were members of the Royal Society.

The two approaches could have met through 'Rosicrucian' alchemy, that is through the Dee alchemical tradition as developed in the German Rosicrucian school. That Newton found bridges between all his studies through such an outlook is a possibility. The more recent Newton scholarship has emphasized the Renaissance type of thinking at the back of Newton's scientific efforts, his belief in the traditions of ancient wisdom concealed in myth, and his confidence that he had himself discovered the true philosophy behind mythology. In their article on 'Newton and the Pipes of Pan', J. E. McGuire and P. M. Rattansi have shown that Newton believed that he had found his system of the universe shadowed forth in Apollo's lyre, with its seven strings.[1] Such musical and cosmic analogies underlie Dee's 'monas' and the emblems of Maier, which combine musical with alchemical modes of expression. 'Rosicrucian' alchemy, musical, mathematical, alchemical, and deeply religious—with a Hebraic and Cabalistic type of piety—is presented visually in that engraving in Khunrath's *Amphitheatrum* of the devout alchemist in profound prayer to Jehova (Pl. 12), his other ways of reaching God through nature being typified in the musical instruments, the architectural mathematics, and the alchemical furnace. With some modifications due to period differences, this engraving might express the inner life, the intense aspiration towards search for God along different avenues, of Isaac Newton.

The function of this chapter, and indeed of the whole of this book, is merely to put together the *historical* pieces through which such thoughts could have moved along historical paths. I believe that such thoughts were behind the German Rosicrucian movement, inspired by Dee, and that they were kept alive in England by those who deplored the failure to support Frederick of the Palatinate. Newton's historical attitudes, his intense preoccupation with apocalyptic prophecy, would have made him intensely aware of the apocalyptic interpretations of the near extinction of Protestantism in Europe brought about by the collapse of Frederick. The approach to Newton through Rosicrucian alchemy might help, not only to unify his physical and alchemical studies, but also to integrate with these the Hebraic piety behind his historical studies.

---

[1] J. E. McGuire and P. M. Rattansi, 'Newton and the Pipes of Pan', *Notes and Records of the Royal Society*, 21 (1966), pp. 108–41. The authors of this article draw attention to Newton's interest in the work of Maier. 'Michael Maier, whose works were deeply studied by Newton, had undertaken a survey of the entire Greek mythology to demonstrate that they represented alchemical secrets. Newton's interpretation of the "harmony of the spheres" is analogous, in that it sees it as a symbolical representation of "physical" secrets' (p. 136).

CHAPTER XV

ROSICRUCIANISM AND FREEMASONRY

The main reason why serious historical studies of the Rosicrucian manifestos and their influence have hitherto been on the whole lacking is no doubt because the whole subject has been bedevilled by enthusiasts for secret societies. There is a vast literature on Rosicrucianism which assumes the existence of a secret society, founded by Christian Rosencreutz, and having a continuous existence up to modern times. In the vague and inaccurate world of so-called 'occultist' writing this assumption has produced a kind of literature which deservedly sinks below the notice of the serious historian. And when, as is often the case, the misty discussion of 'Rosicrucians' and their history becomes involved with the masonic myths, the enquirer feels that he is sinking helplessly into a bottomless bog.

Nevertheless, these questions must be faced by anyone who undertakes an enquiry into Rosicrucianism, and though this book has hitherto concentrated on historical elucidation of the background of the Rosicrucian manifestos, and on tracing their influence—avoiding the secret society question—the time has come when something must be attempted on this aspect of the subject. Though no very certain results may be arrived at, we shall at least be peering through these mists from the vantage ground of a clearer knowledge of the historical situation in which the Rosicrucian movement arose.

The Rosicrucians, do they exist? Are you one? No. Have you ever seen one? No. How often have we heard this debate, with its negative result, as we have made our way through the Rosicrucian literature. The debate still continues. One historian of Freemasonry has divided Rosicrucian theorists into three classes; those who believe that the story of Christian Rosencreutz and the manner of founding the R.C. Fraternity as recounted in the *Fama* is true in fact; those who regard both the society and its founder as purely mythical; those who, without accepting the historical truth of the story of Rosencreutz, believe in the existence of 'the Rosicrucians' as a secret society.[1] No serious person can now believe in the literal truth of the Rosencreutz story, and the view that a real secret society of Rosicrucians existed and was, as it were, veiled in the myth was questioned by Paul Arnold in his book published in 1955.[2]

My researches into the question have not been exhaustive. I have not examined every scrap of the printed literature of the Rosicrucian furore nor have I made a search for evidence possibly hidden in manuscript documents or archives. I can only say that, so far as my own researches have gone, I have found no evidence of a real secret society calling itself 'Rosicrucian', and really in existence as an organized group at the time the manifestos were published and during the time of the furore. There is immense evidence of a passionate search for Rosicrucians but no evidence that they were ever found. Moreover, the Rosicrucian manifestos were highly publicized statements, thrown provocatively out into the world. Since the prime aim of a secret society must ever be to keep itself secret, it would seem an odd thing for a real Rosicrucian secret society to do, to publicize itself so dramatically. The manifestos would appear to be proclamations of enlightenment in the form of an utopist myth about a world in which enlightened beings, almost assimilated to spirits, go about doing good, shedding healing influences, disseminating knowledge in the natural sciences and the arts, and bringing mankind back to its Paradisal state before the Fall. It was thus merely a popular misunderstanding to have assumed that there was a real secret society behind these documents, and the framers of them would seem to have been embarrassed by this misunderstanding. Johann Valentin Andreae made painful efforts to make clear that Christian Rosencreutz and his Fraternity were a fiction.[3]

Yet, we have seen, something real did emerge out of the proclamations of the manifestos. The R.C. Brothers were a fiction but they suggested a reality, the Christian Unions, groups of people who tried to form themselves into societies.[4]

The right way of looking at the question may thus be, to give up the hunt for 'real' Rosicrucians and to ask, instead, whether the Rosicrucian movement *suggested* the formation of secret societies. We have seen that there is the idea of a society for the advancement of learning, such as

[1] A. E. Waite, *The Real History of the Rosicrucians*, London, 1887, pp. 217–18.

[2] Paul Arnold, *Histoire des Rose-Croix*, Paris, 1955. Peuckert, *Die Rosenkreutzer*, is inconclusive on the subject.

[3] See above, pp. 141 ff.

[4] See above, pp. 151 ff.

afterwards materialized in the Royal Society, in the recommendations of the author of the *Fama* that learned men ought to communicate their discoveries to one another and meet in collaboration. Is there also in the manifestos the idea of, or the blueprint for, an international secret society which had, and has, a real existence, namely Freemasonry?

Historical research on the problem of Rosicrucianism and Freemasonry began in Germany in the eighteenth century, and the main results of German research, particularly as expounded in a work by J. G. Buhle published in 1804, were set out in English in an essay by Thomas De Quincey, published in 1824.[1] Though separated from the past by the abyss of the Thirty Years War, which destroyed so much evidence, the German researchers of the time of Buhle were yet nearer to that past than we are, and it is worth while to look at their theories, as transmitted by De Quincey, as representing an early attempt to solve the problem. The argument of Buhle's book is thus resumed by De Quincey.[2]

> To a hoax played off by a young man of extraordinary talents in the beginning of the seventeenth century, but for a more elevated purpose than most hoaxes involve, the reader will find that the whole mysteries of Free-Masonry, as now existing all over the civilised world after a lapse of more than two centuries, are here [i.e. in Buhle's book] distinctly traced: such is the power of a grand and capacious aspiration of philosophic benevolence to embalm even the idlest levities, as amber enshrines straws and insects.

The young man of extraordinary talents is Andreae, assumed by Buhle to be the author of all the Rosicrucian manifestos; the 'hoax' is his account of the R.C. Fraternity, assumed by Buhle to be the origin of Freemasonry. In the last phrase, De Quincey is parodying Buhle's style.

De Quincey, who embellishes and adds to the arguments learned from his German sources, maintains that 'no college or lodge of Rosicrucian brethren . . . can be shown from historical records to have ever been established in Germany.' But he is convinced that when Rosicrucianism was transplanted to England, it became Freemasonry. He solemnly affirms his belief that 'Freemasonry is neither more nor

---

[1] Thomas De Quincey, 'Historico-Critical Inquiry into the Origins of the Rosicrucians and the Freemasons', originally published in *London Magazine*, 1824; reprinted in *Collected Writings*, ed. David Masson, Edinburgh, 1890, XIII, pp. 384–448.

[2] *Ibid.*, p. 386.

29   Elizabeth, Queen of Bohemia, by Gerard Honthorst

30   The Fame of the Royal Society. From Thomas Sprat's *History of the Royal Society*

less than Rosicrucianism as modified by those who transplanted it to England' whence it was re-exported to the other countries of Europe. The person chiefly responsible for transplanting Rosicrucianism to England and giving it a new name was, so states De Quincey, Robert Fludd. The masonic beliefs and practices concerned with mystical interpretation of the building of the Temple at Jerusalem can, thinks De Quincey, already be perceived in the Rosicrucian writings, but when Rosicrucianism was transplanted to England these were attached by Freemasonry to the traditions of the guilds of masons. He therefore concludes with the utmost confidence that:[1]

> The original Free-Masons were a society that arose out of the Rosicrucian mania, certainly within the thirteen years from 1633 to 1646, and probably between 1633 and 1640.

This theory cannot be entirely right, but the way in which it assumes movement or contact between England and Germany through which something was transplanted from the one country to the other, is interesting in view of what we now know about the currents of thought which moved from England to Germany, and vice versa, in the early seventeenth century.

The origin of Freemasonry is one of the most debated, and debatable, subjects in the whole realm of historical enquiry.[2] One has to distinguish between the legendary history of Freemasonry and the problem of when it actually began as an organized institution. According to masonic legend, Freemasonry is as old as architecture itself, going back to Solomon's building of the Temple, and to the guilds of medieval masons who built the cathedrals. At some point, operative masonry, or the actual craft of building, turned into speculative masonry, or the moral and mystical interpretation of building, into a secret society with esoteric rites and teaching. When this actually happened, when the masonic structure and organization came into existence, is not certainly known.

Among the very few early known facts is the date at which Elias Ashmole was admitted to a masonic lodge. Ashmole records in his

---

[1] *Ibid.*, p. 426.

[2] The older literature on history of Freemasonry mingles myth and fact in inextricable confusion. For a more modern and critical approach to the subject, see Douglas Knoop and G. P. Jones, *The Growth of Freemasonry*, Manchester University Press, 1947. The influence of Renaissance Hermetic tradition on masonic mythology is indicated in my *Giordano Bruno and the Hermetic Tradition*, pp. 274, 414-16, 423; in *The Art of Memory*, pp. 303-5, I suggested Renaissance occult forms of the art of memory as a possible influence.

diary that he was admitted to a masonic lodge at Warrington in Lancashire on 16 October 1646.[1] The lodge was already in existence; it was not founded by Ashmole. He gives the names of some other persons who were admitted to it at the same time, one of them being his cousin, Henry Manwaring, who was a Roundhead. Evidently, since Ashmole was a Royalist, members of opposite parties in the civil wars could join in Freemasonry.

Ashmole's note of masonic initiation is said to be 'the earliest known record of speculative masonry in an English lodge'.[2] It is important that this early masonic record comes in connection with the man whose knowledge of Rosicrucianism was discussed in the last chapter, where we saw that Ashmole copied out in his own hand the Rosicrucian manifestos adding to them a formal letter in his own hand admiring their aims and asking to be allowed to join them.[3] This seemed to be a formal exercise, imitating the Rosicrucian tradition in regard to the manifestos, but having no reference to any actually existing group calling themselves Rosicrucians. One now asks oneself the question whether the fact that Ashmole was a Freemason had any bearing on his Rosicrucian exercise. Could it be one possible answer to the problem that quotation and approval of the Rosicrucian manifestos might mean, not that one was a Rosicrucian (if these did not exist) but that one did have some other kind of secret affiliation?

Though Ashmole's masonic initiation in October 1646 is usually taken to be the earliest on record, there is, in fact, a well authenticated earlier one. This is the record of the admission into the mason's lodge of Edinburgh of Robert Moray, on 20 May 1641.[4] Moray did more than, probably, any other individual to foster the foundation of the Royal Society and to persuade Charles II to establish it by his patronage. He was deeply interested in alchemy and chemistry. Thus the two persons of whom we have the earliest certain evidence of membership of masonic lodges were both foundation members of the Royal Society —Moray and Ashmole.

The masonic organization was thus clearly in existence at least twenty years before the foundation of the Royal Society (in 1660). Earlier than this, factual documentation is hard to come by.

There is a hinting reference as early as 1638 to a connection in the

---

[1] Josten, *Ashmole*, I, pp. 33–5.
[2] *Ibid.*, p. 34.
[3] See above, p. 195.
[4] See D. C. Martin, 'Sir Robert Moray', in *The Royal Society*, ed. H. Hartley, p. 246.

public mind between the idea of Rosicrucianism and the idea of Freemasonry. The earliest known reference to the 'Mason Word' occurs in a poem published at Edinburgh in 1638. The poem is a metrical account of Perth and neighbourhood and the reference is as follows:[1]

> For what we do presage is not in grosse,
> For we be brethren of the Rosie Crosse:
> We have the *Mason word* and second sight,
> Things for to come we can foretell aright ...

Perhaps the 'brethren of the Rosie Crosse' are here in the nature of fairies, beings who convey the gift of second sight, but that this possibly purely poetic or literary reference to the Rosy Cross Brothers should occur in the first printed mention of the masonic 'word' is interesting.

The first printed reference to 'Accepted Masons' is found in a masonic pamphlet of 1676, as follows:[2]

> To give notice, that the Modern Green-ribbon'd Caball, together with the Ancient Brotherhood of the Rosy Cross; the Hermetick Adepti and the company of Accepted Masons intend all to dine together on the 31 of November next ...

A comic menu is then described and those who think of going are advised to wear spectacles, 'For otherwise 'tis thought the said Societies will (as hitherto) make their Appearance Invisible.' This is interesting for its suggestion of a whole group of esoteric societies—two of them Freemasons and Rosicrucians—evidently different in membership but having sufficient in common to make it natural for them to dine together. The old joke about 'invisibility' links this reference to the old Rosicrucian tradition.

Later again, in fact as late as 1750, the following statement was made in a letter: 'English Freemasons have copied some ceremonies from Rosicrucians and say they are derived from them and are the same with them.'[3] We are now so late that we have almost reached the middle of the eighteenth century, at about which time, apparently in France, a new 'grade', or set of rituals, was initiated within

[1] Knoop, Jones and Hamer, *Early Masonic Pamphlets*, Manchester, 1945, p. 30.
[2] *Ibid.*, p. 31.
[3] *Ibid.*, p. 235.

Freemasonry. This was called the Rose Cross grade;[1] its mystique was apparently definitely Christian (going further in a Christian direction than the Deist mystique of other grades) and may have been influenced by mysticism of chivalry. This would seem like an acceptance, within masonic tradition itself—though very late—of the idea of a connection between Rosicrucianism and masonry.

These late indications and traditions, interesting though they are, cannot be relied upon for light on our period, the period in the early seventeenth century when the Rosicrucian idea was publicized through the manifestos. What we are asking is still the old question. Were there at that time any Rosicrucians, any real secret organization?

The question has perhaps changed a little since we first replied to it in the negative earlier in this chapter. It might now be expanded as: if there were no Rosicrucians was there perhaps in the background something like an early masonic, or pre-masonic, movement?

The legendary history of masonry, of the actual art of building, is recounted in certain medieval poems (of about 1400) which are valued in Freemasonry as documents belonging to the old operative masonry, the masonry of the craft or the guild, whence speculative masonry—or Freemasonry—claims to derive. In these 'Manuscript Constitutions of Masonry',[2] as these writings are called, masonry, or building, or architecture is identified with geometry. One account maintains that geometry was discovered before the Flood; another states that Abraham taught the Egyptians geometry. In yet another version of the invention of geometry drawn from a classical source (Diodorus Siculus), geometry is said to have been invented by the Egyptians in order to cope with the inundations of the Nile. The invention is attributed to Thoth-Hermes, otherwise Hermes Trismegistus, who is identified with Euclid. Thus the origins of geometry, or masonry, and therefore of Freemasonry, recede into a most distant Hebraic or Egyptian past, and are surrounded by mystiques which clearly relate to the Renaissance conception of 'ancient wisdom', of the *prisci theologi*,[3] or pristine theologians, whence all true wisdom is derived. In the masonic

---

[1] R. F. Gould, *History of Freemasonry*, London, 1886, V, pp. 159–61; revised R. Poole, London, 1951, III, pp. 267–77.

[2] The most important of these 'MS Constitutions of Masonry', or 'Old Charges' are those contained in the *Regius* and *Cooke* manuscripts, both of about 1400; the following quotations from them are taken from Knoop and Jones, *Genesis of Freemasonry*, pp. 62–86.

[3] D. P. Walker, 'The *Prisca Theologia* in France', *Journal of the Warburg and Courtauld Institutes*, XVII (1954), pp. 204–59; D. P. Walker, *The Ancient Theology*, London, 1972; Yates, *Giordano Bruno and the Hermetic Tradition*, pp. 14, 17–18 and *passim*.

mythology, the true ancient wisdom was enshrined in the geometry of the Temple, built by Solomon with the aid of Hiram, King of Tyre. The architect of the Temple was believed to be a certain Hiram Abif (not the same person as Hiram, the king) whose martyrdom forms the theme of symbolic enactment in masonic ritual.

The official source for masonic mythology and mystical history would seem to be the *Constitutions of Freemasons* published by James Anderson in 1725, and which, so I understand, is still treated as an authoritative document for masonic history by Freemasons themselves. It contains a statement to be read at the admission of a new Brother which opens as follows:[1]

> Adam, our first parent, created after the Image of God, the great Architect of the Universe, must have had the Liberal Sciences, particularly Geometry, written on his Heart; for ever since the Fall, we find the Principles of it in the Heart of his Offspring . . .

The history of geometry is then traced throughout Biblical history, culminating in the building of the Temple by Solomon.

As in most histories of Freemasonry, the *Constitutions*, after the account of building, builders, and buildings in the Bible, goes on to give a history of non-Biblical architecture. First, 'the royal art of architecture' spread from the Hebrews to the Greeks. Then Rome learned the art, and became the centre of learning and imperial power, having its zenith under Augustus Caesar 'in whose reign was born God's Messiah, the great Architect of the Church'. Augustus encouraged 'the great VITRUVIUS, the Father of all true Architects to this day'.[2] Augustus was Grand Master of the masonic lodge at Rome and the founder of the Augustan style.

The story then runs rapidly through the loss of 'Roman masonry' in the barbarian invasions, and the rise of the Gothic style, and mentions that, in 'ignorant times', geometry might be 'condemn'd for conjuration'.[3]

Coming to modern, or more recent, times, the account states[4] that Queen Elizabeth was not favourable to architecture but that King James revived the English lodges and recovered the Roman architecture from Gothic ignorance. In Italy brilliant architects had been reviving

[1] James Anderson, *The Constitutions of Freemasons*, 1723; reproduced in facsimile with introduction by L. Vibert, London, 1923, p.1.
[2] *Ibid.*, pp. 24–5.
[3] *Ibid.*, p. 36.
[4] *Ibid.*, pp. 38 ff.

the classical style, which was above all restored by the great Palladio, who is rivalled in England 'by our great Master-Mason Inigo Jones'.[1] Charles I also patronized 'Mr Jones' who is presented as undoubtedly a Freemason, as was also Charles II. Sir Christopher Wren, architect of St Paul's, is mentioned with approbation.

This history does not make clear the point about which definite information is so much needed. When did modern Freemasonry begin, as an organized secret society? Most books on Freemasonry confuse architecture in the Bible, legendary stories, the history of architecture in general, and the history of Freemasonry, after the manner of James Anderson in the *Constitutions* of 1725. But it seems probable—and this point is usually made by masonic historians—that the 'speculative' kind of masonry, and its gradual disassociation from 'operative' masonry, began with the interest in the revived Vitruvius and the revived classical architecture. Though Anderson is not definite about this, it would seem that Inigo Jones is very important in his history, perhaps suggesting that it was in association with the introduction and spread of the 'Augustan style' by Inigo Jones that Freemasonry as an institution, distinct from masonic legend, began in England.

One notices a curious gap in masonic history. Why is it that no mention is made of John Dee, the famous Hermetic philosopher, author of a famous preface to an English translation of Euclid in which he praised 'the great VITRUVIUS'[2] and urged the revival of Euclid, architecture, and all mathematical arts? The English Euclid, with Dee's preface to it, was published in 1570—surely a most memorable monument to the sacred art of geometry, and heralding the revival of classical architecture in England long before Inigo Jones. It is difficult to believe that the Freemasons did not know Dee's preface to the Euclid, with its many quotations from Vitruvius. And indeed it seems pretty clear that James Anderson did know of it, for at more than one point he seems to be almost quoting from it. Compare, for example, Anderson's words on the reign of Augustus as the time when 'God's Messiah, the great Architect of the Church' was born, with Dee's words on Augustus 'in whose daies our Heauenly Archemaster was borne'.[3] Dee, one feels, must have been deliberately left out of official

---

[1] *Ibid.*, p. 39.
[2] The passages on Vitruvius in Dee's preface to the Euclid are quoted in my *Theatre of the World*, pp. 190-7.
[3] Quoted *ibid.*, p. 192.

masonic history.[1] What can have been the reason for this omission? Perhaps the same reason as the one which so often caused his name to be avoided, his reputation for 'conjuring', and Meric Casaubon's damning publication. Though, ironically enough, Dee himself in the Preface deplores the accusation of conjuring brought against him by the ignorant, just as Anderson in the *Constitutions* mentions that, 'in ignorant times', geometry might be 'condemn'd for conjuration'.

There is thus a problem here. How does this problem connect with our problem about Rosicrucianism and Freemasonry?

I have no very clear answer to give to these questions. As I said at the beginning of this chapter, this book is not primarily orientated towards the secret society problem. All that I can do is to try to suggest how the *historical* movements described in this book may present new historical paths along which future investigators might move in the hope of finding new evidence.

Let us suppose—purely as a hypothesis, a historical line along which future investigations might move—that it was in Elizabethan England that an idea of something like what was later the masonic idea had developed, in association with cults of the Queen and of the Dee movement, with which Philip Sidney was associated. In Elizabethan England, bound together by a revived chivalry and by Renaissance esoteric movements, and spiritually organized to resist a dangerous enemy, it seems likely that there would have been secret groupings. When these movements moved abroad, in the wake of the Elector Palatine and his Stuart bride, may they not have included, not only English chivalrous ideas and English alchemical ideas, but also the idea of a kind of pre-masonry, for which John Dee may have been partly responsible, just as he was responsible for so much else in these movements? One should look for possibly masonic mystiques among the writings of the Rosicrucian group, particularly Maier and Andreae, though at this date it would be difficult to differentiate these from general Renaissance mystiques.[2]

The problem is complicated by the fact that, although it seems more than likely that secret societies were developing under the pressures of

---

[1] The omission of Dee from Anderson's *Constitutions* is noted as curious by French, *John Dee*, p. 161 n. 3.

[2] For example, mysticism concerning the proportions of Solomon's Temple underlies early Italian Renaissance architectural theory (see R. Wittkower, *Architectural Principles in the Age of Humanism*, pp. 91, 106, 136), and interest in this subject in Maier and Andreae need not necessarily have anything to do with Freemasonry.

the times, one does not know how many of these societies there were, nor how, if at all, they were related to one another.

As has been said earlier, all the secret movements of the late sixteenth century might have had a secret sympathy with the movements around the Elector Palatine. We know that the Family of Love was a secret society, which undoubtedly had a real existence and organization, arising out of the situation in the Netherlands in the late sixteenth century. We know that many well-known people were secretly members of this sect or society, which allowed its members to belong ostensibly to any religious denomination whilst secretly maintaining their affiliation with the Family. These attitudes of the Family of Love have something in common with those of Freemasonry. We know that secret membership of the Family was widespread among printers, that, for example, the great Antwerp printer, Plantin, was a member of this sect and keen on propagating it through publishing works of those in sympathy with it. It has been suggested earlier[1] that the De Bry family of printers, who had connections with the Plantin firm, might have been Familists, and that the movement of this firm into Palatinate territory where it published, at Oppenheim, works of persons in the 'Rosicrucian' interest—Fludd and Maier—might have been because of secret sympathy with movements in the Palatinate.

Again, we have thought that influences from Giordano Bruno could be detected in the 'Rosicrucian' movement.[2] Bruno, the intensely Hermetic philosopher, who propagated throughout Europe in the late sixteenth century an esoteric movement which demanded a general reformation of the world, in the form of a return to 'Egyptian' religion and good magic, may have formed a secret society, the 'Giordanisti', among Lutheran circles in Germany. Bruno had visited England, where he had probably been in contact with Sidney, and had shown himself sympathetic to the more esoteric aspects of the Elizabethan chivalric cult.[3] Here again is a possible influence on 'Rosicrucianism' mingling with other influences.

One might say that the Familist influences might have represented a secret stream originating in the Netherlands; that a Bruno movement might appeal to secret movements in Italy; and that all such influences might have co-existed with an English esoteric movement, strongly

[1] See above, pp. 72–3.
[2] See above, pp. 82, 85.
[3] *Giordano Bruno and the Hermetic Tradition*, pp. 275 ff.

influenced by John Dee, which was building up the great dash for European 'liberation' through placing Frederick of the Palatinate on the Bohemian throne.

All this is obviously a groping in the dark, suggestions made up of 'ifs' and 'perhapses', yet it is necessary to describe such gropings in order to indicate the difficulty of the theme of this chapter. We know that the later sixteenth century and the early seventeenth century was an age of secret societies, but we do not know their relations to one another nor how they may have differed from one another. The English document of 1676 describes how the Green Ribboned Cabal[1] dined with the Brotherhood of the Rosy Cross, the Hermetic Adepti, and the Accepted Masons, all having in common their 'invisibility'. Perhaps this fragment represents earlier traditions of, so to speak, intercommunion between secret societies, though in the earlier and more terrible times, such relationships would have been deadly serious and full of danger.

If within this complex secret situation around the German Rosicrucian movement, there were an English esoteric influence, perhaps stemming from a masonic movement associated with Dee, perhaps combining with English chivalric influences to give the name 'Rose Cross', there may have been something real behind those mysterious manifestos, something in the nature of a pre-masonic movement.

Let me emphasize again that these gropings are intended only as hypotheses which might guide future investigators along a historical path which has not yet been trodden by those interested in early masonic history, for no one, I believe, has known of' the English influences on the German Rosicrucian movement.

If such influences went out from England to Germany in the early seventeenth century (arriving also via Dee's mission in Bohemia), when would such influences have returned to England? Surely after the crash of 1620. Surely an intense movement of loyalty and sympathy with the King and Queen of Bohemia would have been generated through the terrible events through which they were forced into that long exile at The Hague.

And here it is that this new historical approach may help through indicating what may be quite a new field of enquiry. There were 'Rosicrucian' movements at The Hague, beginning as early as 1622,

---

[1] This was a Whig club of the seventeenth century; see G. M. Trevelyan, *England under the Stuarts*, pp. 378 ff.

and concerning which a certain amount of material is known,[1] and more might be found. It seems possible that organized Freemasonry might have found at The Hague an encouraging soil in which to grow, perhaps out of, or in conjunction with, 'Rosicrucianism', in that atmosphere of loyalty to a lost cause the central figure in which, after the ex-King of Bohemia's death, was the ex-Queen of Bohemia, the royal widow who kept her court for so long at The Hague.

The members of the House of Stuart tended to be carriers of Free-masonry. One has only to think of the Jacobite Freemasonry which surrounded the Pretenders. Perhaps there is one member of the House of Stuart whose milieu has not been sufficiently investigated from this point of view, Elizabeth Stuart, ex-Queen of Bohemia. She had a powerful character and she exerted great influence, possibly in the direction of keeping alive a kind of royalism which even Parliamen-tarians could accept, which could even have something in common with an exiled Bohemian, like Comenius, which might have facilitated the ease with which the Restoration of Charles II was effected. That easy transition from revolution back to royalism has always been a matter for surprise and Freemasonry has been suspected in connection with it.

Our historical researches thus suggest that there was something in J. G. Buhle's theory, though not in the form in which he propounded it. The European phenomenon of Freemasonry almost certainly was connected with the Rosicrucian movement.

Nevertheless, even this provisional and hazy statement is very far from solving the problem, for it is clear that the two movements, though probably related, were not identical. Freemasonry combines an esoteric approach to religion with ethical teaching and emphasis on philanthropy, and in these ways it follows the pattern of the R.C. Brothers, but, as A. E. Waite pointed out, it differs from that pattern in not being interested in reform of arts and sciences, in scientific research, or in alchemy and magic, and in many other ways.[2] From the great

---

[1] Peter Mormius, *Arcana totius naturae secretissimus*, Leyden, 1630, seems to be the representative work for Rosicrucianism at The Hague in the early seventeenth century (I have not myself seen it). In the preface to this work it is stated that the true founder of the Rosicrucian Order was not Christian Rosencreutz but 'Frederick Rose' (see Arnold, *Histoire des Rose-Croix*, pp. 256–7). Another curious episode connected with Rosicrucian-ism in Holland at this time, is that a painter was arrested for being a Rosicrucian, tortured, and imprisoned, but released on the intervention of Charles I of England. See Rudolf and Margot Wittkower, *Born under Saturn*, London, 1963, p. 31.

[2] A. E. Waite, *Real History of the Rosicrucians*, pp. 402 ff. Waite was against the Buhle theory, as was also R. F. Gould (see Gould's *History of Freemasonry*, revised Poole, II, pp. 49–101).

reservoir of spiritual and intellectual power, of moral and reforming vision, represented by the Rosicrucian manifestos, Freemasonry drew off one stream; other streams flowed into the Royal Society, into the alchemical movement, and in many other directions. Our concern in this book is with the Rosicrucian Enlightenment as a whole and its manifold and multiform manifestations, and less with the canalization of some aspects of it into secret societies. The pursuit of secret societies has tended to obscure the importance of the theme. We can never know, for example, whether Francis Bacon was some kind of early Freemason. Nor is it necessary, or indeed important, that we should know such a thing. Much more important it is to trace the influence of the idea of Rosicrucianism, than invent the membership of secret societies.

Yet the theme studied in the present chapter, the theme of secrecy, is of importance, for it connects the Renaissance with the early scientific revolution. The great mathematical and scientific thinkers of the seventeenth century have at the back of their minds Renaissance traditions of esoteric thinking, of mystical continuity from Hebraic or 'Egyptian' wisdom, of that conflation of Moses with 'Hermes Trismegistus' which fascinated the Renaissance. These traditions survived across the period in secret societies, particularly in Freemasonry. Hence it is that we do not know the full content of the minds of early members of the Royal Society unless we take into account the esoteric influences from the Renaissance surviving in their background. Below, or beyond, their normal religious affiliations they would see the Great Architect of the Universe as an all-embracing religious conception which included, and encouraged, the scientific urge to explore the Architect's work. And this unspoken, or secret, esoteric background was a heritage from the Renaissance, from those traditions of Magia and Cabala, of Hermetic and Hebraic mysticism, which underlay 'Renaissance Neoplatonism' as fostered in the Italian Renaissance.

The *Fama* can thus now be seen as the perfect manifesto, combining, as it does, the proclamation of Advancement of Learning in a new enlightened age, with its subtle suggestion of 'invisibility' as the hallmark of the R.C. Brothers.

CHAPTER XVI

THE ROSICRUCIAN ENLIGHTENMENT

A few years ago in a lecture given in the United States I made the following remark:[1]

> I should like to try to persuade sensible people and sensible historians to use the word 'Rosicrucian'. This word has bad associations owing to the uncritical assertions of occultists concerning the existence of a sect or secret society calling themselves Rosicrucians the history and membership of which they claim to establish . . . The word could, I suggest, be used of a certain style of thinking which is historically recognizable without raising the question of whether a Rosicrucian style of thinker belonged to a secret society.

It is in this way that I propose to use 'Rosicrucian' and 'Rosicrucians' in this concluding chapter, as a historical label for a style of thinking such as we have met with in this book.

In the same lecture, I attempted to define the historical position of the Rosicrucian type of thinker, whom I placed midway between the Renaissance and the first, or seventeenth century, phase of the so-called scientific revolution. I said that the Rosicrucian was one fully in the stream of the Renaissance Hermetic-Cabalist tradition, but distinguished from the earlier phases of the movement by his addition of alchemy to his interests. This did not alter the basic adherence of the Rosicrucian to the scheme of 'occult philosophy' as laid down by Cornelius Agrippa. I pointed to John Dee as a typically Rosicrucian thinker, with his combined alchemical and cabalist interests, and I suggested that traces of the Rosicrucian outlook could be detected in Francis Bacon and even in Isaac Newton.

---

[1] 'The Hermetic Tradition in Renaissance Science', *Art, Science, and History in the Renaissance*, ed. Charles S. Singleton, Johns Hopkins Press, Baltimore, 1968, p. 263.

The present book has attempted to provide a historical framework for this line of thinking, and it is as a historical work that I would wish it to be judged. As a historian, I have attempted to open long closed doors through which the Rosicrucian currents of thought once travelled. Realizing that, in order to get any further with this subject, one must tackle the mysterious 'Rosicrucian manifestos', with their proclamation of a new revelation, I plunged into the daunting morass of the Rosicrucian literature, there to make the discovery that the major influence behind the German Rosicrucian movement was undoubtedly John Dee.

One can hardly as yet realize what this means. John Dee now becomes a towering figure in the European scene. His life and work divide into two halves. First, there was his career in England as the magus behind the Elizabethan age, the mathematical magician who inspired the Elizabethan technical advance, and the more esoteric and mystical side of whose thought inspired Sidney and his circle and the Elizabethan poetic movement which they led. Then, in 1583, Dee goes abroad, and he has a second career in central Europe as leader of an alchemical-cabalist movement, sensationally advertised through the reputed successes of Edward Kelley in transmutation. That this movement was a religious movement of some kind, that Dee was during the time in Bohemia in an 'incandescent' state,[1] is now realized, though this second half of Dee's career has not yet been fully studied. Until this has been done, we are not yet in a position to understand the life and work of Dee as a whole.

The Rosicrucian movement in Germany follows on from both these sides of Dee's work. It is in one sense an export of the Elizabethan period and of the inspirations behind it, scientific, mystical, poetic. To the English colouring belongs the name 'Rose Cross', deriving, so I believe, from the red cross of St George and English chivalric traditions. The old tradition whereby 'Rosicrucian' was a word of alchemical import, deriving from *ros* (dew) and *crux*, is encouraged by Dee's *Monas hieroglyphica* with the falling dew on its title-page and the complex allusions to the cross in the 'monas' symbol. Thus 'Rosicrucian' would become a word signifying both English chivalric influences and a Dee influence behind them. In any case, the name of the movement belongs, I believe, into its English side.

The second half of Dee's career is still more important in relation to the Rosicrucian movement, if, as I believe, the Dee movement in

[1] French, *John Dee*, p. 123.

Bohemia was used by Anhalt for building up the Elector Palatine as King of Bohemia.

Thus the historical currents behind the Elector Palatine and his bid for the Bohemian crown bind together the Dee influences coming in from England and also via Bohemia to form the Rosicrucian outburst. Yet this historical web, though it catches the movement, so to speak, is not the cause of the movement which has a much broader sweep than can be fully covered by these historical events.

What, then, did Rosicrucianism stand for?

To the genuine Rosicrucian, the religious side of the movement was always the most important. The Rosicrucian attempted to penetrate to deep levels of religious experience through which his personal religious experience, within his own confessional affiliation, was revived and strengthened. As Dee, and probably also Fludd, conceived it, the movement was to be inclusive of all religious attitudes, and was not necessarily anti-Catholic. The movement as it developed in Germany did, however, take on an anti-Catholic bias, or rather, more particularly, an anti-Jesuit bias. Here it involved an intense piety of a broadly evangelical type through which appeal could be made to all German Protestants, of whatever denomination.

The manifestos stress Cabala and Alchymia as the dominant themes in the movement. The latter gave the movement a turn towards medicine. The R.C. Brothers are healers. Paracelsist physicians like Fludd, Maier, Croll, represent the thought of the movement. But there is in Dee's *Monas* and in Maier's alchemical movement a further aspect which it is difficult to seize and which may represent an approach to nature in which alchemical and cabalist formulations have combined with mathematics to form something new. It may have been this germ in Rosicrucian thought which caused the bearers of some of the greatest names in the history of the scientific revolution to hover round it.

On the other hand, the advancing scientific revolution is also in opposition to the Rosicrucian world, eager to cast off the chrysalis out of which it is emerging. The most notable example of this process of emergence and discard is, of course, to be found in the controversy between Johannes Kepler and Robert Fludd. Though himself still deeply immersed in Hermetic influences, Kepler in his *Harmonice mundi* (1619) claimed to be treating his astronomical work purely as a mathematician, and not *more Hermetico* after the manner of Fludd. He accuses Fludd of resting his numerical and geometrical arguments on the macrocosm-microcosm analogy, and of confusing true mathematicians with 'Chemists, Hermetists, Paracelsists'. These accusations could, of course, apply equally well to Dee and to the whole Rosicrucian school. And Kepler's disapproval of Fludd's use of mathematical diagrams as 'hieroglyphs' could most certainly apply to Dee's 'monas' and all that it implied.

Yet Kepler moved in Andreae's circle, and seems to have been later associated with the Christian Unions. And Kepler, like Fludd, dedicated his great work on harmony to James I of Great Britain. Kepler was employed by the Emperor and would therefore have been, politically, on a different side to the Rosicrucians (he speaks mysteriously, and apparently slightingly, of 'the brothers of the Rosy Cross' in his *Apologia* of 1622). Yet Kepler's association with the Rosicrucian world is so close that one might almost call him a heretic from Rosicrucianism. This book has provided historical material from which a new historical approach to Kepler might be made, but this is too large a subject to be treated here.

To return to the general analysis of the Rosicrucian outlook. Magic was a dominating factor, working as a mathematics-mechanics in the lower world, as celestial mathematics in the celestial world, and as angelic conjuration in the supercelestial world. One cannot leave out the angels in this world view, however much it may have been advancing towards the scientific revolution. The religious outlook is bound up with the idea that penetration has been made into higher angelic spheres in which all religions were seen as one; and it is the angels who are believed to illuminate man's intellectual activities.

In the earlier Renaissance, the magi had been careful to use only the forms of magic operating in the elemental or celestial spheres, using talismans and various rituals to draw down favourable influences from the stars. The magic of a bold operator like Dee, aims beyond the stars, aims at doing the supercelestial mathematical magic, the angel-conjuring magic. Dee firmly believed that he had gained contact with good angels from whom he learned advancement in knowledge. This sense of close contact with angels or spiritual beings is the hallmark of the Rosicrucian. It is this which infuses his technology, however practical and successful and entirely rational in its new understanding of mathematical techniques, with an unearthly air, and makes him suspect as possibly in contact, not with angels, but with devils.

The period during which the Rosicrucian manifestos appeared, and the period of the furore which they aroused, is the time when the Renaissance disappears into convulsions of witch-hunting and wars, to emerge in the years to come—when these horrors were overpast—as enlightenment. I think that our studies in this book have shown that the witch-mania of this terrible period cannot be entirely explained through anthropological studies based on the phenomenon of witchcraft as common to all countries and ages. It is true that the witch-crazes of this period seem mainly to follow the usual patterns, and there is no doubt a sense in which they are basically related to the almost universal human phenomenon. But not all ages, nor all countries, have passed through the experience through which Europe was passing in the early seventeenth century. That experience was that the enormous scientific advances which have made Europe unique in history were at hand. They had almost arrived. When the Rosicrucian felt that he had in Dee's 'monas' something of immense potentiality and power, this was a part of the general feeling that a door was opening in Europe, that great advances were at hand, treasures of knowledge would soon be revealed, like the treasures found through the opening of the tomb of Christian Rosencreutz.

With this there went the sense of danger. The promised advance could appear diabolically dangerous, rather than angelically hopeful, to many. The promised dawn ushers in those terribly dark clouds of witch hysteria, sometimes artificially fomented by those who wished to destroy the movement. The witch-crazes which Descartes so prudently avoids, which Francis Bacon has prudently in mind, are of a somewhat different character from those in less developed countries. They are the reverse side of the scientific advance.

The union of religious with scientific vision took the form in the Rosicrucian movement of that strangely intense alchemical movement, in which alchemical modes of expression seemed best suited to the religious experience. Koyré saw this movement as a natural development out of the animist and vitalist Renaissance philosophies, asking whether alchemy does not provide a symbolism more suited to living religious experience than do the scholastic-Aristotelian doctrines of matter and form. 'Those who seek above all a regeneration of spiritual life are naturally drawn towards doctrines which lay the main stress on the idea of life and propose a vitalistic conception of the universe. And the symbolism of alchemy is as apt for translating (into symbolic form) the realities of the religious life, as that of matter and form. Perhaps more apt, because less used up, less intellectualized, more symbolic through its very nature.'[1] Koyré is speaking of Boehme, but these words can apply to the Rosicrucian alchemical movement, which is so close in spirit to Boehme.

> Teach me, my God and King,
>   In all things thee to see;
> And what I do in anything
>   To do it as for thee!
>
> A man that looks on glass,
>   On it may stay his eye
> Or if he pleaseth, through it pass,
>   And then the heaven espy.
>
> All may of thee partake;
>   Nothing can be so mean,
> Which with this tincture, 'for thy sake',
>   Will not grow bright and clean.
>
> A servant with this clause
>   Makes drudgery divine;
> Who sweeps a room, as for thy laws,
>   Makes that and the action fine
>
> This is the famous stone
>   That turneth all to gold;
> For that which God doth touch and own
>   Cannot for less be told.

So sang George Herbert of his Christian religious experience, and it was such spiritual gold as this that the German Rosicrucian movement sought. In much of the literature of the furore, there is an insistence on the imitation of Christ as taught by Thomas à Kempis as the true 'magnalia' of the alchemical revelation.

The Rosicrucian movement is aware that large new revelations of knowledge are at hand, that man is about to arrive at another stage of advance, far beyond that already achieved. This sense of standing on tiptoe in expectation of new knowledge is most characteristic of the Rosicrucian outlook. And the Rosicrucians, who know that they hold in their hands potentialities for great advance, are concerned to integrate

---

[1] A. Koyré, *La philosophie de Jacob Boehme*, Paris, 1929, p. 45.

these into a religious philosophy. Hence the Rosicrucian alchemy expresses both the scientific outlook, penetrating into new worlds of discovery, and also an attitude of religious expectation, of penetrating into new fields of religious experience.

The question is often asked as to which of the confessional allegiances, or different formulations of Christianity, were most conducive to the advancement of science. Did it advance most under Catholic or under Protestant regimes? And if under Protestant, whether Lutheran or Calvinist?

This question might be formulated in a different way. In my book *Giordano Bruno and the Hermetic Tradition*, I have argued that the main influence on the new turning towards the world in scientific enquiry lay in the religious attitudes fostered in the Hermetic-Cabalist tradition. If this is so (and all my later enquiries have confirmed me in this belief, which is indeed now largely accepted by historians of thought), it would follow that the religious outlook which allowed this tradition to flourish within its sphere of influence would be the one most conducive to scientific advance.

In the early Renaissance, Hermetic and Cabalist studies were not discouraged by the Roman Catholic church, though the problem of magic had always to be carefully negotiated. One of the greatest of the early Christian Cabalists, Egidius of Viterbo, was a cardinal. By the later sixteenth century, it is possible that the tradition was strongest under some forms of Protestantism. A Protestant country which allowed the tradition and did not over-persecute for magic would therefore be a country in which science would develop fairly freely. Such a country was Elizabethan England, and Queen Elizabeth, when she promised John Dee that she would support him in his studies and defend him from persecution, took a step forwards towards the advancement of science.

Compare and contrast what happened in Bohemia. Here was a country in which the tradition making for advancement, the Hermetic-Cabalist tradition as exemplified in the Cabalists and alchemists of Prague, was exceptionally strong. Bohemia was mainly, though not entirely, a Protestant country of the Hussite persuasion. The combination of a Hussite-Protestant type of religious liberalism with very strong infusion of Hermetic-Cabalist tradition should have produced interesting and original results. And when there came in with John Dee's movement an infusion of such traditions as they had developed in Elizabethan England, the results, in original scientific and religious attitudes, might have been phenomenal. But there was no Queen Elizabeth to guarantee freedom to original thinkers; and James I declined to play her role. Instead there was deliberate destruction and repression of a most severe kind. Thus the Bohemian contribution to the new age could only be made indirectly.

As to which type of Protestantism was most conducive to scientific advance, our explorations in this book may suggest that it was not so much the type of Protestantism that mattered as the presence, or absence, of the Hermetic-Cabalist tradition. The Palatinate was a Calvinist country, yet what evidence is there of influence of Calvinist theological doctrines on the movement we have attempted to describe? It was the effort to avoid doctrinal differences, to turn from them to exploration of nature in a religious spirit, which constituted the atmosphere in which science could advance, and would no doubt have advanced in the Palatinate if war had not intervened.

The argument that Puritanism fostered scientific advance has often been put forward. Where this argument might find some support is in the fact that the strong Hebraic, Old-Testament-inspired type of piety of the Puritans and Calvinists was conducive to amalgamation with Cabala, with the mystical side of Judaism. It is obvious that the Puritan worship of Jehova would be conducive to Cabalistic studies. Further, in England in the Parliamentarian period and under Cromwell, there was freedom, toleration of all kinds of scientific and religious attitudes except the Roman Catholic. Since this was the branch which was totally intolerant, its exclusion was not deleterious to freedom for the advancement of science in Puritan England.[1]

The kind of approach which is needed (so it seems to me) for the solution of such problems, has hardly yet been begun. François Secret in his book on Christian Cabala[2] has brought together much material on different attitudes to Cabala in the various divisions of Christianity. He reaches no conclusions, and his book is more in the nature of a bibliography than a book, yet it is suggestive. The Council of Trent put on the index many works on Cabala which had been standard in the Renaissance (such as those by Reuchlin), and tended on the whole, though with reservations, to discourage it. In Protestant countries,

---

[1] The Dee influence would seem to have been rather strongly taken up by the Puritans, see above, pp. 185–7. It spread to Puritanism in the New World through John Winthrop, an alchemist and a follower of Dee; Winthrop used the 'monas' as his personal mark. See R. S. Wilkinson, 'The Alchemical Library of John Winthrop', *Ambix*, XIII (1965), pp. 139–86.

[2] F. Secret, *Les Kabbalistes Chrétiens de la Renaissance*, Paris, 1964.

where of course the Tridentine restrictions did not operate, it could flourish more freely.

A very important aspect of the influence of Cabala, or of Jewish mystical traditions, on European thought in the sixteenth and early seventeenth centuries, is the fact that there had been new developments within the Jewish Cabalist tradition itself. The early Cabala, which had influenced Pico della Mirandola and the Italian Renaissance, had been centred in Spain. After the expulsion of the Jews from Spain in 1492, a new type of Cabala developed, having its centre in Palestine. The new Cabala was spread through Isaac Luria[1] (sixteenth century) and his disciples, who formed a group at Safed, in Palestine. The Lurianic Cabala began to spread in Europe in the late sixteenth and early seventeenth centuries. Lurianic Cabala cultivated and trained the religious imagination by intensive mystical meditation, by magical techniques and cult of the Divine Names, by ecstatic prayer. Its apocalyptic outlook laid stress on the Beginning, as well as on the End, on the return to the Paradisal Beginning as a necessary stage towards the appearance of the End. Prague was a great centre for Jewish Cabalism, and a very remarkable personality, the Rabbi Loew,[2] was prominent in Prague in the late sixteenth century (he died in Prague in 1609). He had a memorable interview with Rudolph II in which the Emperor actually asked the Jew for spiritual advice.

There may well have been influences on John Dee, not only of the older Spanish Cabala incorporated into the Renaissance tradition, but also of the new Lurianic Cabala which was capable of exciting remarkable phenomena of a religious nature. In thinking about the strange, explosive, religious mission of Dee in Bohemia, it is possible that influences of this kind should be taken into account. 'Christian Rosencreutz' describes in the *Fama* travels in the east whence he has returned with a new kind of 'Magia and Cabala' which he incorporates into his own Christian outlook.[3]

The later history of the religious alchemical-Cabalist movement would no doubt be instructive and would throw a retrospective light on our period. The strange figure of Francis Mercury Van Helmont,[4] son of the great alchemist–chemist J. B. Van Helmont, represented in the generation of the Elector Palatine's son, Charles Louis, with whom

---

[1] G. Scholem, *Major Trends in Jewish Mysticism*, London, 1955, pp. 244 ff.
[2] See Frederic Thieberger, *The Great Rabbi Loew of Prague*, London, 1954.
[3] See Appendix, below, pp. 239–41.
[4] See Marjorie Nicolson, *Conway Letters*, London, 1930, pp. 309 ff.

he was closely associated, a remarkable example of the Rosicrucian type of personality. Physician and healer, alchemist and magician, Francis Mercury Van Helmont seems like an R.C. Brother become visible at last. And in his case we know that he was influenced by Lurianic Cabala in Christianized form as propagated by Christian Knorr von Rosenroth, a Lutheran pastor of Silesia. It may be that this combination of religious alchemy with Cabala would be instructive to study as a possible parallel to Dee, alchemy, and Cabala, in the earlier period.

The increase of Cabalist studies seems to me to be a feature of the Hermetic-Cabalist tradition in the later sixteenth and early seventeenth centuries, though the decrees of the Council of Trent operated against such studies in Catholic countries. Paracelsist alchemy was also not encouraged in Catholic countries. Hence the movement expressed in the Rosicrucian manifestos was likely to be anti-Catholic in bias. We have seen that the manifestos are certainly strongly anti-Jesuit.

The Hapsburg-Jesuit alliance which the Rosicrucian movement was up against was not approved by all Catholics. The alliance of the Jesuits with the Hapsburg efforts to achieve European hegemony was entered upon by the Jesuits as the means of achieving that universal victory of Catholicism over Reformation which was the intense desire of the more extreme Counter Reformation enthusiasts, and which seemed on the point of success after 1620. Yet the reigning Pope, Urban VIII, never approved this policy.[1] This was partly because he was politically pro-French and anti-Spanish, but he also set it forth as the view of the Church that the alliance of the Church with the Hapsburgs was deleterious to the Church, and wrong as representing too close an identification of spiritual interests with one dynasty. The Jesuit-Hapsburg combination was disliked by many Catholics, particularly French Catholics. In France, in the sixteenth century, it had destroyed Henry III (though some Jesuits had supported him against the Spanish sympathizers). In Italy, it was the power which was crushing the Renaissance tradition, against which Sarpi had made his stand in Venice, and which had burned Giordano Bruno.

To the Rosicrucians, the Hapsburg-Jesuit combination was simply Antichrist. As we have seen, the Rose Cross fictional Order seemed put forward almost as a mirror image of the Jesuit Order. With their motto of *Jesus mihi omnia*, their mission of healing rather than destroying, the R.C. Brothers are suggested as the true Jesuits (as indeed they are

---

[1] David Ogg, *Europe in the Seventeenth Century*, p. 162; C. V. Wedgwood, *The Thirty Years War*, pp. 191, 336.

called by Adam Haselmayer) in opposition to the false followers of Jesus.

Yet of all the branches of the Roman Catholic Church it was the Jesuits who were most like the Rosicrucians. The Renaissance esoteric influences behind the formation of the Jesuit Order have not yet been fully studied. The Order made great use of the Hermetic tradition in appealing to Protestants and to the many other creeds which it encountered in its missionary work. The Hermetic and occult philosophy of the Jesuits received a tremendous formulation in the work of Athanasius Kircher, whose vast work on Hermetic pseudo-Egyptology was published in 1652, and who constantly cites with profound reverence the supposed ancient Egyptian priest, Hermes Trismegistus.[1] Kircher's work was much used in missionary efforts. He evidently tried to draw in the Dee tradition, for he illustrates an 'Egyptian' version of the 'monas' in one of his volumes.[2]

Through their common attachment to Hermetic tradition, the Jesuits and the 'Rosicrucians' were thus foes with a love-hate relationship through a kind of similarity. We have seen that in the furore the Jesuits tried to draw over Rosicrucian symbolism, suggesting that the two Orders were the same, and manufacturing similar emblematics. So the issues could become confused.

Moreover, the Jesuits most assiduously cultivated the sciences and the arts. Their vast effort in education was directed towards satisfying, within the Church, the thirst for knowledge. Were they initiators, or were they always trying to 'keep up', to intimate that they could take over everything of value in the new movements, whilst eliminating all that displeased them? A careful comparison should be made between the works of Robert Fludd and those of Athanasius Kircher before we can decide whether the Rosicrucian use of Hermetic tradition was more conducive to science than the Jesuit use of it. Probably there was more Cabalist influence in Fludd than in Kircher, and that may be significant.

At any rate, however understood or interpreted, that confrontation between Rosicrucian and Jesuit which we sense in the Rosicrucian movement was a sign of new times, a sign that Europe was moving out of the old world and its classifications into ages in which surviving influences from that world will take new forms. We can already begin to see in that confrontation the emergence of those Masonic *versus*

[1] See *Giordano Bruno and the Hermetic Tradition*, pp. 416 ff.
[2] Reproduced, *ibid.*, Pl. 15 (b).

Jesuit attitudes which were to form one of the most basic, and most secret, of the European patterns right up to the French Revolution.

One way of looking at the explorations in this book is to see them as having uncovered a lost period of European history. Like archaeologists digging down through layers, we have found under the superficial history of the early seventeenth century, just before the outbreak of the Thirty Years War, a whole culture, a whole civilization, lost to view, and not the less important because of such short duration. We may call it a Rosicrucian culture, and examine it from many points of view. In one way of looking at it, it is the Elizabethan age, in its Rosicrucian and Dee-inspired aspects, continued abroad. The Elizabethan age travelled out with the Elector Palatine and his bride, fresh from that wedding full of the splendours of the English Renaissance, out into Germany and Bohemia where it fell over a cliff of disaster. We can watch figures familiar to us in the well-lighted scenes of English history and literature —Henry Wotton, John Donne—as they travel out to that new environment to appear there in a new context. We can see English actors and English chivalric rituals affecting the genesis of a German work of imagination, Andreae's *Chemical Wedding*, which was in turn to influence Goethe who wrote an alchemical allegory based on it. We can see here interweavings of European traditions, connections in it which have been lost to us through the disappearance from history of the Rosicrucian age in the Palatinate. Further reconstruction of that age will no doubt reveal further connections. Michael Maier in his imagery was deliberately reconstructing, or continuing, symbolic themes used in England. John Donne's metaphysical poetry seems in many ways the counterpart of Maier's emblematics, expressing in a different medium a philosophical and religious outlook which may be closely parallel. Donne's Marriage Song, written for the wedding of 'the Lady Elizabeth and Count Palatine', uses imagery about the joining of two phoenixes, about a marriage of sun and moon, which is already in the alchemical vein which was to be so characteristic of their cult in Rosicrucian circles abroad. We have not sufficiently realized what the year 1620 must have meant to Donne and his friend Wotton as they watched those disasters about which nothing could be said owing to the attitude of King James.

Or we can traverse this forgotten piece of historical territory from another direction, one much less familiar to us, the Bohemian angle. The traditions of the court of Rudolph II in Prague were expanding into the Palatinate through Maier and his work. Many of the people involved in the movement at the Bohemian end lost their lives, yet specialists in Bohemian history and culture of this period know much which has not yet been made accessible to the English-speaking reader. When more is known we may understand better the alchemical movement at the Bohemian end, and learn further of the lives and thoughts of men like Daniel Stolcius, and their acceptance of Rosicrucian alchemical themes as part of the build up of the short-lived reign of the King and Queen of Bohemia. This movement, extinguished in Bohemia, had an after life in the alchemical movement in seventeenth-century England, which it would be fascinating to disentangle further.

Or we may think of the German aspect of the movement, how it coincided with a movement towards refreshing Lutheran spiritual life through alchemical religious philosophy as expressed in the life and work of Jacob Boehme. Light will surely be thrown on Boehme through further exploration of the Rosicrucian movement, and of the publications poured out in the Rosicrucian furore. It is to be hoped that the complex and rich subject of the German furore will now receive very serious attention as the expression of a very important phase in European history.

The most striking aspect of the Rosicrucian movement is the one to which the title of this book gives expression, its insistence on a coming Enlightenment. The world, nearing its end, is to receive a new illumination in which the advances in knowledge made in the preceding age of the Renaissance will be immensely expanded. New discoveries are at hand, a new age is dawning. And this illumination shines inward as well as outward; it is an inward spiritual illumination revealing to man new possibilities in himself, teaching him to understand his own dignity and worth and the part he is called upon to play in the divine scheme.

We have seen that the Rosicrucian Enlightenment did in fact shed rays on the seventeenth-century advance, and that many bearers of names famous in that advance seem to have been aware of it. It is hoped that this will demonstrate finally—what indeed has already been realized by many—that the Hermetic-Cabalist tradition as a force in the background of Renaissance science, did not lose that force with the coming of the scientific revolution, that it was still present in the background of the minds of figures formerly taken as fully representative of complete emergence from such influences. What exactly was the part played by Rosicrucian science, and more particularly by Rosicrucian mathematics, in the great advance? These are questions which this book has not attempted to answer.

The Rosicrucian Enlightenment included a vision of the necessity for a reform of society, particularly of education, for a third reformation of religion, embracing all sides of man's activity—and saw this as a necessary accompaniment of the new science. Rosicrucian thinkers were aware of the dangers of the new science, of its diabolical as well as its angelical possibilities, and they saw that its arrival should be accompanied by a general reformation of the whole wide world. This side of the message was perhaps best understood in Parliamentarian England, though circumstances prevented its application, and after the Restoration, science was allowed to develop in isolation from utopia,[1] and apart from the idea of a reformed society, educated to receive it. The comparative disregard of the social and educational possibilities of the movement was surely unfortunate for the future.

Thus the Rosicrucian Enlightenment was indeed, I suggest, an enlightenment, putting forward within its own strange frame of reference of magical and angelic agencies, of prophecy and apocalypse, a movement most of the aspects of which can only be described as enlightened. Though the Enlightenment proper, the *Aufklärung*, seems to introduce a very different atmosphere, yet its rationalism was tinged with illuminism. The words of Comenius in his *Via Lucis*, which has been called 'the Comenian *Fama*', might serve as a text for both the Enlightenments:[2]

If a light of Universal Wisdom can be enkindled, it will be able both to spread its beams thoughout the whole world of the human intellect (just as the radiance of the sun as often as it rises reaches from the east to the west) and to awake gladness in the hearts of men and to transform their wills. For if they see their own destiny and that of the world clearly set before them in this supreme light and learn how to use the means which will unfailingly lead to good ends, why should they not actually use them?

---

[1] On the collapse of utopia after the Restoration, see H. Trevor-Roper, *Religion, the Reformation and Social Change*, pp. 291 ff.
[2] Comenius, *The Way of Light*, trans. Campagnac, p. 30.

THE ROSICRUCIAN MANIFESTOS

The bibliography of the early editions of the manifestos is complicated, and there is no satisfactory modern study. Bibliographical information can be found in the following:

F. Leigh Gardner, *A Catalogue Raisonné of Works on the Occult Sciences*, vol. i: *Rosicrucian Books*, privately printed, 1923, items 23–29.

'Eugenius Philalethes' (Thomas Vaughan), *The Fame and Confession of the Fraternity of the R.C. . . . 1652*, facsimile reprint, ed. F. N. Pryce, privately printed, 1923. In his introduction (pp. 12 ff.), Pryce gives a list of the editions of the manifestos with analyses of their contents.

De Manifesten der Rosenkruisers, ed. Adolf Santing, Amersfoort, 1913. This reprint of the Dutch translation of the *Fama* and the *Confessio*, published in 1617, also contains reprints of the preface to the *Fama* of 1614; the German text of the *Fama* of 1615; the *Confessio* from the original Latin edition of 1615, and the German translation of it from the edition of 1615. Santing's introduction (pp. 13 ff.) gives a list of the editions of the manifestos.

Chymische Hochzeit Christiani Rosencreutz, ed. F. Maack, Berlin, 1913. This reprint of the German text of the *Chemical Wedding* also reprints the German texts of the two manifestos. The introduction and notes are unreliable.

The present note aims only at giving, in non-specialist language, a brief survey of the early editions. The list is almost certainly not complete.

(i) The first item in the bibliography of the manifestos must be the 'reply' to the *Fama* published by Adam Haselmeyer in 1612. The existence of this printed 'reply' of 1612 was reported by W. Begemann in *Monatsheften der Comeniusgesellschaft*, Band VIII (1899). The 'reply' was reprinted in the first edition of the *Fama*. An English translation of the 'reply' by Pryce will be found in Pryce's edition of the *Fame and Confession*, pp. 57–64.

Haselmeyer states that he had seen a manuscript of the *Fama* in 1610.

(ii) The first edition of the *Fama*.

Allgemeine und General Reformation, der gantzen weiten Welt. Beneben der Fama Fraternitatis, dess Löblichen Ordens des Rosenkreutzes, an alle gelehrte und Häupter Europae geschrieben: Auch einer kurtzen Responsion von des Herrn Haselmeyer gestellet, welcher desswegen von den Jesuitern ist gefänglich eingezogen, und auff eine Galleren geschmiedet: Itzo öffentlich in Druck verfetiget, und allen trewen Hertzen comuniceret worden Gedruckt zu Cassel, durch Wilhem Wessell, Anno MDCXIV.

The volume contains the following items:

Epistle to the Reader

The General Reformation (that is the German translation of the extract from Traiano Boccalini's *Ragguagli di Parnaso* (on which see above, pp. 133 ff.)

The *Fama*

Haselmeyer's 'reply'

There was a second edition at Cassel by Wilhelm Wessel, later in 1614, identical with the first except for the addition of another 'reply' to the R.C. Brothers.

(iii) The first edition of the *Confessio*.

Secretioris Philosophiae Consideratio brevis a Philipp a Gabella, Philosophiae St (studioso?) conscripta, et nunc primum una cum Confessione Fraternitatis R.C. in lucem edita Cassellis, Excudebat Guilhelmus Wessellius Ill^{mi}. Princ. Typographus. Anno post natum Christum MDVXV. On the verso of the title-page:—Gen. 27. *De rore Caeli et Pinguedine Terrae det tibi Deus*

The volume contains:

The *Consideratio brevis* by Philip à Gabella, dedicated to Bruno Carolus Uffel, in nine chapters, followed by a prayer. The work is based on John Dee's *Monas hieroglyphica* (see above, pp. 46–7)

The preface to the *Confessio*

The *Confessio Fraternitatis R.C., Ad Eruditos Europae*, in fourteen chapters.

(iv) Later editions of the manifestos. (I do not repeat here the lengthy German titles which are on similar lines to the title of the first edition of the *Fama*, with variations according to contents.)

An edition at Cassel by Wilhelm Wessel in 1615 drops all the additional matter in the two first editions and prints only the two manifestos with their prefaces. The *Fama* is in German as always; the *Confessio*

APPENDIX

is printed in the original Latin, but with a German translation added (divided into chapters, as in the original).

An edition at Frankfurt by Johann Bringer in 1615 includes the *Fama*, the *Confessio* (in another German translation, without division into chapters), Haselmeyer's 'reply' and several other anonymous replies to the *Fama*, and the General Reformation (the Boccalini extract).

An edition at Cassel by Wilhelm Wessel in 1616 reproduces the Frankfurt edition of 1615, with some additional replies and other matter.

An edition at Frankfurt in 1617 by Bringer begins with the *Fama* and the German *Confessio*; the General Reformation is omitted, but the volume contains some new material, including the defence of the Order by 'Julianus de Campis'. After 1617, so far as I know, no further editions of the manifestos were published in Germany in the seventeenth century.

(v) English translations of the manifestos.

It is stated in both the *Fama* and the *Confessio* that the *Fama* was 'set forth in five languages' (see below, pp. 250, 254). Except for the Dutch translation printed, probably, at Amsterdam in 1617 (and reprinted by Santing), no other traces of early printed translations have come to light. Early translations into other languages were presumably circulated in manuscript.

There were certainly English translations circulating in manuscript long before Vaughan's publication of 1652. Vaughan states in his preface that he was following a translation by 'an unknown hand'. Pryce has shown in his introduction to *The Fame and Confession* (pp. 3–8) that the translation printed by Vaughan corresponds very closely to a manuscript translation in Scots dialect preserved among the papers of the Earl of Crawford and Balcarres and dated 1633. Pryce thinks that both the Crawford manuscript and the manuscript copied by Vaughan descended from an original which must have been earlier than 1633.

The English translation in manuscript which Ashmole possessed and from which he made a copy (see above, pp. 194–5) was probably earlier than this.

In the interests of scholarship it would be desirable that there should be a reprint of the whole of the contents of the volumes containing the first editions of the *Fama* and the *Confessio*, together with an English translation of all the contents. It would then be

237

possible for students to make a detailed study of the context in which the manifestos appeared. In the following pages, only the *Fama* and the *Confessio* are reprinted, as they appear in the English translation published by Thomas Vaughan in 1652, with some modernization of spelling and punctuation and with the addition of a few notes. The translation is far from perfect (particularly that of the *Confessio*), but its minor inaccuracies and confusions do not obscure the general drift and meaning.

FAMA FRATERNITATIS

or a

DISCOVERY OF THE FRATERNITY OF THE MOST NOBLE ORDER OF THE ROSY CROSS

Seeing the only wise and merciful God in these latter days hath poured out so richly his mercy and goodness to mankind, whereby we do attain more and more to the perfect knowledge of his Son Jesus Christ and Nature, that justly we may boast of the happy time, wherein there is not only discovered unto us the half part of the world, which was heretofore unknown and hidden, but he hath also made manifest unto us many wonderful, and never heretofore seen, works and creatures of Nature, and moreover hath raised men, imbued with great wisdom, who might partly renew and reduce all arts (in this our age spotted and imperfect) to perfection; so that finally man might thereby understand his own nobleness and worth, and why he is called Microcosmus, and how far his knowledge extendeth into Nature.

Although the rude world herewith will be but little pleased, but rather smile and scoff thereat; also the pride and covetousness of the learned is so great, it will not suffer them to agree together; but were they united, they might out of all those things which in this our age God doth so richly bestow upon us, collect *Librum Naturae*, or a perfect method of all arts: but such is their opposition, that they still keep, and are loth to leave the old course, esteeming Porphyry,[1] Aristotle, and Galen, yea and that which hath but a mere show of learning, more than the clear and manifested light and truth; who if they were now living, with much joy would leave their erroneous doctrines. But here is too great weakness for such a great work. And although in theology, physic, and the mathematics, the truth doth oppose[2] itself, nevertheless

[1] A mistake for 'Popery'. The German original reads 'the Pope'.
[2] The German original reads 'doth manifest itself'.

the old enemy by his subtlety and craft doth show himself in hindering every good purpose by his instruments and contentious wavering people. To such an intent of a general reformation, the most godly and highly illuminated father, our brother, C.R. a German, the chief and original of our Fraternity, hath much and long time laboured, who by reason of his poverty (although descended of noble parents) in the fifth year of his age was placed in a cloister, where he had learned indifferently the Greek and Latin tongues, who (upon his earnest desire and request) being yet in his growing years, was associated to a brother, P.A.L. who had determined to go to the Holy Land.

Although this brother died in Cyprus, and so never came to Jerusalem, yet our brother C.R. did not return, but shipped himself over, and went to Damasco, minding from thence to go to Jerusalem; but by reason of the feebleness of his body he remained still there, and by his skill in physic he obtained much favour with the Turks. In the meantime he became by chance acquainted with the wise men of Damascus in Arabia, and beheld what great wonders they wrought, and how Nature was discovered unto them; hereby was that high and noble spirit of brother C.R. so stirred up, that Jerusalem was not so much now in his mind as Damascus; also he could not bridle his desires any longer, but made a bargain with the Arabians, that they should carry him for a certain sum of money to Damascus; he was but of the age of sixteen years when he came thither, yet of a strong Dutch constitution. There the wise received him (as he himself witnesseth) not as a stranger, but as one whom they had long expected; they called him by his name, and showed him other secrets out of his cloister, whereat he could not but mightily wonder. He learned there better the Arabian tongue, so that the year following he translated the book M. into good Latin, which he afterwards brought with him. This is the place where he did learn his physic, and his mathematics, whereof the world hath just cause to rejoice, if there were more love, and less envy. After three years he returned again with good consent, shipped himself over Sinus Arabicus into Egypt, where he remained not long, but only took better notice there of the plants and creatures. He sailed over the whole Mediterranean sea for to come unto Fez, where the Arabians had directed him. And it is a great shame unto us, that wise men, so far remote the one from the other, should not only be of one opinion, hating all contentious writings, but also be so willing and ready under the seal of secrecy to impart their secrets to others.

Every year the Arabians and Africans do send one to another, enquiring one of another out of their arts, if happily they had found out some better things, or if experience had weakened their reasons. Yearly there came something to light, whereby the mathematics, physic, and magic (for in those are they of Fez most skilful) were amended. As there is nowadays in Germany no want of learned men, magicians, Cabalists, physicians, and philosophers, were there but more love and kindness among them, or that the most part of them would not keep their secrets close only to themselves. At Fez he did get acquaintance with those which are commonly called the Elementary Inhabitants, who revealed unto him many of their secrets. As we Germans likewise might gather together many things, if there were the like unity, and desire of searching out secrets amongst us.

Of these of Fez he often did confess that their Magia was not altogether pure, and also that their Cabala was defiled with their religion; but notwithstanding he knew how to make good use of the same, and found still more better grounds for his faith, altogether agreeable with the harmony of the whole world, and wonderfully impressed in all periods of times. And thence proceedeth that fair concord, that, as in every several kernel is contained a whole good tree or fruit, so likewise is included in the little body of man the whole great world, whose religion, policy, health, members, nature, language, words and works, are agreeing, sympathizing, and in equal tune and melody with God, heaven, and earth. And that which is disagreeing with them is error, falsehood, and of the Devil, who alone is the first, middle, and last cause of strife, blindness, and darkness in the world. Also, might one examine all and several persons upon the earth, he should find that which is good and right, is always agreeing with itself; but all the rest is spotted with a thousand erroneous conceits.

After two years brother C.R. departed the city of Fez, and sailed with many costly things into Spain, hoping well (that since) he himself had so well and so profitably spent his time in his travel, that the learned in Europe would highly rejoice with him, and begin to rule and order all their studies according to those sound and sure foundations. He therefore conferred with the learned in Spain, showing unto them the errors of our arts, and how they might be corrected, and from whence they should gather the true *Indicia* of the times to come, and wherein they ought to agree with those things that are past; also how the faults of the Church and the whole *Philosophia Moralis* was to be amended. He showed them new growths, new fruits, and beasts, which did concord with old philosophy, and prescribed them new *Axiomata*, whereby all things might fully be restored. But it was to them a laughing matter; and being a new thing unto them, they feared that their great name should be lessened, if they should now again begin to learn and acknowledge their many years errors, to which they were accustomed, and wherewith they had gained them enough. Who-so loveth unquietness, let him be reformed.

The same song was also sung to him by other nations, the which moved him the more because it happened to him contrary to his expectations, being ready then bountifully to impart all his arts and secrets to the learned, if they would have but undertaken to write the true and infallible *Axiomata*, out of all faculties, sciences, and arts, and whole Nature, as that which he knew would direct them, like a globe or circle, to the only middle point and *Centrum*, and (as is usual among the Arabians) it should only serve to the wise and learned as a rule. That also there might be a Society in Europe, which might have gold, silver, and precious stones, sufficient for to bestow them on kings, for their necessary uses and lawful purposes; with which such as be governors might be brought up, for to learn all that which God hath suffered man to know, and thereby to be enabled in all times of need to give their counsel unto those that seek it, like the heathen oracles. Verily we must confess that the world in those days was already big with those great commotions, labouring to be delivered of them; and did bring forth painful, worthy men, who broke with all force through darkness and barbarism, and left us who succeeded to follow them: and assuredly they have been the uppermost point *in trigono igneo*, whose flame now should be more and more bright, and shall undoubtedly give to the world the last light.

Such a one likewise hath Theophrastus (Paracelsus) been in vocation and callings, although he was none of our Fraternity, yet nevertheless hath he diligently read over the book M: whereby his sharp *ingenium* was exalted; but this man was also hindered in his course by the multitude of the learned and wise-seeming men, that he was never able peacefully to confer with others of his knowledge and understanding he had of Nature. And therefore in his writing he rather mocked these busy bodies, and doth not show them altogether what he was: yet nevertheless there is found with him well grounded the aforenamed *Harmonia*, which without doubt he had imparted to the learned, if he had not found them rather worthy of subtle vexation, than to be instructed in greater arts and sciences; he then with a free and careless life lost his time, and left unto the world their foolish pleasures.

But that we do not forget our loving father, brother C.R., he after many painful travels, and his fruitless true instructions, returned again into Germany, the which he (by reason of the alterations which were shortly to come, and of the strange and dangerous contentions) heartily loved. There, although he could have bragged with his art, but specially of the transmutations of metals, yet did he esteem more Heaven, and the citizens thereof, Man, than all vain glory and pomp.

Nevertheless he built a fitting and neat habitation, in which he ruminated his voyage, and philosophy, and reduced them together in a true memorial. In this house he spent a great time in the mathematics, and made many fine instruments, *ex omnibus hujus artis partibus*, whereof there is but little remaining to us, as hereafter you shall understand. After five years came again into his mind the wished for reformation; and in regard he doubted of the aid and help of others, although he himself was painful, lusty, and unwearying, he undertook, with some few joined with him, to attempt the same. Wherefore he desired to this end, to have out of his first cloister (to the which he bare a great affection) three of his brethren, brother G.V., brother J.A., and brother J.O., who besides that, they had some more knowledge in the arts, than in that time many others had, he did bind those three unto himself, to be faithful, diligent, and secret; as also to commit carefully to writing, all that which he should direct and instruct them in, to the end that those which were to come, and through especial revelation should be received into this Fraternity, might not be deceived of the least syllable and word.

After this manner began the Fraternity of the Rose Cross; first, by four persons only, and by them was made the magical language and writing, with a large dictionary, which we yet daily use to God's praise and glory, and do find great wisdom therein; they made also the first part of the book M. But in respect that that labour was too heavy, and the unspeakable concourse of the sick hindered them, and also whilst his new building (called *Sancti spiritus*) was now finished, they concluded to draw and receive yet others more into their Fraternity; to this end was chosen brother R.C., his deceased father's brother's son, brother B. a skilful painter, G. and P.D. their secretary, all Germans except J.A., so in all they were eight in number, all bachelors and of vowed virginity; by those was collected a book or volume of all that which man can desire, wish, or hope for.

Although we do now freely confess, that the world is much amended within an hundred years, yet we are assured that our *Axiomata* shall unmovably remain unto the world's end, and also the world in her highest and last age shall not attain to see anything else; for our *Rota* takes her beginning from that day when God spake *Fiat*, and shall end when he shall speak *Pereat*; yet God's clock striketh every minute, where ours scarce striketh perfect hours. We also steadfastly believe, that if our brethren and fathers had lived in this our present and clear light, they would more roughly have handled the Pope, Mahomet, scribes, artists, and sophisters, and had showed themselves more helpful, not simply with sighs, and wishing of their end and consummation.

When now these eight brethren had disposed and ordered all things in such manner, as there was not now need of any great labour, and also that everyone was sufficiently instructed, and able perfectly to discourse of secret and manifest philosophy, they would not remain any longer together, but as in the beginning they had agreed, they separated themselves into several countries, because that not only their *Axiomata* might in secret be more profoundly examined by the learned, but that they themselves, if in some country or other they observed anything, or perceived some error, they might inform one another of it.

Their agreement was this: First, That none of them should profess any other thing than to cure the sick, and that *gratis*. 2. None of the posterity should be constrained to wear one certain kind of habit, but therein to follow the custom of the country. 3. That every year upon the day C. they should meet together in the house *S. Spiritus*, or write the cause of his absence. 4. Every brother should look about for a worthy person, who, after his decease, might succeed him. 5. The word C.R. should be their seal, mark, and character. 6. The Fraternity should remain secret one hundred years. These six articles they bound themselves one to another to keep, and five of the brethren departed, only the brethren B. and D. remained with the father, *Fra.* R.C., a whole year; when these likewise departed. Then remained by him his cousin and brother J.O. so that he hath all the days of his life with him two of his brethren. And although that as yet the Church was not cleansed, nevertheless we know that they did think of her, and what with longing desire they looked for. Every year they assembled together with joy, and made a full resolution of that which they had done; there must certainly have been great pleasure, to hear truly and without invention related and rehearsed all the wonders which God had poured out here and there through the world. Everyone may hold it out for certain, that such persons as were sent, and joined together by God, and the heavens, and chosen out of the wisest of men, as have lived in many ages, did live together above all others in highest unity, greatest secrecy, and most kindness one towards another.

After such a most laudable sort they did spend their lives, and although they were free from all diseases and pain, yet notwithstanding they could not live and pass their time appointed of God. The first of this Fraternity which died, and that in England, was J.O., as brother C. long before had foretold him; he was very expert, and well learned in Cabala, as his book called H. witnesseth. In England he is much spoken of, and chiefly because he cured a young Earl of Norfolk of the leprosy. They had concluded, that as much as possibly could be, their burial place should be kept secret, as at this day it is not known unto us what is become of some of them, yet everyone's place was supplied with a fit successor. But this we will confess publicly by these presents to the honour of God, that what secret soever we have learned out of the book M. (although before our eyes we behold the image and pattern of all the world) yet are there not shown unto us our misfortunes, nor hour of death, the which only is known to God himself, who thereby would have us keep in a continual readiness. But hereof more in our Confession, where we do set down 37 reasons wherefore we now do make known our Fraternity, and proffer such high mysteries, and without constraint and reward. Also we do promise more gold than both the Indies bring to the King of Spain; for Europe is with child and will bring forth a strong child, who shall stand in need of a great godfather's gift.

After the death of J.O., brother R.C. rested not, but as soon as he could, called the rest together (and as we suppose) then his grave was made. Although hitherto we (who were the latest) did not know when our loving father R.C. died, and had no more but the bare names of the beginners, and all their successors, to us, yet there came into our memory a secret, which through dark and hidden words, and speeches of the 100 years, brother A., the successor of D. (who was of the last and second row and succession, and had lived amongst many of us) did impart unto us of the third row and succession. Otherwise we must confess, that after the death of the said A. none of us had in any manner known anything of brother R.C. and of his first fellow-brethren, than that which was extant of them in our philosophical

Bibliotheca, amongst which our *Axiomata* was held for the chiefest, *Rota Mundi* for the most artificial, and *Protheus* the most profitable. Likewise we do not certainly know if these of the second row have been of the like wisdom as the first, and if they were admitted to all things. It shall be declared hereafter to the gentle Reader, not only what we have heard of the burial of R.C., but also made manifest publicly by the foresight, sufferance, and commandment of God, whom we most faithfully obey, that if we shall be answered discreetly and Christian-like, we will not be afraid to set forth publicly in print our names and surnames, our meetings, or anything else that may be required at our hands.

Now the true and fundamental relation of the finding out of the high illuminated man of God, *Fra.* C.R.C. is this. After that A. in *Gallia Narbonensis* was deceased, then succeeded in his place our loving brother N.N. This man after he had repaired unto us to take the solemn oath of fidelity and secrecy, he informed us *bona fide* that A. had comforted him in telling him that this Fraternity should ere long not remain so hidden, but should be to all the whole German nation helpful, needful, and commendable; of the which he was not in any wise in his estate ashamed of. The year following, after he had performed his school right and was minded now to travel, being for that purpose sufficiently provided with Fortunatus' purse, he thought (he being a good architect) to alter something of his building and to make it more fit. In such renewing he lighted upon the memorial table which was cast of brass, and containeth all the names of the brethren, with some few other things. This he would transfer in another more fitting vault; for where or when *Fra.* R.C. died, or in what country he was buried, was by our predecessors concealed and unknown to us. In this table stuck a great nail somewhat strong, so that when he was with force drawn out, he took with him an indifferently big stone out of the thin wall, or plastering, of the hidden door, and so, unlooked for, uncovered the door. Wherefore we did with joy and longing throw down the rest of the wall, and cleared the door, upon which was written in great letters, *Post 120 annos patebo*, with the year of the Lord under it. Therefore we gave God thanks and let it rest that same night, because we would first overlook our *Rotam*. But we refer ourselves again to the Confession, for what we here publish is done for the help of those that are worthy, but to the unworthy (God willing) it will be small profit. For like as our door was after so many years wonderfully discovered, also there shall be opened a door to Europe (when the wall is removed) which already doth begin to appear, and with great desire is expected of many.

In the morning following we opened the door, and there appeared to our sight a vault of seven sides and corners, every side five foot broad, and the height of eight foot. Although the sun never shined in this vault, nevertheless it was enlightened with another sun, which had learned this from the sun, and was situated in the upper part in the center of the ceiling. In the midst, instead of a tombstone, was a round altar covered over with a plate of brass, and thereon this engraven:

A.C.R.C. Hoc universi compendium unius mihi sepulchrum feci[1]

Round about the first circle, or brim, stood,

Jesus mihi omnia.[2]

In the middle were four figures, inclosed in circles, whose circumscription was,

1 *Nequaquam vacuum.*

2 *Legis Jugum.*

3 *Libertas Evangelii.*

4 *Dei gloria intacta.*[3]

This is all clear and bright, as also the seven sides and the two *Heptagoni*: so we kneeled altogether down, and gave thanks to the sole wise, sole mighty and sole eternal God, who hath taught us more than all men's wits could have found out, praised be his holy name. This vault we parted in three parts, the upper part or ceiling, the wall or side, the ground or floor.

Of the upper part you shall understand no more of it at this time, but that it was divided according to the seven sides in the triangle, which was in the bright center;[4] but what therein is contained, you shall God willing (that are desirous of our society) behold the same with your own eyes; but every side or wall is parted into ten figures, every one with their several figures and sentences, as they are truly shown and set forth *Concentratum* here in our book.

The bottom again is parted in the triangle,[5] but because therein is

---

[1] For *unius* read *vivus*. 'This compendium of the universe I made in my lifetime to be my tomb.'

[2] 'Jesus, all things to me.'

[3] 'A vacuum exists nowhere. The Yoke of the Law. The Liberty of the Gospel. The whole Glory of God.'

[4] 'but that it was divided into triangles running from the seven sides to the bright light in the centre.'

[5] 'The floor is again divided into triangles.'

described the power and the rule of the inferior governors,[1] we leave
to manifest the same, for fear of the abuse by the evil and ungodly
world. But those that are provided and stored with the heavenly
antidote, they do without fear or hurt tread on and bruise the head of
the old and evil serpent, which this our age is well fitted for. Every side
or wall had a door or chest, wherein there lay divers things, especially
all our books, which otherwise we had. Besides the *Vocabular* of
Theoph: Par. Ho.[2] and these which daily unfalsifieth we do participate.[3]
Herein also we found his *Itinerarium* and *vitam*, whence this relation for
the most part is taken. In another chest were looking-glasses of divers
virtues, as also in another place were little bells, burning lamps, and
chiefly wonderful artificial songs, generally all done to that end, that if
it should happen after many hundred years the Order or Fraternity
should come to nothing, they might by this only vault be restored
again.

Now as yet we had not seen the dead body of our careful and wise
father, we therefore removed the altar aside, there we lifted up a strong
plate of brass, and found a fair and worthy body, whole and un-
consumed, as the same is here lively counterfeited, with all his orna-
ments and attires. In his hand he held a parchment book, called I., the
which next unto the Bible is our greatest treasure, which ought to be
delivered to the censure of the world. At the end of this book standeth
this following *Elogium*:

Granum pectori Jesu insitum.
C. Ros. C. ex nobili atque splendida Germaniae R.C. familia oriundus,
vir sui seculi divinis revelationibus subtilissimis imaginationibus, indefessis
laboribus ad coelestia, atque humana mysteria; arcanave admissus
postquam suam (quam Arabico, & Africano itineribus Collegerat) plusquam
regiam, atque imperatoriam Gazam suo seculo nondum convenientem,
posteritati eruendam custodivisset & jam suarum Artium, ut & nominis,
fides acconjunctissimos herides instituisset, mundum minitum omnibus
motibus magno illi respondentem fabricasset hocque tandem preteritarum,
praesentium, & futurarum, rerum compendio extracto, centenario major
non morbo (quem ipse nunquam corpore expertus erat, nunquam alios
infestare sinebat) ullo pellente sed spiritu Dei evocante, illuminatam
animam (inter Fratrum amplexus & ultima oscula) fidelissimo creatori Deo

[1] The stars.
[2] Theophrastus Paracelsus ab Hohenheim.
[3] 'And which we daily communicate unfalsified.'

reddidisset, Pater dilectissimus, Fra: suavissimus, praeceptor fidelissimus, amicus integerimus, a suis ad 120 annos hic absconditus est.[1]

Underneath they had subscribed themselves,

1 *Fra. I.A., Fr. C.H. electione Fraternitatis caput*[2]
2 *Fr. G.V. M.P.C.*
3 *Fra. R.C. Iunior haeres S. Spiritus*
4 *Fra. B.M., P.A. Pictor & Architectus*
5 *Fr. G.G. M.P.I. Cabalista*
　　　Secundi Circuli
1 *Fra. P.A. Successor, Fr. I.O. Mathematicus*
2 *Fra. A. Successor Fra. P.D.*
3 *Fra. R. Successor patris C.R.C. cum Christo triumphant.*[3]

At the end was written

Ex Deo nascimur, in Jesu morimur, per spiritum sanctum reviviscimus.[4]

At that time was already dead brother I.O. and Fra. D. but their burial place where is it to be found? We doubt not but our Fra. Senior hath the same, and some especial thing laid in earth, and perhaps likewise hidden. We also hope that this our example will stir up others more diligently to enquire after their names (whom we have therefore published) and to search for the place of their burial; for the most part of them, by reason of their practise and physic, are yet known, and praised among very old folks; so might perhaps our Gaza be enlarged, or at least be better cleared.

[1] 'A grain buried in the breast of Jesus. C, Ros. C. sprung from the noble and renowned German family of R.C.; a man admitted into the mysteries and secrets of heaven and earth through the divine revelations, subtle cogitations and unwearied toil of his life. In his journeys through Arabia and Africa he collected a treasure surpassing that of Kings and Emperors; but finding it not suitable for his times, he kept it guarded for posterity to uncover, and appointed loyal and faithful heirs of his arts and also of his name. He constructed a microcosm corresponding in all motions to the macrocosm and finally drew up this compendium of things past, present, and to come. Then, having now passed the century of years, though oppressed by no disease, which he had neither felt in his own body nor allowed to attack others, but summoned by the Spirit of God, amid the last embraces of his brethren he rendered up his illuminated soul to God his Creator. A beloved Father, an affectionate Brother, a faithful Teacher, a loyal Friend, he was hidden here by his disciples for 120 years.' (Translated by F. N. Pryce.)
From the various indications given, the date at which the tomb is supposed to have been discovered works out as 1604. According to the *Confessio* (see below, p. 255), Brother R.C. was born in 1378 and lived for 106 years. He therefore died in 1484. His tomb was discovered 120 years after his death—that is, in 1604.
[2] 'by the choice of Fr.C.H., head of the Fraternity'.
[3] *Triumphantis.*
[4] 'We are born of God, we die in Jesus, we live again through the Holy Spirit.'

Concerning *Minutum Mundum,* we found it kept in another little altar, truly more fine than can be imagined by any understanding man; but we will leave him undescribed, until we shall truly be answered upon this our true hearted *Fama.* And so we have covered it again with the plates, and set the altar thereon, shut the door, and made it sure, with all our seals. Besides by instruction and command of our *Rota,* there are come to sight some books, among which is contained M. (which were made instead of household care by the praise-worthy M.P.). Finally we departed the one from the other, and left the natural heirs in possession of our jewels. And so we do expect the answer and judgment of the learned, or unlearned.

Howbeit we know after a time there will now be a general reformation, both of divine and human things, according to our desire, and the expectation of others. For it is fitting, that before the rising of the sun, there should appear and break forth Aurora, or some clearness, or divine light in the sky. And so in the mean time some few, who shall give their names, may join together, thereby to increase the number and respect of our Fraternity, and make a happy and wished for beginning of our *Philosophical Canons,* prescribed to us by our brother R.C., and be partakers with us of our treasures (which never can fail or be wasted), in all humility and love to be eased of this world's labour, and not walk so blindly in the knowledge of the wonderful works of God.

But that also every Christian may know of what religion and belief we are, we confess to have the knowledge of Jesus Christ (as the same now in these last days, and chiefly in Germany, most clear and pure is professed, and is nowadays cleansed and void of all swerving people, heretics, and false prophets), in certain noted countries maintained, defended and propagated. Also we use two Sacraments, as they are instituted with all forms and ceremonies of the first reformed Church. In *Politia* we acknowledge the Roman Empire and *Quartam Monarchiam* for our Christian head; albeit we know what alterations be at hand, and would fain impart the same with all our hearts to other godly learned men; notwithstanding our hand-writing which is in our hands, no man (except God alone) can make it common, nor any unworthy person is able to bereave us of it. But we shall help with secret aid this so good a cause, as God shall permit or hinder us. For our God is not blind, as the heathen Fortune, but is the Church's ornament, and the honour of the Temple. Our Philosophy also is not a new invention, but as Adam after his fall hath received it, and as Moses and Solomon used it. Also she ought not much to be doubted of, or contradicted by other opinions, or meanings; but seeing the truth is peaceable, brief, and always like herself in all things, and especially accorded by with *Jesus in omni parte* and all members. And as he is the true Image of the Father, so is she his Image. It shall not be said, this is true according to Philosophy, but true according to Theology.[1] And wherein Plato, Aristotle, Pythagoras and others did hit the mark, and wherein Enoch, Abraham, Moses, Solomon did excel, but especially wherewith that wonderful book the Bible agreeth. All that same concurreth together, and makes a sphere or Globe, whose total parts are equidistant from the Centre, as hereof more at large and more plain shall be spoken of in Christianly conference.

But now concerning (and chiefly in this our age) the ungodly and accursed gold-making, which hath gotten so much the upper hand, whereby under colour of it, many runagates and roguish people do use great villanies and cozen and abuse the credit which is given them. Yea nowadays men of discretion do hold the transmutation of metals to be the highest point and *fastigium* in philosophy, this is all their intent and desire, and that God would be most esteemed by them, and honoured, which could make great store of gold, and in abundance, the which with unpremeditate prayers, they hope to attain of the all-knowing God, and searcher of all hearts. We therefore do by these presents publicly testify, that the true philosophers are far of another mind, esteeming little the making of gold, which is but a *parergon*; for besides that they have a thousand better things.

And we say with our loving father R.C.C. *Phy: aurum nisi quantum aurum*, for unto them the whole nature is detected: he doth not rejoice that he can make gold, and that, as saith Christ, the devils are obedient unto him; but is glad that he seeth the heavens open, and the angels of God ascending and descending, and his name written in the book of life. Also we do testify that under the name of Chymia many books and pictures are set forth in *Contumeliam gloriæ Dei*, as we will name them in their due season, and will give to the pure-hearted a Catalogue, or register of them. And we pray all learned men to take heed of these kind of books; for the enemy never resteth but soweth his weeds, till a stronger one doth root it out. So according to the will and meaning of *Fra C.R.C.* we his brethren request again all the learned in Europe who shall read (sent forth in five languages) this our *Famam* and *Confessionem*, that it would please them with good deliberation to ponder this our

[1] '... but false in Theology.'

offer, and to examine most nearly and most sharply their arts, and behold the present time with all diligence, and to declare their mind, either *Communicatio consilio*, or *singulatim* by print.

And although at this time we make no mention either of names or meetings, yet nevertheless everyone's opinion shall assuredly come to our hands, in what language so ever it be; nor anybody shall fail, who so gives his name, but to speak with some of us, either by word of mouth, or else, if there be some let, in writing. And this we say for a truth, that whosoever shall earnestly, and from his heart, bear affection unto us, it shall be beneficial to him in goods, body, and soul; but he that is false-hearted, or only greedy of riches, the same first of all shall not be able in any manner of wise to hurt us, but bring himself to utter ruin and destruction. Also our building (although one hundred thousand people had very near seen and beheld the same) shall for ever remain untouched, undestroyed, and hidden to the wicked world.

SUB UMBRA ALARUM TUARUM JEHOVA

CONFESSIO FRATERNITATIS

or

THE CONFESSION OF THE LAUDABLE FRATERNITY OF THE MOST HONORABLE ORDER OF THE ROSY CROSS, WRITTEN TO ALL THE LEARNED OF EUROPE

Whatsoever is published, and made known to everyone, concerning our Fraternity, by the foresaid *Fama*, let no man esteem lightly of it, nor hold it as an idle or invented thing, and much less receive the same, as though it were only a mere conceit of ours. It is the Lord Jehovah (who seeing the Lord's Sabbath is almost at hand, and hastened again, his period or course being finished, to his first beginning) doth turn about the course of Nature; and what heretofore hath been sought with great pains, and daily labour, is now manifested unto those who make small account, or scarcely once think upon it; but those which desire it, it is in a manner forced and thrust upon them, that thereby the life of the godly may be eased of all their toil and labour, and be no more subject to the storms of inconstant Fortune; but the wickedness of the ungodly thereby, with their due and deserved punishment, be augmented and multiplied.

Although we cannot be by any suspected of the least heresy, or of any wicked beginning, or purpose against the worldly government, we do condemn the East and the West (meaning the Pope and Mahomet) blasphemers against our Lord Jesus Christ, and offer and present with a good will to the chief head of the Roman Empire our prayers, secrets, and great treasures of gold.

Yet we have thought good, and fit for the learned's sakes, to add somewhat more to this, and make a better explanation if there be anything too deep, hidden, and set down over dark in the *Fama*, or for certain reasons were altogether omitted, and left out; hoping herewith the learned will be more addicted unto us, and be made far more fit and willing for our purpose.

Concerning the alteration and amendment of Philosophy. we have (as much as at this present is needful) sufficiently declared, to wit, that the same is altogether weak and faulty; yet we doubt not, although the most part falsely do allege that she (I know not how) is sound and strong, yet notwithstanding she fetches her last breath and is departing.

But as commonly, even in the same place or country where there breaketh forth a new and unaccustomed disease, Nature also there discovereth a medicine against the same; so there doth appear for so manifold infirmities of Philosophy the right means, and unto our Patria sufficiently offered, whereby she may become sound again, which is now to be renewed and altogether new.

No other Philosophy we have, than that which is the head and sum, the foundations and contents of all faculties, sciences, and arts, the which (if we well behold our age) containeth much of Theology and medicine, but little of the wisdom of the law, and doth diligently search both heaven and earth: or, to speak briefly thereof, which doth manifest and declare sufficiently Man, whereof all learned who will make themselves known unto us, and come into our brotherhood, shall find more wonderful secrets by us than heretofore they did attain unto, and did know, or are able to believe or utter.

Wherefore, to declare briefly our meaning hereof, we ought to labour carefully that there be not only a wondering at our meeting and adhortation, but that likewise everyone may know, that although we do not lightly esteem and regard such mysteries and secrets, we nevertheless hold it fit, that the knowledge thereof be manifested and revealed to many.

For it is to be taught and believed, that this our unhoped (for), willing offer will raise many and divers thoughts in men, unto whom (as yet) be unknown *Miranda sexta aetatis*, or those which by reason of the course of the world, esteem the things to come like unto the present, and are hindered through all manner of importunities of this our time, so that they live no otherwise in the world, than blind fools, who can, in the clear sun-shine day discern and know nothing, than only by feeling.

Now concerning the first part, we hold this, that the meditations, knowledge and inventions of our loving Christian Father (of all that, which from the beginning of the world, Man's wisdom, either through God's revelation, or through the service of the angels and spirits, or through the sharpness and depth of understanding, or through long observation, use, and experience, hath found out, invented, brought forth, corrected, and till now hath been propagated and transplanted) are so excellent, worthy and great, that if all books should perish, and by God's almighty sufferance, all writings and all learnings should be lost, yet the posterity will be able only thereby to lay a new foundation, and bring truth to light again; the which perhaps would not be so hard to do as if one should begin to pull down and destroy the old ruinous building, and then to enlarge the fore court, afterwards bring lights in the lodgings, and then change the doors, stair, and other things according to our intention.

But to whom would not this be acceptable, for to be manifested to everyone rather than to have it kept and spared, as an especial ornament for the appointed time to come?

Wherefore should we not with all our hearts rest and remain in the only truth (which men through so many erroneous and crooked ways do seek) if it had only pleased God to lighten unto us the sixth *Candelabrium*? Were it not good that we needed not to care, not to fear hunger, poverty, sickness and age?

Were it not a precious thing, that you could always live so, as if you had lived from the beginning of the world, and, moreover, as you should still live to the end thereof? Were it not excellent you dwell in one place, that neither the people which dwell beyond the River Ganges in the Indies could hide anything, nor those which live in Peru might be able to keep secret their counsels from thee?

Were it not a precious thing, that you could so read in one only book, and withal by reading understand and remember, all that which in all other books (which heretofore have been, and are now, and hereafter shall come out) hath been, is, and shall be learned and found out of them?

How pleasant were it, that you could so sing, that instead of stony rocks you could draw the pearls and precious stones, instead of wild beasts, spirits, and instead of hellish Pluto, move the mighty princes of the world.

O ye people, God's counsel is far otherwise, who hath concluded now to increase and enlarge the number of our Fraternity, the which we with such joy have undertaken, as we have heretofore obtained this great treasure without our merits, yea without our hopes, and thoughts, and purpose with the like fidelity to put the same in practise, that neither the compassion nor pity of our own children (which some of us in the Fraternity have) shall draw us from it, because we know these unhoped for goods cannot be inherited, nor by chance be obtained.

If there be some body now, which on the other side will complain of our discretion, that we offer our treasures so freely, and without any difference to all men, and do not rather regard and respect more the godly, learned, wise, or princely persons, than the common people; those we do not contradict, seeing it is not a slight and easy matter; but withal we signify so much, that our *Arcana* or secrets will no ways be common, and generally made known. Although the *Fama* be set forth in five languages, and is manifested to everyone, yet we do partly very well know that the unlearned and gross wits will not receive nor regard the same; as also the worthiness of those who shall be accepted into our Fraternity are not esteemed and known of us by Man's carefulness, but by the Rule of our Revelation and Manifestation. Wherefore if the unworthy cry and call a thousand times, or if they shall offer and present themselves to us a thousand times, yet God hath commanded our ears, that they should hear none of them: yea God hath so compassed us about with his clouds, that unto us his servants no violence or force can be done or committed; wherefore we neither can be seen or known by anybody, except he had the eyes of an eagle. It hath been necessary that the *Fama* should be set forth in everyone's mother tongue, because those should not be defrauded of the knowledge thereof, whom (although they be unlearned) God hath not excluded from the happiness of this Fraternity, the which shall be divided and parted into certain degrees; as those which dwell in the city of Damcar[1] in Arabia, who have a far different politick order from the other Arabians. For there do govern only wise and understanding men, who by the king's permission make particular laws; according unto which example also the government shall be instituted in Europe (whereof we have a description set down by our Christianly Father) when first is done and come to pass that which is to precede. And thenceforth our Trumpet shall publicly sound with a loud sound, and great noise, when namely the same (which at this present is shown

[1] Damascus.

254

by few, and is secretly, as a thing to come, declared in figures and pictures) shall be free and publicly proclaimed, and the whole world shall be filled withal. Even in such manner as heretofore, many godly people have secretly and altogether desperately pushed at the Pope's tyranny, which afterwards, with great, earnest, and especial zeal in Germany, was thrown from his seat, and trodden underfoot, whose final fall is delayed, and kept for our times, when he also shall be scratched in pieces with nails, and an end be made of his ass's cry, by a new voice.[1] The which we know is already reasonably manifest and known to many learned men in Germany, as their writings and secret congratulations do sufficiently witness the same.

We could here relate and declare what all the time, from the year of Our Lord 1378 (in which year our Christian Father was born) till now, hath happened, where we might rehearse what alterations he hath seen in the world these one hundred and six years of his life, which he hath left to our brethren and us after his decease to peruse. But brevity, which we do observe, will not permit at this present to make rehearsal of it, till a more fit time. At this time it is enough for those which do not despise our declaration, having therefore briefly touched it, thereby to prepare the way for their acquaintance and friendship with us.

Yet to whom it is permitted that he may see, and for his instruction use, those great letters and characters which the Lord God hath written and imprinted in heaven and earth's edifice, through the alteration of government, which hath been from time to time altered and renewed, the same is already (although as yet unknown to himself) ours. And as we know he will not despise our inviting and calling, so none shall fear any deceit, for we promise and openly say, that no man's uprightness and hopes shall deceive him, whosoever shall make himself known unto us under the seal of secrecy, and desire our Fraternity.

But to the false hypocrites, and to those that seek other things than wisdom, we say and witness by these presents publicly, we cannot be made known, and be betrayed unto them; and much less they shall be able to hurt as any manner of way without the will of God; but they shall certainly be partakers of all the punishment spoken of in our *Fama*; so their wicked counsels shall light upon themselves, and our treasures shall remain untouched and unstirred, until the Lion doth

---

[1] 'by the new voice of a roaring lion' (according to Pryce, this reading is found in the Frankfurt, 1617, edition).

come, who will ask them for his use, and employ them for the confirmation and establishment of his kingdom. We ought therefore here to observe well, and make it known unto everyone, that God hath certainly and most assuredly concluded to send and grant to the world before her end, which presently thereupon shall ensue, such a truth, light, life and glory, as the first man Adam had, which he lost in Paradise, after which his successors were put and driven, with him, to misery. Wherefore there shall cease all servitude, falsehood, lies, and darkness, which by little and little, with the great world's revolution, was crept into all arts, works, and governments of men, and have darkened the most part of them. For from thence are proceeded an innumerable sort of all manner of false opinions and heresies, that scarce the wisest of all was able to know whose doctrine and opinion he should follow and embrace, and could not well and easily be discerned; seeing on the one part they were detained, hindered, and brought into errors through the respect of the philosophers and learned men, and on the other part through true experience. All the which, when it shall once be abolished and removed, and instead thereof a right and true rule instituted, then there will remain thanks unto them which have taken pains therein. But the work itself shall be attributed to the blessedness of our age.

As we now willingly confess, that many principal men by their writings will be a great furtherance unto this Reformation which is to come; so we desire not to have this honour ascribed to us, as if such work were only commanded and imposed upon us. But we confess, and witness openly with the Lord Jesus Christ, that it shall first happen that the stones shall arise, and offer their service, before there shall be any want of executors and accomplishers of God's counsel; yea, the Lord God hath already sent before certain messengers, which should testify his will, to wit, some new stars, which do appear and are seen in the firmament in *Serpentario* and *Cygno*, which signify and give themselves known to everyone, that they are powerful *Signacula* of great weighty matters.[1] So then, the secret hid writings and characters

[1] On the 'new stars' in the constellations Serpentarius and Cygnus, see Johannes Kepler, *De stella nova in pede Serpentarii: De stella incognita Cygni*, Prague, 1606 (reprinted *Gesammelte Werke*, ed. M. Caspar, I, pp. 146 ff.). Since the new stars appeared in 1604, the reference to them here again emphasizes the date 1604 as significant. This is the year in which Rosencreutz's tomb is supposed to have been discovered (see above, p. 248, n. 1).

Peuckert (*Die Rosenkreutzer*, pp. 53 ff.) discusses this passage. I would suggest that the religious significance of the date 1604 (the date of the new stars and of the discovery of the tomb) may be connected with some formation, of the 'Militia Evangelica' in that year. See above, pp. 33–6.

are most necessary for all such things which are found out by men. Although that great book of nature stands open to all men, yet there are but few that can read and understand the same. For as there is given to man two instruments to hear, likewise two to see, and two to smell, but only one to speak, and it were but vain to expect speech from the ears, or hearing from the eyes. So there hath been ages or times which have seen, there have also been ages that have heard, smelt, and tasted. Now there remains yet that which in short time, honour shall be likewise given to the tongue, and by the same; what before times hath been seen, heard, and smelt, now finally shall be spoken and uttered forth, when the World shall awake out of her heavy and drowsy sleep, and with an open heart, bare-head, and bare-foot, shall merrily and joyfully meet the new arising Sun.

These characters and letters, as God hath here and there incorporated them in the Holy Scriptures, the Bible, so hath he imprinted them most apparently into the wonderful creation of heaven and earth, yea in all beasts. So that like as the mathematician and astronomer can long before see and know the eclipses which are to come, so we may verily foreknow and foresee the darkness of obscurations of the Church, and how long they shall last. From the which characters or letters we have borrowed our magic writing, and have found out, and made, a new language for ourselves, in the which withall is expressed and declared the nature of all things. So that it is no wonder that we are not so eloquent in other languages, the which we know that they are altogether disagreeing to the language of our forefathers, Adam and Enoch, and were through the Babylonical confusion wholly hidden.

But we must also let you understand that there are yet some Eagles' Feathers in our way, the which do hinder our purpose. Wherefore we do admonish everyone for to read diligently and continually the Holy Bible, for he that taketh all his pleasures therein, he shall know that he prepared for himself an excellent way to come to our Fraternity. For as this is the whole sum and content of our rule, that every letter or character which is in the world ought to be learned and regarded well; so those are like unto us, and are very near allied unto us, who do make the Holy Bible a rule of their life, and an aim and end of all their studies: yea to let it be a compendium and content of the whole world. And not only to have it continually in the mouth, but to know how to apply and direct the true understanding of it to all times and ages of the world. Also, it is not our custom to prostitute and make so common the Holy Scriptures; for there are innumerable expounders of the same;

some alleging and wresting it to serve for their opinion, some to scandal it, and most wickedly do liken it to a nose of wax, which alike should serve the divines, philosophers, physicians, and mathematicians, against all the which we do openly witness and acknowledge, that from the beginning of the world there hath not been given unto men a more worthy, a more excellent, and more admirable and wholesome Book than the Holy Bible. Blessed is he that hath the same, yet more blessed is he who reads it diligently, but most blessed of all is he that truly understandeth the same, for he is most like to God, and doth come most near to him. But whatsoever hath been said in the *Fama* concerning the deceivers against the transmutation of metals,[1] and the highest medicine in the world, the same is thus to be understood, that this so great gift of God we do in no manner set at naught, or despise it. But because she bringeth not with her always the knowledge of Nature, but this bringeth forth not only medicine, but also maketh manifest and open unto us innumerable secrets and wonders. Therefore it is requisite, that we be earnest to attain to the understanding and knowledge of philosophy. And moreover, excellent wits ought not to be drawn to the tincture of metals, before they be exercised well in the knowledge of Nature. He must needs be an insatiable creature, who is come so far, that neither poverty nor sickness can hurt him, yea, who is exalted above all other men, and hath rule over that, the which doth anguish, trouble and pain others, yet will give himself again to idle things, as to build houses, make wars, and use all manner of pride, because he hath gold and silver infinite store.

God is far otherwise pleased, for he exalteth the lowly, and pulleth down the proud with disdain; to those which are of few words, he sendeth his holy Angel to speak with them, but the unclean babblers he driveth in the wilderness and solitary places. The which is the right reward of the Romish seducers, who have vomited forth their blasphemies against Christ, and as yet do not abstain from their lies in this clear shining light. In Germany all their abominations and detestable tricks have been disclosed, that thereby he may fully fulfil the measure of sin, and draw near to the end of his punishment. Therefore one day it will come to pass, that the mouth of those vipers will be stopped and the three double horn[2] will be brought to nought, as thereof at our meeting shall more plain and at large be discoursed.

For conclusion of our Confession, we must earnestly admonish you,

[1] That is, against false alchemists. See the passage in the *Fama*, above, p. 250.
[2] 'triple crown'.

that you put away, if not all, yet the most books written by false Alchemists, who do think it but a jest, or a pastime, when they either misuse the Holy Trinity, when they do apply it to vain things, or deceive the people with most strange figures, and dark sentences and speeches, and cozen the simple of their money; as there are nowadays too many such books set forth, which the Enemy of man's welfare doth daily, and will to the end, mingle among the good seed, thereby to make the Truth more difficult to be believed, which in herself is simple, easy, and naked, but contrarily Falsehood is proud, haughty, and coloured with a kind of lustre of seeming godly and of humane wisdom. Ye that are wise eschew such books, and turn unto us, who seek not your moneys, but offer unto you most willingly our great treasures. We hunt not after your goods with invented lying tinctures, but desire to make you partakers of our goods. We speak unto you by parables, but would willingly bring you to the right, simple, easy and ingenuous exposition, understanding, declaration, and knowledge of all secrets. We desire not to be received of you, but invite you unto our more than kingly houses and palaces, and that verily not by our own proper motion, but (that you likewise may know it) as forced unto it, by the instigation of the Spirit of God, by his admonitions, and by the occasion of this present time.

What think you, loving people, and how seem you affected, seeing that you now understand and know, that we acknowledge ourselves truly and sincerely to profess Christ, condemn the Pope, addict ourselves to the true Philosophy, lead a Christian life, and daily call, entreat and invite many more unto our Fraternity, unto whom the same Light of God likewise appeareth? Consider you not at length how you might begin with us, not only by pondering the Gifts which are in you, and by experience which you have in the word of God, beside the careful consideration of the imperfection of all arts, and many other unfitting things, to seek for an amendment therein; to appease God, and to accommodate you for the time wherein you live. Certainly if you will perform the same, this profit will follow, that all those goods which Nature hath in all parts of the world wonderfully dispersed, shall at one time altogether be given unto you, and shall easily disburden you of all that which obscureth the understanding of man, and hindereth the working thereof, like unto the vain eccentrics and epicycles.

But those pragmatical and busy-headed men, who either are blinded with the glittering of gold, or (to say more truly) who are now honest, but by thinking such great riches should never fail, might easily be corrupted, and brought to idleness, and to riotous proud living, those we desire that they would not trouble us with their idle and vain crying. But let them think, that although there be a medicine to be had which might fully cure all diseases, nevertheless those whom God hath destined to plague with diseases, and to keep under the rod of correction, such shall never obtain any such medicine.

Even in such manner, although we might enrich the whole world, and endue them with learning, and might release it from innumerable miseries, yet shall we never be manifested and made known unto any man, without the especial pleasure of God; yea, it shall be so far from him whosoever thinks to get the benefit and be partaker of our riches and knowledge, without and against the will of God, that he shall sooner lose his life in seeking and searching for us, than to find us, and attain to come to the wished happiness of the Fraternity of the Rosy Cross.